FREE Study Skills DVD Offer

Dear Customer,

Thank you for your purchase from Mometrix! We consider it an honor and a privilege that you have purchased our product and we want to ensure your satisfaction.

As a way of showing our appreciation and to help us better serve you, we have developed a Study Skills DVD that we would like to give you for FREE. This DVD covers our *best practices* for getting ready for your exam, from how to use our study materials to how to best prepare for the day of the test.

All that we ask is that you email us with feedback that would describe your experience so far with our product. Good, bad, or indifferent, we want to know what you think!

To get your FREE Study Skills DVD, email freedvd@mometrix.com with *FREE STUDY SKILLS DVD* in the subject line and the following information in the body of the email:

- The name of the product you purchased.
- Your product rating on a scale of 1-5, with 5 being the highest rating.
- Your feedback. It can be long, short, or anything in between. We just want to know your impressions and experience so far with our product. (Good feedback might include how our study material met your needs and ways we might be able to make it even better. You could highlight features that you found helpful or features that you think we should add.)
- Your full name and shipping address where you would like us to send your free DVD.

If you have any questions or concerns, please don't hesitate to contact me directly.

Thanks again!

Sincerely,

Jay Willis
Vice President
jay.willis@mometrix.com
1-800-673-8175

Six Sigma Black Belt Study Guide

Six Sigma Black Belt Exam Prep Secrets

Practice Test Question Book

Detailed Answer Explanations

Updated for the Third Edition Handbook

Written and edited by the Six Sigma Black Belt Secrets Test Prep Staff

Printed in the United States of America

This paper meets the requirements of ANSI/NISO Z39.48-1992 (Permanence of Paper).

Paperback
ISBN 13: 978-1-5167-1246-5
ISBN 10: 1-5167-1246-3

Dear Future Exam Success Story

First of all, **THANK YOU** for purchasing Mometrix study materials!

Second, congratulations! You are one of the few determined test-takers who are committed to doing whatever it takes to excel on your exam. **You have come to the right place.** We developed these study materials with one goal in mind: to deliver you the information you need in a format that's concise and easy to use.

In addition to optimizing your guide for the content of the test, we've outlined our recommended steps for breaking down the preparation process into small, attainable goals so you can make sure you stay on track.

We've also analyzed the entire test-taking process, identifying the most common pitfalls and showing how you can overcome them and be ready for any curveball the test throws you.

Standardized testing is one of the biggest obstacles on your road to success, which only increases the importance of doing well in the high-pressure, high-stakes environment of test day. Your results on this test could have a significant impact on your future, and this guide provides the information and practical advice to help you achieve your full potential on test day.

Your success is our success

We would love to hear from you! If you would like to share the story of your exam success or if you have any questions or comments in regard to our products, please contact us at **800-673-8175** or **support@mometrix.com**.

Thanks again for your business and we wish you continued success!

Sincerely,
The Mometrix Test Preparation Team

TABLE OF CONTENTS

Introduction

Thank you for purchasing this resource! You have made the choice to prepare yourself for a test that could have a huge impact on your future, and this guide is designed to help you be fully ready for test day. Obviously, it's important to have a solid understanding of the test material, but you also need to be prepared for the unique environment and stressors of the test, so that you can perform to the best of your abilities.

For this purpose, the first section that appears in this guide is the **Secret Keys**. We've devoted countless hours to meticulously researching what works and what doesn't, and we've boiled down our findings to the five most impactful steps you can take to improve your performance on the test. We start at the beginning with study planning and move through the preparation process, all the way to the testing strategies that will help you get the most out of what you know when you're finally sitting in front of the test.

We recommend that you start preparing for your test as far in advance as possible. However, if you've bought this guide as a last-minute study resource and only have a few days before your test, we recommend that you skip over the first two Secret Keys since they address a long-term study plan.

If you struggle with **test anxiety**, we strongly encourage you to check out our recommendations for how you can overcome it. Test anxiety is a formidable foe, but it can be beaten, and we want to make sure you have the tools you need to defeat it.

Secret Key #1 – Plan Big, Study Small

There's a lot riding on your performance. If you want to ace this test, you're going to need to keep your skills sharp and the material fresh in your mind. You need a plan that lets you review everything you need to know while still fitting in your schedule. We'll break this strategy down into three categories.

Information Organization

Start with the information you already have: the official test outline. From this, you can make a complete list of all the concepts you need to cover before the test. Organize these concepts into groups that can be studied together, and create a list of any related vocabulary you need to learn so you can brush up on any difficult terms. You'll want to keep this vocabulary list handy once you actually start studying since you may need to add to it along the way.

Time Management

Once you have your set of study concepts, decide how to spread them out over the time you have left before the test. Break your study plan into small, clear goals so you have a manageable task for each day and know exactly what you're doing. Then just focus on one small step at a time. When you manage your time this way, you don't need to spend hours at a time studying. Studying a small block of content for a short period each day helps you retain information better and avoid stressing over how much you have left to do. You can relax knowing that you have a plan to cover everything in time. In order for this strategy to be effective though, you have to start studying early and stick to your schedule. Avoid the exhaustion and futility that comes from last-minute cramming!

Study Environment

The environment you study in has a big impact on your learning. Studying in a coffee shop, while probably more enjoyable, is not likely to be as fruitful as studying in a quiet room. It's important to keep distractions to a minimum. You're only planning to study for a short block of time, so make the most of it. Don't pause to check your phone or get up to find a snack. It's also important to **avoid multitasking**. Research has consistently shown that multitasking will make your studying dramatically less effective. Your study area should also be comfortable and well-lit so you don't have the distraction of straining your eyes or sitting on an uncomfortable chair.

The time of day you study is also important. You want to be rested and alert. Don't wait until just before bedtime. Study when you'll be most likely to comprehend and remember. Even better, if you know what time of day your test will be, set that time aside for study. That way your brain will be used to working on that subject at that specific time and you'll have a better chance of recalling information.

Finally, it can be helpful to team up with others who are studying for the same test. Your actual studying should be done in as isolated an environment as possible, but the work of organizing the information and setting up the study plan can be divided up. In between study sessions, you can discuss with your teammates the concepts that you're all studying and quiz each other on the details. Just be sure that your teammates are as serious about the test as you are. If you find that your study time is being replaced with social time, you might need to find a new team.

Secret Key #2 – Make Your Studying Count

You're devoting a lot of time and effort to preparing for this test, so you want to be absolutely certain it will pay off. This means doing more than just reading the content and hoping you can remember it on test day. It's important to make every minute of study count. There are two main areas you can focus on to make your studying count:

Retention

It doesn't matter how much time you study if you can't remember the material. You need to make sure you are retaining the concepts. To check your retention of the information you're learning, try recalling it at later times with minimal prompting. Try carrying around flashcards and glance at one or two from time to time or ask a friend who's also studying for the test to quiz you.

To enhance your retention, look for ways to put the information into practice so that you can apply it rather than simply recalling it. If you're using the information in practical ways, it will be much easier to remember. Similarly, it helps to solidify a concept in your mind if you're not only reading it to yourself but also explaining it to someone else. Ask a friend to let you teach them about a concept you're a little shaky on (or speak aloud to an imaginary audience if necessary). As you try to summarize, define, give examples, and answer your friend's questions, you'll understand the concepts better and they will stay with you longer. Finally, step back for a big picture view and ask yourself how each piece of information fits with the whole subject. When you link the different concepts together and see them working together as a whole, it's easier to remember the individual components.

Finally, practice showing your work on any multi-step problems, even if you're just studying. Writing out each step you take to solve a problem will help solidify the process in your mind, and you'll be more likely to remember it during the test.

Modality

Modality simply refers to the means or method by which you study. Choosing a study modality that fits your own individual learning style is crucial. No two people learn best in exactly the same way, so it's important to know your strengths and use them to your advantage.

For example, if you learn best by visualization, focus on visualizing a concept in your mind and draw an image or a diagram. Try color-coding your notes, illustrating them, or creating symbols that will trigger your mind to recall a learned concept. If you learn best by hearing or discussing information, find a study partner who learns the same way or read aloud to yourself. Think about how to put the information in your own words. Imagine that you are giving a lecture on the topic and record yourself so you can listen to it later.

For any learning style, flashcards can be helpful. Organize the information so you can take advantage of spare moments to review. Underline key words or phrases. Use different colors for different categories. Mnemonic devices (such as creating a short list in which every item starts with the same letter) can also help with retention. Find what works best for you and use it to store the information in your mind most effectively and easily.

Secret Key #3 – Practice the Right Way

Your success on test day depends not only on how many hours you put into preparing, but also on whether you prepared the right way. It's good to check along the way to see if your studying is paying off. One of the most effective ways to do this is by taking practice tests to evaluate your progress. Practice tests are useful because they show exactly where you need to improve. Every time you take a practice test, pay special attention to these three groups of questions:

- The questions you got wrong
- The questions you had to guess on, even if you guessed right
- The questions you found difficult or slow to work through

This will show you exactly what your weak areas are, and where you need to devote more study time. Ask yourself why each of these questions gave you trouble. Was it because you didn't understand the material? Was it because you didn't remember the vocabulary? Do you need more repetitions on this type of question to build speed and confidence? Dig into those questions and figure out how you can strengthen your weak areas as you go back to review the material.

Additionally, many practice tests have a section explaining the answer choices. It can be tempting to read the explanation and think that you now have a good understanding of the concept. However, an explanation likely only covers part of the question's broader context. Even if the explanation makes sense, **go back and investigate** every concept related to the question until you're positive you have a thorough understanding.

As you go along, keep in mind that the practice test is just that: practice. Memorizing these questions and answers will not be very helpful on the actual test because it is unlikely to have any of the same exact questions. If you only know the right answers to the sample questions, you won't be prepared for the real thing. **Study the concepts** until you understand them fully, and then you'll be able to answer any question that shows up on the test.

It's important to wait on the practice tests until you're ready. If you take a test on your first day of study, you may be overwhelmed by the amount of material covered and how much you need to learn. Work up to it gradually.

On test day, you'll need to be prepared for answering questions, managing your time, and using the test-taking strategies you've learned. It's a lot to balance, like a mental marathon that will have a big impact on your future. Like training for a marathon, you'll need to start slowly and work your way up. When test day arrives, you'll be ready.

Start with the strategies you've read in the first two Secret Keys—plan your course and study in the way that works best for you. If you have time, consider using multiple study resources to get different approaches to the same concepts. It can be helpful to see difficult concepts from more than one angle. Then find a good source for practice tests. Many times, the test website will suggest potential study resources or provide sample tests.

Practice Test Strategy

When you're ready to start taking practice tests, follow this strategy:

UNTIMED AND OPEN-BOOK PRACTICE

Take the first test with no time constraints and with your notes and study guide handy. Take your time and focus on applying the strategies you've learned.

TIMED AND OPEN-BOOK PRACTICE

Take the second practice test open-book as well, but set a timer and practice pacing yourself to finish in time.

TIMED AND CLOSED-BOOK PRACTICE

Take any other practice tests as if it were test day. Set a timer and put away your study materials. Sit at a table or desk in a quiet room, imagine yourself at the testing center, and answer questions as quickly and accurately as possible.

Keep repeating timed and closed-book tests on a regular basis until you run out of practice tests or it's time for the actual test. Your mind will be ready for the schedule and stress of test day, and you'll be able to focus on recalling the material you've learned.

Secret Key #4 – Pace Yourself

Once you're fully prepared for the material on the test, your biggest challenge on test day will be managing your time. Just knowing that the clock is ticking can make you panic even if you have plenty of time left. Work on pacing yourself so you can build confidence against the time constraints of the exam. Pacing is a difficult skill to master, especially in a high-pressure environment, so **practice is vital**.

Set time expectations for your pace based on how much time is available. For example, if a section has 60 questions and the time limit is 30 minutes, you know you have to average 30 seconds or less per question in order to answer them all. Although 30 seconds is the hard limit, set 25 seconds per question as your goal, so you reserve extra time to spend on harder questions. When you budget extra time for the harder questions, you no longer have any reason to stress when those questions take longer to answer.

Don't let this time expectation distract you from working through the test at a calm, steady pace, but keep it in mind so you don't spend too much time on any one question. Recognize that taking extra time on one question you don't understand may keep you from answering two that you do understand later in the test. If your time limit for a question is up and you're still not sure of the answer, mark it and move on, and come back to it later if the time and the test format allow. If the testing format doesn't allow you to return to earlier questions, just make an educated guess; then put it out of your mind and move on.

On the easier questions, be careful not to rush. It may seem wise to hurry through them so you have more time for the challenging ones, but it's not worth missing one if you know the concept and just didn't take the time to read the question fully. Work efficiently but make sure you understand the question and have looked at all of the answer choices, since more than one may seem right at first.

Even if you're paying attention to the time, you may find yourself a little behind at some point. You should speed up to get back on track, but do so wisely. Don't panic; just take a few seconds less on each question until you're caught up. Don't guess without thinking, but do look through the answer choices and eliminate any you know are wrong. If you can get down to two choices, it is often worthwhile to guess from those. Once you've chosen an answer, move on and don't dwell on any that you skipped or had to hurry through. If a question was taking too long, chances are it was one of the harder ones, so you weren't as likely to get it right anyway.

On the other hand, if you find yourself getting ahead of schedule, it may be beneficial to slow down a little. The more quickly you work, the more likely you are to make a careless mistake that will affect your score. You've budgeted time for each question, so don't be afraid to spend that time. Practice an efficient but careful pace to get the most out of the time you have.

Secret Key #5 – Have a Plan for Guessing

When you're taking the test, you may find yourself stuck on a question. Some of the answer choices seem better than others, but you don't see the one answer choice that is obviously correct. What do you do?

The scenario described above is very common, yet most test takers have not effectively prepared for it. Developing and practicing a plan for guessing may be one of the single most effective uses of your time as you get ready for the exam.

In developing your plan for guessing, there are three questions to address:

- When should you start the guessing process?
- How should you narrow down the choices?
- Which answer should you choose?

When to Start the Guessing Process

Unless your plan for guessing is to select C every time (which, despite its merits, is not what we recommend), you need to leave yourself enough time to apply your answer elimination strategies. Since you have a limited amount of time for each question, that means that if you're going to give yourself the best shot at guessing correctly, you have to decide quickly whether or not you will guess.

Of course, the best-case scenario is that you don't have to guess at all, so first, see if you can answer the question based on your knowledge of the subject and basic reasoning skills. Focus on the key words in the question and try to jog your memory of related topics. Give yourself a chance to bring the knowledge to mind, but once you realize that you don't have (or you can't access) the knowledge you need to answer the question, it's time to start the guessing process.

It's almost always better to start the guessing process too early than too late. It only takes a few seconds to remember something and answer the question from knowledge. Carefully eliminating wrong answer choices takes longer. Plus, going through the process of eliminating answer choices can actually help jog your memory.

Summary: Start the guessing process as soon as you decide that you can't answer the question based on your knowledge.

How to Narrow Down the Choices

The next chapter in this book (**Test-Taking Strategies**) includes a wide range of strategies for how to approach questions and how to look for answer choices to eliminate. You will definitely want to read those carefully, practice them, and figure out which ones work best for you. Here though, we're going to address a mindset rather than a particular strategy.

Your chances of guessing an answer correctly depend on how many options you are choosing from.

How many choices you have	How likely you are to guess correctly
5	20%
4	25%
3	33%
2	50%
1	100%

You can see from this chart just how valuable it is to be able to eliminate incorrect answers and make an educated guess, but there are two things that many test takers do that cause them to miss out on the benefits of guessing:

- Accidentally eliminating the correct answer
- Selecting an answer based on an impression

We'll look at the first one here, and the second one in the next section.

To avoid accidentally eliminating the correct answer, we recommend a thought exercise called **the $5 challenge**. In this challenge, you only eliminate an answer choice from contention if you are willing to bet $5 on it being wrong. Why $5? Five dollars is a small but not insignificant amount of money. It's an amount you could afford to lose but wouldn't want to throw away. And while losing $5 once might not hurt too much, doing it twenty times will set you back $100. In the same way, each small decision you make—eliminating a choice here, guessing on a question there—won't by itself impact your score very much, but when you put them all together, they can make a big difference. By holding each answer choice elimination decision to a higher standard, you can reduce the risk of accidentally eliminating the correct answer.

The $5 challenge can also be applied in a positive sense: If you are willing to bet $5 that an answer choice *is* correct, go ahead and mark it as correct.

Summary: Only eliminate an answer choice if you are willing to bet $5 that it is wrong.

Which Answer to Choose

You're taking the test. You've run into a hard question and decided you'll have to guess. You've eliminated all the answer choices you're willing to bet $5 on. Now you have to pick an answer. Why do we even need to talk about this? Why can't you just pick whichever one you feel like when the time comes?

The answer to these questions is that if you don't come into the test with a plan, you'll rely on your impression to select an answer choice, and if you do that, you risk falling into a trap. The test writers know that everyone who takes their test will be guessing on some of the questions, so they intentionally write wrong answer choices to seem plausible. You still have to pick an answer though, and if the wrong answer choices are designed to look right, how can you ever be sure that you're not falling for their trap? The best solution we've found to this dilemma is to take the decision out of your hands entirely. Here is the process we recommend:

Once you've eliminated any choices that you are confident (willing to bet $5) are wrong, select the first remaining choice as your answer.

Whether you choose to select the first remaining choice, the second, or the last, the important thing is that you use some preselected standard. Using this approach guarantees that you will not be enticed into selecting an answer choice that looks right, because you are not basing your decision on how the answer choices look.

This is not meant to make you question your knowledge. Instead, it is to help you recognize the difference between your knowledge and your impressions. There's a huge difference between thinking an answer is right because of what you know, and thinking an answer is right because it looks or sounds like it should be right.

Summary: To ensure that your selection is appropriately random, make a predetermined selection from among all answer choices you have not eliminated.

Test-Taking Strategies

This section contains a list of test-taking strategies that you may find helpful as you work through the test. By taking what you know and applying logical thought, you can maximize your chances of answering any question correctly!

It is very important to realize that every question is different and every person is different: no single strategy will work on every question, and no single strategy will work for every person. That's why we've included all of them here, so you can try them out and determine which ones work best for different types of questions and which ones work best for you.

Question Strategies

Read Carefully

Read the question and answer choices carefully. Don't miss the question because you misread the terms. You have plenty of time to read each question thoroughly and make sure you understand what is being asked. Yet a happy medium must be attained, so don't waste too much time. You must read carefully, but efficiently.

Contextual Clues

Look for contextual clues. If the question includes a word you are not familiar with, look at the immediate context for some indication of what the word might mean. Contextual clues can often give you all the information you need to decipher the meaning of an unfamiliar word. Even if you can't determine the meaning, you may be able to narrow down the possibilities enough to make a solid guess at the answer to the question.

Prefixes

If you're having trouble with a word in the question or answer choices, try dissecting it. Take advantage of every clue that the word might include. Prefixes and suffixes can be a huge help. Usually they allow you to determine a basic meaning. Pre- means before, post- means after, pro - is positive, de- is negative. From prefixes and suffixes, you can get an idea of the general meaning of the word and try to put it into context.

Hedge Words

Watch out for critical hedge words, such as *likely, may, can, sometimes, often, almost, mostly, usually, generally, rarely,* and *sometimes.* Question writers insert these hedge phrases to cover every possibility. Often an answer choice will be wrong simply because it leaves no room for exception. Be on guard for answer choices that have definitive words such as *exactly* and *always.*

Switchback Words

Stay alert for *switchbacks.* These are the words and phrases frequently used to alert you to shifts in thought. The most common switchback words are *but, although,* and *however.* Others include *nevertheless, on the other hand, even though, while, in spite of, despite, regardless of.* Switchback words are important to catch because they can change the direction of the question or an answer choice.

FACE VALUE

When in doubt, use common sense. Accept the situation in the problem at face value. Don't read too much into it. These problems will not require you to make wild assumptions. If you have to go beyond creativity and warp time or space in order to have an answer choice fit the question, then you should move on and consider the other answer choices. These are normal problems rooted in reality. The applicable relationship or explanation may not be readily apparent, but it is there for you to figure out. Use your common sense to interpret anything that isn't clear.

Answer Choice Strategies

ANSWER SELECTION

The most thorough way to pick an answer choice is to identify and eliminate wrong answers until only one is left, then confirm it is the correct answer. Sometimes an answer choice may immediately seem right, but be careful. The test writers will usually put more than one reasonable answer choice on each question, so take a second to read all of them and make sure that the other choices are not equally obvious. As long as you have time left, it is better to read every answer choice than to pick the first one that looks right without checking the others.

ANSWER CHOICE FAMILIES

An answer choice family consists of two (in rare cases, three) answer choices that are very similar in construction and cannot all be true at the same time. If you see two answer choices that are direct opposites or parallels, one of them is usually the correct answer. For instance, if one answer choice says that quantity *x* increases and another either says that quantity *x* decreases (opposite) or says that quantity *y* increases (parallel), then those answer choices would fall into the same family. An answer choice that doesn't match the construction of the answer choice family is more likely to be incorrect. Most questions will not have answer choice families, but when they do appear, you should be prepared to recognize them.

ELIMINATE ANSWERS

Eliminate answer choices as soon as you realize they are wrong, but make sure you consider all possibilities. If you are eliminating answer choices and realize that the last one you are left with is also wrong, don't panic. Start over and consider each choice again. There may be something you missed the first time that you will realize on the second pass.

AVOID FACT TRAPS

Don't be distracted by an answer choice that is factually true but doesn't answer the question. You are looking for the choice that answers the question. Stay focused on what the question is asking for so you don't accidentally pick an answer that is true but incorrect. Always go back to the question and make sure the answer choice you've selected actually answers the question and is not merely a true statement.

EXTREME STATEMENTS

In general, you should avoid answers that put forth extreme actions as standard practice or proclaim controversial ideas as established fact. An answer choice that states the "process should be used in certain situations, if…" is much more likely to be correct than one that states the "process should be discontinued completely." The first is a calm rational statement and doesn't even make a definitive, uncompromising stance, using a hedge word *if* to provide wiggle room, whereas the second choice is a radical idea and far more extreme.

Benchmark

As you read through the answer choices and you come across one that seems to answer the question well, mentally select that answer choice. This is not your final answer, but it's the one that will help you evaluate the other answer choices. The one that you selected is your benchmark or standard for judging each of the other answer choices. Every other answer choice must be compared to your benchmark. That choice is correct until proven otherwise by another answer choice beating it. If you find a better answer, then that one becomes your new benchmark. Once you've decided that no other choice answers the question as well as your benchmark, you have your final answer.

Predict the Answer

Before you even start looking at the answer choices, it is often best to try to predict the answer. When you come up with the answer on your own, it is easier to avoid distractions and traps because you will know exactly what to look for. The right answer choice is unlikely to be word-for-word what you came up with, but it should be a close match. Even if you are confident that you have the right answer, you should still take the time to read each option before moving on.

General Strategies

Tough Questions

If you are stumped on a problem or it appears too hard or too difficult, don't waste time. Move on! Remember though, if you can quickly check for obviously incorrect answer choices, your chances of guessing correctly are greatly improved. Before you completely give up, at least try to knock out a couple of possible answers. Eliminate what you can and then guess at the remaining answer choices before moving on.

Check Your Work

Since you will probably not know every term listed and the answer to every question, it is important that you get credit for the ones that you do know. Don't miss any questions through careless mistakes. If at all possible, try to take a second to look back over your answer selection and make sure you've selected the correct answer choice and haven't made a costly careless mistake (such as marking an answer choice that you didn't mean to mark). This quick double check should more than pay for itself in caught mistakes for the time it costs.

Pace Yourself

It's easy to be overwhelmed when you're looking at a page full of questions; your mind is confused and full of random thoughts, and the clock is ticking down faster than you would like. Calm down and maintain the pace that you have set for yourself. Especially as you get down to the last few minutes of the test, don't let the small numbers on the clock make you panic. As long as you are on track by monitoring your pace, you are guaranteed to have time for each question.

Don't Rush

It is very easy to make errors when you are in a hurry. Maintaining a fast pace in answering questions is pointless if it makes you miss questions that you would have gotten right otherwise. Test writers like to include distracting information and wrong answers that seem right. Taking a little extra time to avoid careless mistakes can make all the difference in your test score. Find a pace that allows you to be confident in the answers that you select.

KEEP MOVING

Panicking will not help you pass the test, so do your best to stay calm and keep moving. Taking deep breaths and going through the answer elimination steps you practiced can help to break through a stress barrier and keep your pace.

Final Notes

The combination of a solid foundation of content knowledge and the confidence that comes from practicing your plan for applying that knowledge is the key to maximizing your performance on test day. As your foundation of content knowledge is built up and strengthened, you'll find that the strategies included in this chapter become more and more effective in helping you quickly sift through the distractions and traps of the test to isolate the correct answer.

Now it's time to move on to the test content chapters of this book, but be sure to keep your goal in mind. As you read, think about how you will be able to apply this information on the test. If you've already seen sample questions for the test and you have an idea of the question format and style, try to come up with questions of your own that you can answer based on what you're reading. This will give you valuable practice applying your knowledge in the same ways you can expect to on test day.

Good luck and good studying!

Organization-Wide Planning and Deployment

LEAN AND SIX SIGMA

Lean and Six Sigma are process and quality improvement methodologies used across the globe, most often in businesses. The central philosophy of lean is to eliminate waste. Waste is considered to be anything that is not essential to produce or deliver the product or service desired by the customer. The central philosophy of Six Sigma is to reduce variation in a process. Variation from the customer's requirements or expectations reflects a reduction in quality. Both approaches seek to give the customer exactly what they desire with as little error or waste as possible.

	Lean	Six Sigma
Goal	Reduce waste	Reduce variation
Focus	Process flow oriented	Problem oriented
Tools	More visual-based tools	More statistical tools
Outcome	Consistent process output Higher quality Satisfied customers	Smoother process flow Less waste Satisfied customers

CENTRAL CONCEPTS OF LEAN

Lean is a concept that focuses on reducing all elements of a process that lack value to the customer. These elements are defined in lean as wastes. There are seven types of waste common to processes. Lean is commonly applied in manufacturing but can also apply to services. Lean emphasizes the optimization of flow in a process. Similar to Six Sigma, there are five key steps to a lean system:

Lean step	Features
Define value	Defining the attributes or features that are valuable to the customer. Voice of the customer tools may be used.
Identify the value stream	Mapping the process entirely using value stream mapping. Identify value-added and non-value-added parts of the process from the customer's perspective.
Create flow	Creating unhindered movement of raw inputs to valuable outputs as consistently as possible. Reducing cycle time. Tools such as total productive maintenance are used.
Create customer pull	Becoming rapidly responsive to customer demand only when the customer asks.
Achieve perfection	Relentless improvements in removing non-value-added wastes, optimal flow, and meeting customer demand instantly.

CENTRAL CONCEPTS OF SIX SIGMA AND PROBLEM-SOLVING TOOLS

Six Sigma initiatives and projects generally use several common concepts. The most essential of these include support of decision-making through statistics, management commitment, following the DMAIC process, and skill-based teamwork. Statistically supported decision making, as the namesake of the process, is clearly evident in the Six Sigma body of knowledge. Teams use statistics to validate hypotheses of preventative improvement approaches to variation reduction. The organization and its management must also provide the support and resources to allow Six Sigma teams to function effectively and capture quality improvements and organizational change. The DMAIC process is the pattern through which such improvements can be realized. The hierarchy of stakeholders, belts, and contributors to Six Sigma projects gives the process its repeatability and cultural longevity. The end results of these efforts include higher quality, lower variation, increased customer satisfaction, better profit margins, and sustainable competitive advantage.

Six Sigma concept	Example tools
Statistical decision-making	Hypothesis testing, design of experiments, standard deviation
Management commitment	Stakeholder analysis, strategic planning, project selection, IRR, KPIs, balanced scorecard, project NPV
DMAIC-type processes	Quality function deployment, SIPOC, measurement systems, ANOVA, control charting, design for Six Sigma
Skill-based teamwork	Charters, black belts, green belts, team dynamics
Quantifiable results	Return on investment, defects per million units or 6σ, net sales, COGS

Aligning Six Sigma Objectives with Organizational Goals

Six Sigma initiatives are essential to meeting organizational goals. Both concepts are interdependent in the organizations that are aware of their need to initiate a Six Sigma effort. Organizations have overarching goals of gaining and satisfying customers, responding to internal and external influences, generating a profit, pleasing stakeholders to the organization, and developing the workforce. Six Sigma initiatives are often undertaken to help drive improvement towards those overarching goals. Six Sigma is skill-based teamwork supported by management that uses the DMAIC process and statistical decision-making to drive out customer dissatisfaction and process variation to achieve improvement or maximized business outcomes.

Screening and Selecting Improvement Projects

Organizations work with resource constraints, some organizations more so than others. Resources such as human, fiscal, and strategic will impact which improvement concepts become accepted and started as projects. Deciding how best to use those limited resources is essential to the black belt, master black belt, and their relevant stakeholders. Tools must be used that can identify key variables, relate those variables to the organization's strategy, and validate the most likely resource usage and quantifiable outcomes. While revenue generation is a potential outcome to a Six Sigma project, such projects are more commonly related to operating expenses. Operational expense savings can be in areas such as materials, labor costs, scrap, customer claims, and capacity improvement. Financial measures such as NPV, IRR, and operating expenses can be used to rank improvement projects. Other measures such as strategic fit, customer satisfaction gained, and OEE may be used to rank and select the projects to begin.

Interrelationship Between Six Sigma, Lean, and Theory of Constraints

The three approaches to quality improvement have five core principles which define them. Like an engineer's toolbox, using the best tools from each discipline can make any project a success. Many of the tools within each are complementary. Where one approach is weak, another provides the tools to eliminate the weakness. All systems are focused on reducing and eliminating that which does not matter to the customer and stakeholders. Six Sigma reduces variation, lean reduces waste, and theory of constraints reduces process bottlenecks. Six Sigma increases output quality, lean improves process flow time, and theory of constraints increases throughput.

Relationships Between Business Systems and Processes

Business systems are a collection of interacting forces that implement processes and coordinate resources and supporting services to help processes succeed and improve. Business systems are managed from a broader perspective in an organization, often by executives and directors. The processes that exist within business systems can be production or service lines that directly supply customers with desired goods and services. Business systems also include non-value-added functions separate from product processes but still necessary to operate the business. The system can negatively impact the organization's ability to service customers if continuous improvement is not an essential element to the system function. A process is a less complex set of sub-processes and/or tasks that create a good or service. Six Sigma professionals are keenly focused on process improvement while being aware of how the business system can influence improvement efforts, both positively and negatively.

Value of Strategic Planning in Successful Continuous Improvement

Strategic planning provides company management with a clear future path towards goals and objectives that meet stakeholder or shareholder expectations. Strategic planning comes in many forms. The basic process of planning begins with analyzing the current internal operations and external competitive environment. The analysis is used to create the future goals and objectives, often 3-5 years in the future. Lastly, the current and future state are bridged with defined initiatives, projects, tasks, and metrics that all serve to keep the organization moving towards the goals. The plan takes the current state and builds a process for improvement to achieve the future state. This cycle often repeats due to the constant flux of internal and external forces. The strategic planning process is essentially a continuous improvement effort with executive commitment and execution from all levels of the organization.

Hoshin-Kanri (X-Matrix)

Hoshin-Kanri is a term derived from Japanese, roughly meaning "management direction." The tool is a common version of top-down strategic planning that begins with executives setting organizational goals and objectives and lower layers of the organization creating aligned goals and objectives. The Hoshin-Kanri process identifies strategies, time boundaries, measurements, and contingency plans that correspond to each objective. Each objective at each level has an accountable team member responsible for success. The process is sustained through regular performance reviews and adjustment measures where needed. The entire organization becomes aligned to the vision of leadership. Hoshin-Kanri is adaptable to long-, mid-, and short-term strategic planning. The final visual of the strategy is documented in an X-matrix. Objectives, strategies, tactics, and targets are all listed clockwise in a four-sided matrix and each item pair is ranked A through D as an indicator of how well each element supports the original objective.

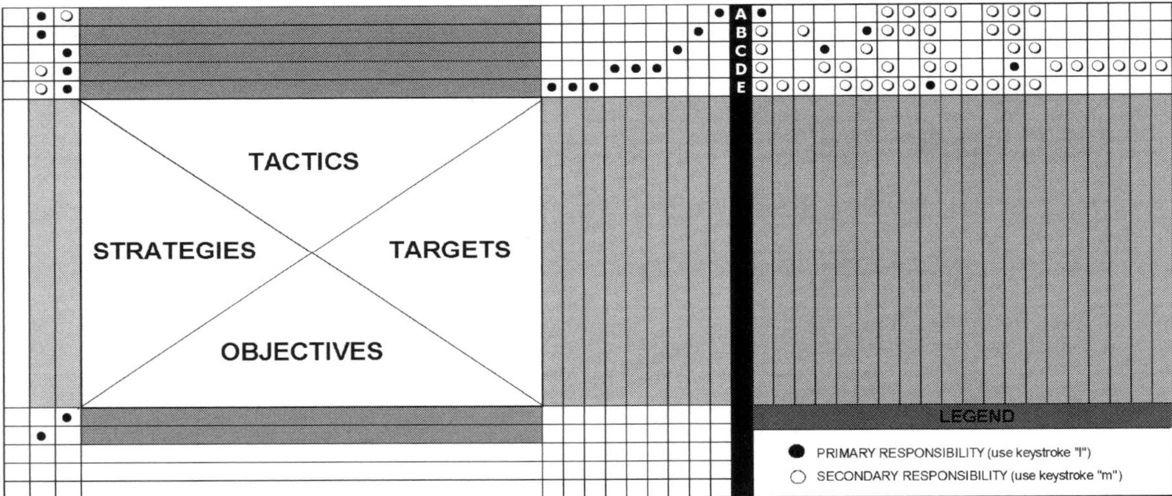

Use of Portfolio Analysis in Strategic Business Development

Portfolio analysis identifies the key elements and features to existing product and service lines to help a company develop new strategic products and services. Strategic business units (SBUs) or product groups within an organization often cross-utilize common operating practices. Modules are defined around these common practices and plotted in a matrix against the defined units. SBUs that have common modules allow for strategic benefits in resource sharing and optimization. Future product lines or business units can be customized to use existing modules, expanding scale and scope economies, and becoming a competitive advantage to new market entry.

	Modules			
SBU or product line	**Developers**	**Contractors**	**Marketing**	**Licensing**
Accounting software	Yes		Yes	Yes
Tax preparation services		Yes	Yes	
Audit support services		Yes	Yes	
Point of sale analytics	Yes		Yes	Yes
Government contracts	Yes	Yes		Yes

SWOT Analysis

SWOT stands for strengths, weaknesses, opportunities, and threats. The strategic planning tool uses internal and external competitive data to determine the most significant conditions under each element. A SWOT analysis is an essential strategic planning tool. It compares the internal competencies and external forces to maximize an organization's advantages and preserve its operation. Strengths and weaknesses reflect the internal environment, while opportunities and threats represent the external competitive environment. Each element is paired to each of the other elements by permutation and the conditions are compared in order to devise strategies that can expand or protect competitive advantage. For example, strengths and opportunities are analyzed together to generate offensive strategies. Threats and weaknesses are analyzed together to form defensive strategies. Analyzing strengths-to-threats and opportunities-to-weaknesses will generate transformative change opportunities.

PEST Analysis

PEST stands for political, economic, social, and technological. Like a SWOT analysis, a PEST tool allows an organization to assess stimuli and factors that will impact its competitive advantage and profitability. PEST analyses look at macro-scale factors that can impact the organization, for better or for worse. Often, PEST and SWOT analyses are used in combination to further advance strategic planning. PEST elements are external in nature and comparable to the opportunities and threats elements from SWOT.

Political	Public funding availability, regulatory hurdles, political stability, and labor
Economic	Market factors such as inflation, rates, trade, and regulatory imposed costs
Social	Social trends, demographics, culture, customs and beliefs
Technological	Advancements, research and development, rate of change

Business Continuity Planning

Business continuity serves as an organization's lifeboat should a catastrophic or unexpected event occur and disrupt business activities. Examples of negative disruptions include recalls, loss of material supply, data hacking, natural disasters, work stoppage, civil unrest, violence, and economic turmoil. Positive disruptions include unexpected rises in demand and sudden spikes in market share. Planning can follow an approach similar to FMEA or a fishbone diagram. The key components of continuity planning include:

- Perform a risk assessment to define what the types of failures might be for various business activities.
- Rank failure possibilities using scales for likelihood of occurrence and severity to the business operations. Perform these rankings for each business unit assessed.
- Execute corrective and preventative actions for the identified risks, starting with the highest ranked.
- Develop contingency plans for all probable disruptions, including step-by-step actions for leaders to take in each event.
- Test and reassess each plan routinely.

Leadership Roles and Responsibilities for Six Sigma Black Belts

Black belts play a central leadership role in the Six Sigma process. Many Six Sigma professionals serve in this role in their organizations, often working full-time on improvement projects. Black belts have two primary roles: to lead improvement efforts and to mentor green belts and lower-level professionals in Six Sigma. Black belts are expected to be competent in statistical methods, leading improvement teams in reducing variation, and coaching green belts into skilled improvement leaders ready to become black belts themselves. Black belts are able to identify the correct tools and methods for problem solving using the DMAIC and DFSS methods.

Deming's 14 Points for Transformation of Western Management Practices

Deming's most famous list of quality advice is very consistent with his 14 points for quality improvement. His belief that quality is the reason for success in business and society led him to create the 14 transformational points. A **constancy of purpose** for quality improvement; a **new quality philosophy**; and strong, lasting **leadership** form the first three points. Another point involves increasing **quality engagement** within a company. **Driving out fear** and **removing barriers** between departments—especially those that undermine employee workmanship—drive transformation. Several points focus on elimination of detrimental practices such as **eliminating quotas** and slogans for employees and **eliminating numerical goals** for management. Additional points focus on eliminating the mindset that quality can be achieved through **inspection** and that business should be **awarded based on cost, not quality**. The final points focus on taking action and sustaining improvements. **Action** is a necessary step to realizing improvements. By encouraging **training** and **self-improvement** of all employees, an improved culture is sustained. The final point is that a continuous improvement culture is an **ongoing system**.

Influence of Various Roles Within Improvement Teams

Black belts are often the most active contributors to Six Sigma improvement efforts. They often have the most improvement expertise in an organization and are very effective with a wide range of tools. Master black belts, though less common across industries, also hold very significant influence over improvement efforts, especially when managing several black belts. Champions, though not actively involved in the day-to-day improvement activities, can be very highly influential to allocating resources to projects, getting organizational buy-in, or clearing bureaucratic road-blocks in the organization to allow improvements to move forward. Green belts are less influential in the big decision making of projects, but can be highly influential when task-based employees working in a process are responsible to work with the proposed improvements. Green belts can help with implementing improvements in the process steps and overcome problems in implementation.

Organizational Roadblocks

Organizational roadblocks are often created in response to the resistance to change. Many organizations experience such resistance and the struggles of overcoming the resistance to allow breakthrough improvements to occur. The history of an organization and the workforce that runs it will mold the company's culture for better or for worse. As a company experiences patterns of evolution and revolution in how management, external influences, and internal workforces or processes interact, the resistance to improvement and acceptance of change will rise and fall.

Strategies for Effective Change Management

The seven strategies for effective change management are:

1. Communicate to the organization the case for change. Build awareness for that case.
2. Define the mission and vision for the change. Describe how success will look.
3. Establish the measurement system and goals for ongoing improvements in the short, mid, and long term.
4. Eliminate barriers to effective change. Catalyze and nurture the forces that drive the right changes.
5. Share and communicate on early success and progress within the team. Build confidence.
6. Sustain the achievements made through control measures such as auditing.
7. Build agile systems in the organization. Be prepared for future change.

Causes of Six Sigma Project Failure

Though there can be many reasons why projects fail, the most common reasons center around management, financial, execution, analysis, and DMAIC control. A critical element to the success of lean Six Sigma improvement initiatives is committed support from top leadership. Without this support, projects never have a chance to be successful. Furthermore, without management providing the capital and human resources needed to realize improvements, projects will fail and improvements will stall. Projects can also fail when the intended improvement opportunity (whether in cost savings or quality improvement) are misrepresented or not achieved as planned. When well-planned and validated projects are poorly executed in the implementation phase, final results can be poor or non-existent. Lastly, if well-designed and well-implemented improvements are not sustained, the old pre-improvement state will return.

Stakeholder Analysis and Impact Process

Stakeholders are groups or individuals that have a vested interest in the actions and outcomes of a business, organization, or team. Stakeholders can be external or internal to the organization or team, as well as primary or secondary. Primary stakeholders are more significantly affected by actions, while secondary ones are indirectly affected. Stakeholders to lean Six Sigma projects often include customers, executives, co-workers, engineering staff, R&D staff, unions, suppliers, and the industry itself, among many others.

A stakeholder analysis serves to include the needs and interests of stakeholders in the organization's decision-making process. A stakeholder impact analysis (SIA) tool is used to compile all relevant interests and concerns, evaluate the resulting claims those stakeholders may make, and prioritize each interest. Identifying the strategic challenge that each interest creates allows this analysis to be transferred into strategic planning. Other examples of stakeholder analysis tools include an influence/importance matrix, a multi-criteria decision making (MCDM) matrix, and a reverse stakeholder impact analysis (RSIA).

Multi-criteria Decision Making for Stakeholder Impact Analysis

Stakeholder Criteria	Weight	Hospital #1		Hospital #2		Hospital #3	
		Rating	Score	Rating	Score	Rating	Score
Emergency Services	0.25	3	0.75	2	0.50	4	1.00
Specialty Doctors	0.1	4	1.00	1	0.25	3	0.75
Ethical Practices	0.1	4	1.00	4	1.00	1	0.25
Customer Service	0.05	3	0.75	2	0.50	3	0.75
Proximity to Home	0.05	1	0.25	1	0.25	4	1.00
Bedside Manners	0.1	3	0.75	2	0.50	2	0.50
Outpatient Services	0.025	3	0.75	1	0.25	2	0.50
In-Network Providers	0.15	3	0.75	4	1.00	1	0.25
Medical Error Rate	0.1	4	1.00	4	1.00	1	0.25
Doctor to Patient Ratio	0.025	3	0.75	3	0.75	2	0.50
National Reputation	0.05	2	0.50	2	0.50	3	0.75
TOTAL	1.00	➡	8.25		6.50		6.50

Deming's Seven Deadly Diseases That Obstruct Business Success

Deming's seven diseases are led by the disease of **lacking a constancy of purpose**. In other words, the company does not have a mission and management has no vision to keep the company in business for the long-term—undermining stability and job security for employees. **Mobility of management** is considered a disease because achievement of the company's purpose is eroded when management is not committed to the longer-term success of the company. Job-hopping never allows for strong quality systems. A strong **focus on short-term profits** without awareness of long-term stability creates weak quality and productivity systems. **Merit rankings and annual reviews** undermine employee engagement and add detrimental competition and fear in the company. Because many important performance indicators may be unknown or unknowable, rigid **focus on visible figures alone** is a disease. Lastly, **excess healthcare costs** borne by the company get passed to the customer as cost of goods sold. Failure costs—termed **warranty costs**—are resources wasted on what could have been prevented.

Change Readiness Assessments

Change readiness assessments are performed by a black belt, master black belt or champion to understand how willing and capable a team or organization is to permitting the improvement to be pursued. The assessment gauges the target culture's receptiveness to change and can help in creating communications and strategies to overcome resistance to strong valid improvements. A resistance assessment model maps out the points of success necessary for improvement efforts and a score or assessment of how well the studied organization meets these expectations. An organization may often establish the readiness assessment as a milestone for beginning a project or initiative with a certain organization or team if scores are weak.

Benefits of Using Communication Plans for Organization Improvement

Communication plans serve to define the most effective and wide-reaching avenues of communicating the need for change, the goals and steps to the project, and the project outcomes. Critical elements of the communication plan include stakeholder awareness of the need for change and the problems facing the organization if no change is made. Much like a problem statement, these awareness efforts should focus on objective evidence and be limited on discussing premature solutions. Communication of the needs and how the improvement team(s) are progressing are important steps towards achieving improvement plans.

Deming's 14 Points for Quality Improvement

Deming's 14 points for quality improvement can be grouped into five phases and thought of as a cycle: commitment, team management, measurements, action, and communication. Commitment starts with senior management that takes **full dedication to quality** and its improvement. Management must make all **employees aware and engaged in quality** across the organization. Giving **reward and recognition** reinforces management's commitment to the work of the contributors. Team approaches to quality improvement begin with an established **quality committee** routinely overseeing a goal of zero defects. Quality **improvement teams** are staffed with contributors from key departments. From there, leadership and stakeholders determine measurement approaches, including a **cost of quality system** and the best means to identify **where current and likely quality issues exist**. Measurement of **individual development goals** is encouraged by senior leadership towards all employees. Next, the teams take action. Leadership declares a **zero-defects day** to set the new standard in the organization. Teams then **take formal action** on the identified deficiencies. **Communication of team challenges** and **training** on achieved improvements round out the cycle and help control the achievements. **Repeating the cycle** ensures a continuous improvement culture.

Joseph Juran and Statistical Quality Control

Juran's philosophy on quality included a high regard for management's role in driving quality control, quality planning, and quality improvement. These three concepts, termed the Juran Trilogy, were viewed by Juran as essential to effective modern and future management success. Juran's quality management course, titled "Managing for Quality," emphasized this trilogy as well as the increasing influence of quality in business and management. While at Bell Systems in the 1920s, Juran wrote and published an early concept of statistical quality control. Juran had 10 key points to his quality philosophy.

Juran's 10 Quality Points
Make the organization aware of the improvement need
Establish improvement goals
Organize teams for the effort

Juran's 10 Quality Points
Train and educate the teams
Execute improvement projects
Document and report results
Reward and recognize performance
Communicate
Compete for successes using measurements
Sustain momentum

Contributions to Quality and Continuous Improvement Made by W. Edwards Deming

Deming began his career in quality assurance within the US government. With the Department of Agriculture and the War Department, Deming was a champion and trainer of the new discipline of statistical quality control. Deming's work for the US War Department in rebuilding Japanese industrial activity was his most famous achievement. Japanese industrial quality became arguably the best in the world after following Deming's guidance. Like other famous quality figures, Deming promoted his 14 points for quality change. The Deming prize was created through the Japanese Union of Scientists and Engineers (JUSA) as a global quality award in total quality management. The Deming prize became the first premier industry quality award and further motivated quality efforts in Japan.

Philip Crosby and 14 Steps to Improvement

Philip Crosby introduced the term "zero defects" into the field of quality assurance. Crosby's most notable contribution was his 14 steps to quality improvement. Crosby's steps were strikingly similar to Deming's 14 points.

Management must clearly demonstrate its commitment to quality
A dedicated quality improvement team is established
Develop quality measurements
Understand the cost of quality and its use as a managerial tool
Raise quality awareness
Develop a defect identification and resolution process
Zero defects planning for all aspects of the organization
Train all managers and supervisors in quality and zero-defect principles
Hold a zero-defects day to announce the culture change
Goals and objectives are set by organization towards zero defects
Reporting system for employees to update management on goal progress
Develop a reward and recognition system for achievement
Capture knowledge and experiences through quality councils
Continuously reassess and repeat process for improvement

Armand Feigenbaum and Total Quality Control Process

Feigenbaum is best known for creating the total quality control (TQC) philosophy. The main goal of TQC is to have an entire organization aligned with common, customer-driven quality practices. The vision of TQC was that it spans all levels and units of an organization. He was an early champion for the use of cost-of-quality tools. Feigenbaum had four main principles of TQC:

- Competition requires continuous improvement to sustain competitive advantages
- Quality can be achieved without detriment to costs
- Innovation needs strong quality systems
- Management commitment is key in aligning the organization towards high-quality standards

Contributions to Quality and Continuous Improvement

Kaoru Ishikawa

Ishikawa was a central leader in the Japanese quality movement in the mid-20th century. After training under Deming, he developed the total quality control principles. Ishikawa's total quality control stressed quality as a responsibility for all employees, working in groups with full cooperation and not alone, and middle management bearing significant criticism. Ishikawa emphasized quality over profits and customers over producing firm. He routinely stressed the need for four audit types, including audit by top management, audit by division head, quality division audit, and mutual audits. He is credited with developing quality circles and the fishbone cause-and-effect diagram.

Genichi Taguchi

Taguchi is most known for his work on design of experiments, robustness, quality loss functions, the signal-to-noise ratio, and statistical design approaches. His famous quality loss-function linked minimizing process variation to minimizing the cost of quality loss. Achieving both goals, Taguchi argued, would maximize customer satisfaction, minimize loss waste, and be a benefit to society. He championed fractional factorial design of experiments to drive parameter design and tolerance design. Taguchi realized robust parameter design involved minimizing the effect of noise variables on control variables in a process. Taguchi popularized his advancements as the Taguchi methods in the 1980s in the United States.

Baldrige National Quality Award

The Baldrige Award of the United States is presented annually to the organization that best meets predefined criteria demonstrating excellence in quality management and performance. The criteria are divided into several key sections that assess the influence of quality in an organization and the results that are achieved. Sections in the criteria for performance excellence include:

- Senior leadership
- Strategy
- Customer focus
- Measurement, analysis, and learning management
- Workforce engagement
- Operations design
- Performance against competitors

Awards may be presented annually to three companies in each of six industry categories: education, healthcare, manufacturing, nonprofit, service company, and small business.

Porter's Five Forces Model

Michael Porter's five forces model describes five influential, qualitative, competitive forces that can influence an organization's strategy on pricing and profit. Some forces may drive pricing down while others influence higher pricing. Assessing the competitive industry forces allows a company to set economic strategy. The five forces include:

- Rivalry among existing firms
- Threat of new entrants
- Bargaining power of suppliers
- Bargaining power of buyers
- Threat of substitute goods or services

Force	Elements of Force	Example
Rivalry among existing firms	Differentiation, switching costs, number of competitors, slow growth	Competing soft drink brands
Bargaining power of suppliers	Availability, switching costs, relative size of buyer to seller	Few airplane suppliers drive up costs of new planes
Threat of new entrants	Regulation, economies of scale, brand loyalty, learning curve, high capital requirements.	Automobile manufacturing has large scale economies, regulation, and capital barriers
Bargaining power of buyers	Large buyer to selling firm, little switching costs for buyer, minimal differentiation of goods, brand power	Big box retailers holding purchasing power over goods manufacturers
Threat of substitute goods or services	Quality, relative price and performance, switching costs, availability	Private label brands, luxury versus non-luxury goods.

Six Sigma Black Belts Versus Master Black Belts

Both positions must demonstrate proficiency in lean Six Sigma concepts and must be capable of leading improvement projects and coach other Six Sigma professionals. Black belts lead projects with mid-level contributors such as green belts, engineers, line workers, and other stakeholders. Master black belts are responsible for leading a wide array of black belts, projects, and organizational improvement efforts. Master black belts have demonstrated advanced skills, many years of successful projects, and strong capabilities in leading other black belts. There are often different certifications for each belt.

Role of Six Sigma Green Belt

Green belts are trained in essential elements of lean and Six Sigma for the support of black belt-led projects. Green belts are nearly always performing lean Six Sigma project work in addition to their normal job duties. Green belts are tasked in improvement projects to provide highly capable task execution towards completion of the improvement. However, black belts are more skilled in team facilitation and statistical methods. Green belt training and certification can also be a very comprehensive way to strengthen the skills of an improvement or quality team.

Deming's Four Components to Organizational System Transformation

Deming's philosophy on the transformation of the systems of an organization centers on the main idea that all parts of an organization affect one another. The first component is systems appreciation. This means that if changes are made in one area, they are likely to impact another part of the business. The second component is knowledge of variation. It is important for an organization to know the difference between for-cause and random-cause variation and when to take action on that variation. The third component is to have a theory of knowledge. An organization must hypothesize and theorize about their operation and be able to test those theories in order to gain useful knowledge. The fourth component focuses on human psychology. All people respond to stimuli differently and have differing needs of acceptance and appreciation. Organizations need to account for those differences in systems transformation.

Organizational Process Management and Measures

Organizational Benchmarking

The most commonly used types of benchmarking include competitive, functional, internal, process, strategic, and generic. Competitive benchmarking focuses on direct competition within the same industry, while functional compares a firm's activity to a non-competitor in another industry performing similar functions. Similarly, process benchmarking compares a more specific internal process to that of an external entity. Internal benchmarking compares similar internal processes and business systems to an internal gold standard. Strategic benchmarking uses elements of collective strategic planning to create oriented improvements. Generic benchmarking looks at adopting best practices and higher performance approaches from firms in dissimilar industries that have solved similar problems to the firm.

Competitive, Process, and Internal Benchmarking

Competitive benchmarking is the comparison of an organization against a direct competitor, operating in either a local, regional, national, or global scale. The nature of the competition to an organization determines the scope and reach of the competitive benchmarking performed. It all depends on what the organization considers its market competition.

Process benchmarking and the related practice of generic benchmarking assess the performance of a defined process within the organization against that of another organization. An example would include comparing the checkout process of a competing retail store. The related generic benchmarking approach compares the organization to best-in-class performance of a variety of functions in order to draw in such practices for internal improvement.

Internal benchmarking compares internal divisions or functions against each other to attempt to improve low performers. An example of internal benchmarking would be the comparison of snack food manufacturing lines across dozens of sister factories creating the same products.

Caveats of Benchmarking an Organizational Process

The most critical caveat of benchmarking is the risk that what is adopted and adapted from other organizations may not be suitable for the seeking firm's culture and strategy. It can be enticing and satisfying to find best practices and plug them into one's organization hoping for great returns on investment, but the benchmarking process does not work that way. A firm must evaluate benchmarking results weighted against the culture, strategy, and developmental state of the organization. Another critical caveat is the protection of sensitive information when benchmarking or sharing with other firms. What seems like an innocent collaboration between firms can quickly change to a weakening of competitive advantage without non-disclosure or protective measures in place.

Process Steps in Organizational Benchmarking

Though several similar but distinct processes for organizational benchmarking exist, the approaches follow very similar common steps. Ironically, the most common approaches have many parallels to the DMAIC process. In benchmarking, early steps are taken to define the current process to be evaluated. This phase also can include scope, problem statement exercises, and team formation. Measurement and analysis steps in benchmarking approaches include compiling the right data both internally and externally from valid sources. This research must support well-planned and valid analyses. The analysis steps can include looking for gaps, comparing performance to the benchmark firm, or process comparisons. Implementation of best practices can include simple task execution, idea testing, and financial analysis for the ideal improvements to accept. Finally, controlling the benchmarked improvements is often performed through KPIs, strategic plan reviews, and repeating the benchmarking process as an ongoing cycle of competitive advantage protection.

Setting Performance Measures and Goals from the Benchmarking Process

Setting performance goals from valid benchmarking efforts eliminates the need for erroneous and illogical goal setting. Tying performance goals to the benchmark creates strategic and competitive meaning to such targets. The benchmark is often used as the default level of performance to be obtained. Improvement from that benchmark by an achievable degree is considered a target. Processes or business systems that reach the target are significantly exceeding the baseline benchmark. A stretch goal may be included to provide an extra incentive for the organization to maximize its improvement effort where possible. Whatever the objective, validation to benchmarking results provides meaning to previously irrational measures of organizational success.

Balanced Scorecards in an Organization

Balanced scorecards are the result of strategic planning and allow an organization to measure and analyze performance against critical success factors, both financial and non-financial (such as customer-focused). It is a way to link short-term actions with long-term goals. Financial measures give owners, shareholders, and stakeholders a view of the value and expenses, while non-financial can give stakeholders a perspective on customer value, operational performance, and quality. A balanced scorecard supports executive decision making in areas such as business planning, organizational learning, rewarding performance, and establishing the vision. Using the right mix of KPIs, both financial and non-financial, supports an organization's balanced scorecard goals.

KPIs and SMARTc3 Objectives

Key performance indicators (KPIs) are measurements used by organizations to monitor achievement against the important factors that lead to business success. KPIs may take many forms, but are often based on financial, customer, and process criteria. KPIs are the result of the critical success factors derived from strategic planning. SMARTc3 objectives are also used to link critical success factors to business results. These objectives are defined by the acronym and demonstrate that the objective measurement is clear. The SMARTc3 acronym is:

- **Specific** – clearly define the point of the objective
- **Measurable** – the organization should be capable of measuring their performance
- **Achievable** – performance must not be unattainable
- **Relevant** – don't have the organization work toward a meaningless objective
- **Timed** – define the time boundaries for achieving the objective
- **Caveat** – define the scope and limitations to the objective
- **3 – Three levels of success** – give baseline and stretch goals for achievement.

Example: Within 2 years, reduce the cost per patient treated within the hospital by 2% of 2015 levels without sacrificing quality of care, patient safety, and satisfaction. Two percent for good, 2.5% for very good, and 3% for outstanding.

Customer Loyalty Metrics

Customer loyalty metrics can provide objective evidence of how committed customers are to a company or brand. Though there are many types of loyalty metrics, those most commonly used focus on capturing and repeating customers. Effective measurement can be a starting point for validating specific sales improvement efforts.

Loyalty Metric	Description
Referrals	Referral rate represents the transfer of strong loyalty feelings from one customer to that of another. Customer-to-customer relationships are often highly trusting. Referrals can yield an expansion of high loyal customer base.
Retention	Retention rate demonstrates how valuable an organization or business is to a customer and how willing those customers are to stay affiliated with that business.
Renewal	Renewal metrics can show the extent of customer participation or membership in programs offered by a company.
Repeat	Repeat customer metrics have maximum value when they represent repeat sales, where the typical duration of purchase by that same customer between sales is long.
Churn	Churn represents customer turn-over. Churn = (1-Retention). Churn can help an organization focus on the reasons why customers leave.
Complimentary effect	Also called "share of the wallet," this metric refers to the gain companies experience when loyal customers to one brand also boost sales of a complimentary brand.

Leading Indicators, Current Indicators, and Lagging Indicators

Leading indicators are business performance metrics that foreshadow the actual quality or profitability actions that occur. Leading indicators often occur outside of the core process elements in an organization and eventually make an impact on the process. Current indicators are those that are directly witnessed in the process. Lagging indicators are those that occur after a process generates output, sometimes months later. In a manufacturing process, examples of leading indicators may include raw material quality and supplier reliability. Current indicators may include in-process yield and statistical process control. Lagging indicators can include customer complaints, changes in market share, and warranty costs.

Connecting Performance Measures to Organizational Strategies

The connection of performance measures to organizational strategies is commonly referred to as "creating a line of sight" between the two processes. The execution and coordination of the organization to achieve the strategic plan will be best tracked and achieved through performance measures. Success in the strategy is a matter of objective fact and less subjective opinion when linkage exists. This can be especially important for publicly traded organizations that rely on positive market results and shareholder satisfaction. Various measures such as financial, operational, HR, customer-focused, and quality will all be key indicators of successful strategy execution.

Revenue Growth, Profit Margin, and Market Share

Revenue growth is defined as the change in income that will be realized as the result of a strategy, initiative, or project. Profit margin is a percentage of revenue the firm keeps from sales after deducting costs and operating expenses. Profit margins may be predetermined before a process or product is designed by a firm. Desired profit margins may also influence the erosion in the short term of quality programs meant to sustain profits in the long term. Market share is defined as the proportion of business revenue obtained by a firm from a defined market of an estimated maximum revenue potential. Share very much depends on how the market is defined. Data for calculating these three values is often available within the accounting and sales functions of an organization.

Revenue growth	$\frac{\text{Change in revenue}}{\text{Previous revenue}} \times 100 = \%\text{ revenue growth}$ $\text{Compound annual growth rate (CAGR)} = \left(\frac{\text{Ending revenue}}{\text{Initial revenue}}\right)\left(\frac{1}{\text{years}}\right) - 1$
Profit margin	$\text{Profit margin} = \frac{\text{net income}}{\text{Revenue}} \times 100$
Market share	$\%\text{ Market share} = \frac{\text{firm revenue}}{\text{Total market revenue}} \times 100$

NPV and ROI in Project Selection

Net present value (NPV) is a common financial measure in project selection. NPV gives the change in organizational value that is expected to occur as a result of undertaking a project. Projects with higher positive value NPVs should be prioritized over lower positive and negative NPVs. Positive NPV values indicate that the revenue likely to be created from the project adequately covers the costs to implement the project. Return on investment (ROI) represents how well a project or organization will replenish the initial investment made to launch or create the project or product. Large and positive ROI values indicate that the return will be beneficial and substantial. ROI values are most effective at prioritizing projects. Financial statements and an organization's controller can often provide these financial figures. It is important to include finance and accounting colleagues on improvement project teams as well.

$\text{NPV (project)} = \frac{-I_0 + \sum F_t}{(1 + k + p)^t}$ Where I_0 = initial cash investment at time 0 F_t = net cash flow over period t k = required return rate p_t = inflation rate over time t	$\text{ROI (project)} = \frac{\text{Income}}{\text{Cost}}\text{ x (100\%)}$

Cost-Benefit Analysis

A cost-benefit analysis summarizes the expenditures and the gains from a choice or plan and shows the net result between both categories. A cost-benefit analysis can be either financial with hard costs and cash flows or more colloquial with estimates and non-financial items such as indirect benefits and soft costs. The net results of the cost-benefit analysis are used to demonstrate the financial benefit of performing a project or task versus another competing project. Champions and executives are responsible for allocating resources to projects likely to have positive returns on investment.

For example, a continuous improvement project may require labor, new parts, and training expenses of $15,000 NPV in the calendar year in order to implement an effective SPC weight control program for finished packages. The estimated operations savings (benefit) from doing the project is estimated at $150,000 NPV. The net cost-benefit is significantly positive, implying quantifiable benefit for every cost dollar.

$$\frac{\Sigma(\text{Net Present Value of Benefits})}{\Sigma(\text{Net Present Value of Costs})} = \frac{\$150{,}000}{\$15{,}000} = 10.0$$

Hard and Soft Costs

Hard costs are defined as those that can be considered tangible savings in current expenses in an operation. Operating profit increases as a result of saving hard costs through improvement projects. Hard cost savings have three key features:

- A 12-month expenditure history as a baseline state
- Existing expenses must be predetermined through budget process
- A measured impact on the operating profit of the business

Examples of hard costs include raw material costs and labor expenses

Soft costs are considered avoidance costs. By making improvements in a business, certain costs such as failure, waste, customer claims, and market recalls can be avoided. Soft costs may seem abstract, but historical data does provide good supporting evidence on their value. Key types of soft costs include:

- Budgeted costs that have not yet been recorded
- Non-budgeted costs that can be reduced through efficiency or productivity improvements

Cost of Quality

Quality costs are those that are incurred on an organization for a process or good when not meeting customer quality expectations. Cost of quality financial systems provide management with monetary figures on how well quality expectations are achieved. Four types of quality costs are based on their degree of lead or lag.

- **Preventative costs** – costs incurred in advance of producing or delivering a product or service. Because these costs are most likely to minimize other lagging costs, preventative is most desirable. Examples include design for Six Sigma, auditing, engineering, and training.
- **Appraisal costs** – costs incurred during the process to assure the final product meets expectations. Examples include raw material testing, finished product inspection, and calibrations.
- **Internal failure costs** – costs incurred after a product or service is completed, determined to fail expectations, but while still in control of the operation. Examples include the common waste categories in lean, scrap and rework, holds, and low-grading for poor quality.
- **External failure costs** – costs incurred when failure product is identified in the marketplace and out of direct control of the producing operation. Examples include warranty costs, customer complaints, recalls, and returned products. These costs are least desirable.

EBITDA and EBIT

EBITDA is a financial acronym for earnings before interest, tax, depreciation, and amortization. It is often equivalent to operating profitability, performance, or cash flow. EBITDA equals revenue minus expenses. Though they are effective for internal managers and leaders, public financial statements do not generally include these measures because they do not fully explain the financial prospects of an organization to an investor. Management often uses EBITDA as a financial performance measure for business units or factories that do not have control over broader financial situations like tax and depreciation of assets. EBITDA is often tied to mid-level management bonuses and incentives. EBIT stands for earnings before interest and tax. EBIT equals revenue minus broader operating expenditures. EBIT is used as a broader metric on the core operations and does include depreciation and amortization as well as any non-operating profits.

Revenue	**(in millions $)**
Sales	**$45,050**
Operation expenses	
Cost of goods sold	$25,100
Selling, general and administrative (SGA) costs	$10,600
Operating profit (EBITDA)	**$9,350**
Depreciation	$1,500
Amortization	$670
Earnings before interest and tax (EBIT)	**$7,180**
Interest expense	$950
Tax expense	$1,405
Net profit	**$4,825**

COGS, Operating Expenses, and Operating Profit

Costs of goods sold (COGS) is a financial measure that includes the expenses necessary to create the goods ordered by a customer. These direct costs often include raw materials and labor costs and exclude indirect costs—or operating expenses—such as quality assurance and marketing. COGS is the difference between starting and ending goods inventory plus any additional raw material purchases made in the same timeframe. Operating expenses are the sum of all expenses not directly involved in creating a product or service. The intangible value of operating expenses can often be overlooked. Operating profit is equivalent to EBIT and represents the profit generated from the core competencies of the business and excluding profit raised by other means such as investments or futures hedging.

$$\text{Operating Profit (EBIT)} = \text{Revenue} - \text{COGS} - (\text{Operating Expenses} - \text{Depreciation} - \text{Amortization})$$

Calculating Improvement Project Savings

Lean Six Sigma projects very often have attainable operational expense savings that coincide with quality improvements. Defining the amount of estimated savings often depends upon the business process, inputs, and outputs being improved. These operational savings are often tracked in hard costs. Customer-focused projects can also have revenue-centered improvement benefits as well as intangibles that are harder to quantify. Black belts often create tracking tools to estimate the potential savings or benefit of various project ideas using financials and process data unique to the processes being analyzed. Viable projects on such a list can be filtered and projects can be selected based on relevance to strategy.

Some examples of operational expense savings are generally focused on throughput, waste reduction, defect reduction, downtime, WIP reduction, inventory reduction, labor balancing and effectiveness, customer claims, yields, and capacity growth.

Cost Curves in Cost of Quality Analytics

Cost curves are useful in cost of quality financial programs because they approximate where quality reduction efforts show diminishing returns on investment. The traditional curves also show how continued investment is needed for achieving high quality results. Though spending on preventive costs is far better than spending on failure costs, the curves demonstrate a diminishing return to quality improvement and no net benefit as achieved quality level approaches perfection. More contemporary curve analyses do not indicate a diminished return on quality investment. Rather, cost of quality continues to be reduced as quality level increases.

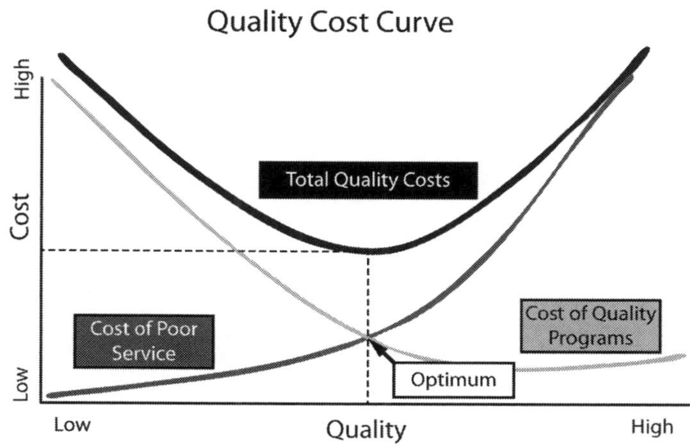

Team Management

Types of Teams

Virtual teams are represented by members that may or may not always be physically present with each other as they work on the project. Virtual implies dispersed and remote members performing team tasks at varying times, locations, and paces. Telecommunications and internet tools facilitate flexible virtual teamwork. Strong team charters and commitment to a common vision and goals ensures that virtual work remains effective. Cross-functional teams are composed of members that bring a variety of different yet essential expertise, points of view, and skills to the team. Self-directed teams are considered functionally autonomous and often lack a defined leader. The vision and the purpose of the team drive its actions and performance rather than one person alone. Self-directed teams are often ones that have worked together for a long time and have strong team dynamics.

Examples of Team Types		
Virtual	**Cross-functional**	**Self-directed**
A sales and operations voice of the customer project performing various qualitative studies across the country.	Stakeholders from sales, marketing, operations, manufacturing, quality assurance, and maintenance participated in a house of quality project.	Customer complaint investigation and response teams.

Six Sigma Project Champion

The Six Sigma champion is often a senior executive or leader that provides strategic guidance to black belts and their projects. The champion holds a firm stake in the success of the improvement efforts, clears organizational hurdles, reduces inertia, and removes barriers to aid the improvement efforts. Champions are able to direct necessary resources to project teams and obtain broader organization support for such improvements. Champions are often consulted or informed of project progress and should receive regular updates from black belts and project leaders. Champions are often very knowledgeable about the benefits of lean Six Sigma in quality improvements.

Factors That Influence Team Member Selection

The effective selection of team members is a critical task for the champion and black belts. Foremost, members should be considered who have enough time and focus to dedicate to the work of the project team. Conflicting workload and schedule do not make for an effective member of the team. The team member should have a desire to want to see an improvement in the process being addressed, or at least be open to change in the process. Those lacking this trait will often undermine the work of the team. The team members should have applicable skills and knowledge that will be beneficial to the work. Not every member needs to be an expert in all aspects of the scope, but each contributes a valuable insight that drives success. Subject matter experts, process line workers, and financial staff are often good examples of specialized skills that contribute to overall success. Lastly, members must be effective at working in teams. Individuals that bristle at team decisions, meetings, documented processes, and validated plans may not be ready for team improvement projects.

Factors That Predict Team Success

Awareness of the common factors used in successful lean Six Sigma improvement projects can help a team or black belts ensure an easier path to success for their own projects. The most common factors focus on themes such as performance indicators, planning, and training. Many of these factors are established during the define phase of DMAIC.

Two early prerequisites to success are management commitment and resources. Without support from top leadership and champions, improvement efforts will not make an impact and will not be sustained. Furthermore, teams that have well-defined goals, objectives, and performance indicators will be more focused on executing projects that help them reach those targets. Having an unambiguous purpose will keep the team focused as well. Strong team norms and training are essential to make the group work well together. Norms such as meeting facilitation, project charters, defined rules, and routine meetings are all supportive actions.

Team Motivational Techniques Used in Lean Six Sigma Projects

Hard and creative improvement work can cease without positive motivation for the workers performing the projects. Many project members are participating on top of their normal assigned duties. A very effective way for champions and black belts to prevent demotivated teams is to be honest and supportive of the team's efforts through actions. Enforcing commitment to the lean Six Sigma processes for improvement projects also prevents demotivation when teams encounter resistance. Two common motivational factors are rewards and recognition. Rewards are given following extraordinary contributions by the team or its individual members towards the success of the project. Common rewards include money, time off with pay, or a percentage of the project dollar savings. Recognition serves to have strong project contributors receive notoriety among their work peers for their efforts. More simply, recognition can be direct acknowledgement of individuals from their supervisors. Recognition can include awards, positive feedback, announcements to the firm regarding the work, or promotions.

Stages of Team Development (FSNPA)

The five stages of team development are forming, storming, norming, performing, and adjourning. Understanding the features of and transition between each step can help project leaders achieve high performance quickly. Development begins in a general environment of individual actions and transitions to an environment of interdependence within the team before finally adjourning to independence again.

- Forming features members getting acquainted and learning the social norms within the group. Relationships are built and leaders emerge.
- Storming is characterized by emotion, tension, and conflict as those early assumptions are tested. Resolving problems and moving through this phase is critical to the team's success.
- Norming features team members agreeing on standards of practice within the team and roles are better defined. Cohesiveness and communication are strengths of this stage.
- Performing stages show a mature, organized, and effective team. Motivation is high and leadership focuses on team self-management and strategy. Members complement each other's skills and weaknesses to achieve agile high performance.
- Adjourning ends the team's work and frees members to join new project teams. Recognition is a well-deserved part of this phase.

Impact of Team Communication Plans on Success of Improvement Projects

Communication plans for improvement projects are essential and should not be overlooked by teams, especially when large multi-site participation is involved. A team communication plan is very similar to a project charter. Elements such as goals and objectives help recipients of the communication understand the context. Continuous adherence to the plan is necessary to facilitate the project. While the formal plan is ideal, there are several supporting methods used to deliver the message to participants and stakeholders on a continuing basis. Examples include member status updates consolidated into one report, avenues of constructive feedback, action registers for tasks, meeting minutes captured and shared soon after meetings, and A3 or closeout summaries that capture the project results. Improvement efforts are most effective when using both internal and external communications plans. Internal ground rules that facilitate teamwork complement external status reporting to key stakeholders.

Internal Team Communication Plan

Responsible person	Deliverable	Recipient(s)	Means	Frequency
Team leader	Project status update	Executives, champion	Board meeting presentation	Monthly
Green belt	Document meeting minutes	Team members and champion	Template posted to intranet	After every weekly meeting
Champion	Feedback reports	Team leader	One-on-one interview	Every 8 weeks or as needed

Situational Team Leadership Approaches Used in Six Sigma Improvement Projects

Four common team leadership approaches are based on the degree of supportive behaviors and degree of directive behaviors used by a leader upon their team members. Supportive behavior is described as emotional and social guidance and leadership. Directive behavior is described as detailing tasks, time-frames for completion, and responsibilities to a team. Coaching leadership methods are best suited for those with high supportive and directive behavior. Team leaders must take a coaching approach to members who show good competence but are weakly motivated to contribute their best. Supporting leadership methods are best for members who are competent but hesitant to commit their highest levels of performance. Delegation leadership is used on top performers. Highly competent and motivated contributors need little influence and can have important work delegated to them. Lastly, directing leadership is reserved for enthusiastic novices on the team. Their motivation is very high, but their competence is a weakness. It is the team leader's job to balance personnel management according to these dimensions.

Conflict Awareness and Resolution Matrix

The conflict matrix represents degrees of assertiveness and cooperation that, in combination, will address potential ways to address conflict within improvement teams. Themes emerge from these dimensions when highs and lows are paired in combinations. Each theme is a useful approach for resolving conflict under certain conditions. Knowing the optimal conditions for using a certain approach will help defuse conflict effectively.

Low cooperation paired with low assertiveness represents an avoiding approach, where removing oneself from the conflict leads to resolution of insignificant issues. High assertiveness with low cooperation yields a competitive resolution approach; this dominant approach should be used with caution. High assertiveness with high cooperation creates a collaborative resolution method. Collaboration is necessary when strong support exists for both sides of the conflict and middle ground is necessary. Finally, low assertiveness with high cooperation is a deferential method. The individual doesn't have a preference for the outcome and surrenders to others to resolve the conflict.

		Cooperation	
		Low	High
Assertiveness	High	Competition	Collaboration
	Low	Avoidance	Accommodation

Overcoming Negative Group Dynamics

Negative group dynamics are behaviors of one or more members of a team that can have various degrees of detrimental impact on the progress of the team itself towards the desired outcomes. A black belt leading lean Six Sigma improvements will draw a variety of stakeholders and colleagues into improvement projects. Project leadership must be aware of such negative behaviors and be ready to use behavioral techniques to undermine the negative behavior and keep the team focused on the charter.

An example of a negative group behavior would include team members accepting opinions and outcomes without reliable results. This behavior is common in organizations that frequently jump from crisis to crisis looking for quick solutions. A black belt can overcome this behavior by steering the team to move forward with deliverable steps only after the data validates that progression can occur. Also, the leader can play the devil's advocate and seek reliable outside reviewers to support team decisions before allowing advancement of the project phase.

Groupthink

Groupthink is a phenomenon where members of a group uniformly agree on a decision or idea due to peer influence rather than through critical evaluation and ethical reasoning. Groupthink can be common where teams have dominating leaders or members that are easily influenced. Groupthink can lead to poor or inadequate decision making. Common indicators that groupthink is occurring include:

- Rationalization – where members devise justification for irrational decisions
- Self-censorship – members deliberately fail to raise concerns with decisions
- Negative stereotyping – often of outsiders
- Illusions of invulnerability – feelings of being above criticism open the team to high risk taking
- Illusions of group morality – leads to ignoring ethical considerations due to misbelief that all group actions are moral
- Illusions of unanimity – Silence is considered agreement.
- Peer pressure – conformance through intimidation by other group members.
- Mind-guarding – group members protect the group from outside thoughts and influence that may disrupt the unanimity.

Benefits of Meeting Management Through Agendas

Effective meetings for projects or continuous teams help individual contributors know the topics for discussion. The term "agenda" is used here not in the negative connotation, but in the definition of a pre-set list of points to be discussed in the meeting time. Written agendas also help contributors effectively prepare for the meeting in advance. Clarity on the content of the meeting adds intrinsic value to the time spent in the meeting. Without a defined agenda, the meeting may diverge on tangents, side topics, and not accomplish that which the meeting organizer intended. Often, effective meeting organizers will distribute an agenda ahead of the planned meeting and give approximate time frames to be spent discussing each topic. This practice helps the organizer stay on track with the meeting, complete the expected content, and not waste the time of the participants. Meeting participants are often welcome to suggest topics for the meeting agenda as well.

QUALITY IMPROVEMENT TEAM MEETING
WHERE/WHEN: Tuesday 8:00am to 8:50am in the Large Conference Room
AGENDA:
Opening welcome, roll call (5 minutes)
Review of last month project metrics (5 minutes)
Review of quality metrics (5 minutes)
Discussion of old business (10 minutes)
Discussion of new business (10 minutes)
Open discussion time (10 minutes)
Finalize action items (2 minutes)
Adjourn

Effective Meeting Minutes and Action Plans

Project or team meeting minutes are essential forms of communication in continuous improvement efforts and regular business. They serve as a formal means of communication as well as a record of actions discussed and executed. Clarity among team members regarding discussions, plans, participants, past and future actions, and responsibilities all ensure such team efforts progress effectively. The essential parts of meeting minutes include old business, new business, and action items. Old business content describes status updates and progress made on the topics discussed at the previous meeting. New business content describes upcoming or potential activity by the team. This helps prepare the team for future action. The action items section documents the tasks that individual participants are responsible to complete and the agreed timeframe for completion. In short, action lists document who does what by when. Other pre-requisite components of effective meeting minutes include timestamps (date, start/end times, next meeting time), participant names, and relevant addendums of context information.

Nominal Group Technique

The nominal group technique can translate improvement ideas from a brainstorming event into a smaller list of preferred choices for action. The technique begins with all project team members agreeing on a non-redundant set of improvement ideas, grouping ideas together where repeating. Each person then ranks each idea in descending order of best to worst. The rankings are added together from all participants and those choices with the highest ranking (lowest total score) are selected to implement or test. In short, the highest priority ideas are acted upon first.

Idea	Person 1	Person 2	Person 3	Person 4	Total score	Net rank
A	1	2	1	1	5	1
B	4	4	3	3	14	4
C	3	1	2	2	8	2
D	2	3	4	3	12	3

Multi-Voting in Improvement Projects

Multi-voting is a tool used to prioritize the improvement approach(es) most preferred by a team. Typically used after a team brainstorm session, the team lists all suggested improvement approaches and each team member votes for their top choice. A facilitator eliminates the desired number of options below a vote-count threshold. A second round of voting is done on the remaining options. After another reduction in available options, a final round of voting may be done to narrow the list to the desired minimum. The remaining options carry the most preference to the team members and should be pursued first. A drawback to this method includes the risk of groupthink and negative influence on members casting votes.

Performing a Needs Assessment for Training with a Team or Organization

A training needs assessment documents the gaps that exist between the desired state of performance and the current state of performance for an individual or team. Executing a project plan or organization-wide strategic plan often requires persons involved to be competent in the skills that will achieve those plans. A leader performing a training needs analysis would begin by understanding the body of knowledge necessary for the target employee in order to meet the desired outcome. Data must be compiled—both objective and subjective—to complete a thorough assessment of individual or team performance and build a training plan.

Modes of Learning and Adult Learner Training Delivery Theories

Modes of learning are the approaches by which a trainer can effectively impart knowledge upon trainees based on the best-fit method of trainee learning. Effective training depends upon how the trainee receives and learns the information. One method may not suit all trainees. Examples of learning modes differ by degrees of physical and sensory stimuli. Methods such as self-directed learning and workbooks are minimally interactive but can supplement other learning. Methods such as lectures, discussions, and case study review all provide more interactivity with trainers or experts. On-the-job training, simulations, experience, and coaching provide the highest levels of interactivity for learning. The ideal combination of approaches depends on the learners themselves.

Adult learning behaviors are uniquely important for continuous improvement training delivery. The motivations and preferences for adults are different than youth. Adults are often motivated by career, social, and performance goals while having various constraints such as schedule, family responsibilities, and inattentiveness to non-work concepts. Often, learning is more effective for adults when it can be related to their existing job or workplace challenges. Preferred training delivery methods can also vary among different age groups of adult workers.

Evaluating Training for Effectiveness

Training program evaluation for effectiveness is an often-overlooked practice in organizations. While many assume that training offerings are sufficient, the applicability and value of training can vary and be ill-suited to an organization or individual. Without evaluation, such weaknesses cannot be found until after the training has been delivered. Evaluation and linkage to strategic planning is essential to effective training delivery. A checklist approach to evaluating training programs can be used. Evaluation criteria are generally bulked into categories of validation, delivery, and outcome. Validation-type criteria can include content, accuracy, and semantics. Delivery-type criteria include format, progression, conveyance to trainees, and logistical features. Outcome-focused criteria include learning styles, ownership, and evaluation.

Activity Network Diagrams

Activity network diagrams (AND) are visual representations of the sequence of project tasks as nodes and their interrelationships. ANDs are an effective way to map the critical path of a project and schedule the sequential tasks required. The diagram is also referred to as an arrow diagram. Steps in a project are mapped out with arrows directing through the flow of the tasks and showing precursor and downstream relationships. Each task has a precedence task that supports the layout of the diagram; without precedence, the diagram would not flow logically. Knowing the duration of each task, in combination with precedence, will allow for the longest continuous duration to be highlighted in the diagram. This would represent the critical path (highlighted in green).

Task	Precursor	Time
A	None	10 days
B	None	18 days
C	a	5 days
D	b	10 days
E	b	6 days
F	c	17 days
G	d	11 days
H	e	10 days
I	f, g	12 days
J	h	19 days

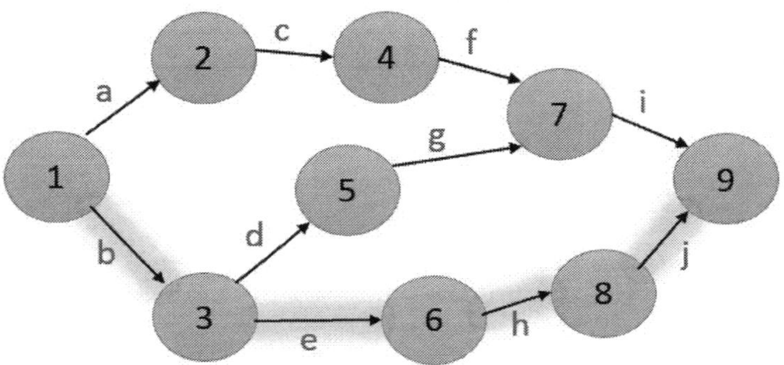

PDPCs

Process decision program charts (PDPCs) are one of the seven essential management planning tools. PDPCs are a form of contingency analysis, where the objectives and corresponding tasks to be completed in a project are listed along with all relevant and significant ways that the task could fail. Each failure is assigned a contingency plan in order to hedge against task failure. These contingencies can be planned in advance so that, in the event of failure, the contingencies can be executed and the project is likely to remain on course and not derail. PDPCs are similar to a fault tree analysis and can be considered a lighter version of a FMEA. The failure modes in a PDPC and their likely frequencies are often obtained from prior experience. PDPCs are very advantageous for situations where failure likelihood is unknown. Having contingencies available mitigates the risk of project failure. Supporting data for failures and contingencies can also be found from subject matter experts, technical whitepapers related to the tasks, or stakeholders involved in the project.

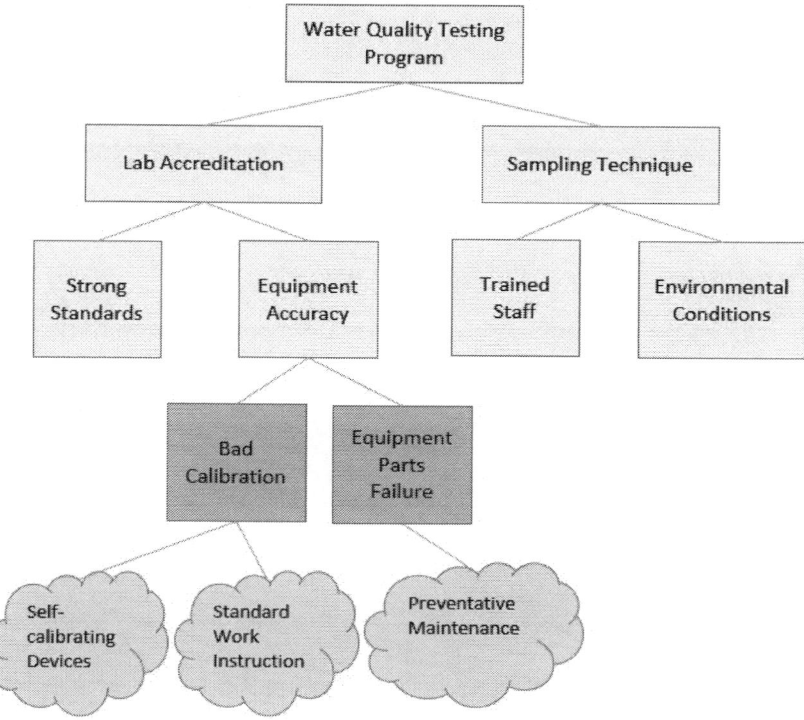

Matrix Diagrams

Matrix diagrams serve to give insight into the relationships between different datasets facing an improvement project. It is an essential management tool that comes in many forms based on how many types of sources are to be analyzed. By comparing relevant datasets amongst each other using any of several diagram methods, a team can gain useful information and knowledge for improvement or strategic planning. The six types of matrix diagrams used in lean Six Sigma include X, Y, C, L, T, and Roof-type diagrams. For example, an L-shaped diagram often summarizes specifications and can be represented as:

	Particle size (mm)	**Density (kg/m³)**	**Appearance**
Resin A	0.4	116.2	Smooth and tan color
Resin B	0.7	70.0	Grainy with pink color
Resin C	1.0	15.0	Coarse with white color

Prioritization Matrices

Prioritization matrices involve giving weight (or prioritization) to certain criteria over others to determine the best options among several choices. Weighting criteria act as a multiplier for each ranking of an option. Depending on the intended result, the highest or lowest scoring option would be considered the priority choice. Prioritization matrices can be used in selecting ideal projects, root causes, or choices from a list of many. After weights are agreed upon or determined by leadership or an outside source, options are assessed, ranked, and multiplied by each weight criteria. The results can be summarized in an L-diagram and the top priority option(s) are clear.

	Criteria			
	Particle size (mm)	**Density (kg/m³)**	**Appearance**	**Total weighted rank**
Weight	0.80	0.15	0.05	
Resin A	1 x 0.80 = 0.80	3 x 0.15 = 0.45	2 x 0.05 = 0.10	1.35
Resin B	2 x 0.80 = 1.6	2 x 0.15 = 0.30	1 x 0.05 = 0.05	1.95
Resin C	3 x 0.80 = 2.4	1 x 0.15 = 0.15	3 = 0.05 = 0.15	2.70

Tree Diagrams

Tree diagrams are related to the work breakdown structure (WBS) in project management and to flow diagrams. Tree diagrams are a type of flow diagram where all of the necessary components and sub-components of a goal or objective are mapped out to their smallest tasks. The orientation of the tree can depend on the type of quality tool using the diagram. Tree diagrams are created from a clear task or objective as a starting point. Subtasks and activities are then created within single or multiple layers until all granular components of the starting task or objective are mapped out. Tasks, subtasks, and activities are linked using connecting lines. The final tree is verified to ensure that the right elements were captured and no items can be further broken down in to subparts. A benefit of tree diagrams includes clear understanding of the elements and relationships of those elements in a process.

Interrelationship Diagraphs

Interrelationship diagraphs help a team map out how various factors within a complex problem are interrelated by cause and effect. Knowing the interrelationships can help a team plan out improvement tasks more effectively and understand how improvements may impact other parts of a process. All concepts and aspects of a project are spread out visually and each item is organized based on the impact they would create on other concepts if they are changed by the team. Impact of change is indicated by an arrow towards the factors that would bear the impact. Similar to a fishbone diagram, all elements of the diagraph would lead to a final intended goal or result.

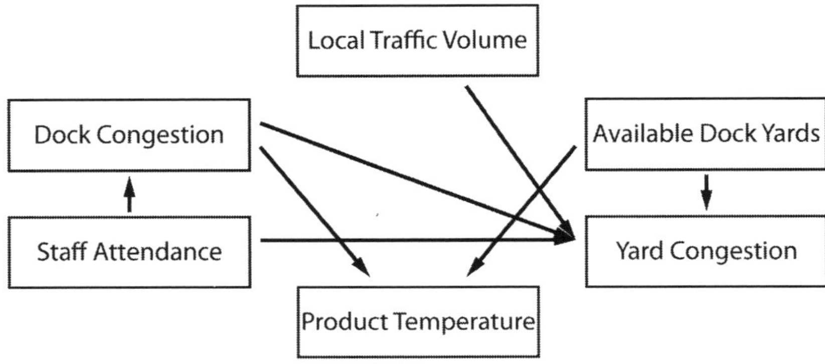

Affinity Diagrams

Affinity diagrams are commonly created as mind maps to group similar ideas from a brainstorming session. Broader categorical descriptions are created where several ideas can be grouped together. This process helps focus the group efforts towards a smaller set of manageable themes or lines of work. Another example of affinity diagraming is found in the Ishikawa fishbone diagram. The root cause analysis tool includes broader categories of man, material, method, machine, measurement, and environment. These categories often contain several examples of contributing causes related to each category. Categorization allows team members to more effectively process the improvement approaches mentally.

Creating an affinity diagram

- Generate all ideas from brainstorming
- Document all ideas on cards or sticky notes
- Session participants group similar ideas into common clusters
- Discussion among the group regarding clusters precedes final determination of affinity groupings.

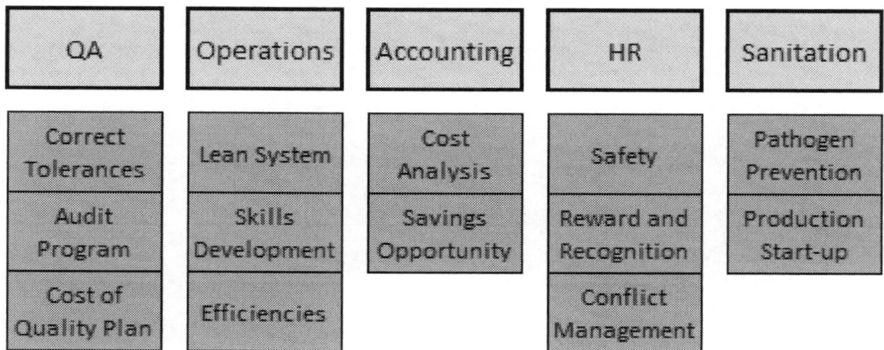

PDCA Cycle

PDCA stands for plan-do-check-act and may also be referred to as plan-do-study-act or PDSA. W. E. Deming created the PDSA process improvement tool, building upon the PDCA work of Shewhart. PDCA is an ongoing cycle of improvement phases where improvements are planned, enacted, and then assessed for effectiveness. Planning includes developing measurement tools to be able to assess the improvements. The assessment determines the next course of action, whether that is to modify the improvements or move on to another project. The cycle continues as a tool for long-term continuous improvement in an organization. The check and study steps have the same intent.

The improvement needs to be evaluated closely, objectively, and without bias in order to be confident that the improvement supports the desired outcomes.

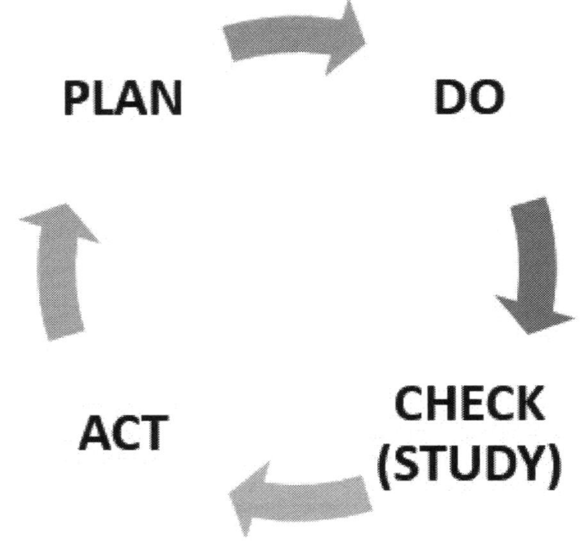

FFA

The force field analysis (FFA) helps a team visualize and assess the factors that are driving change. It is also called the Lewin's model. Such forces can often be considered to drive or resist that change and thus are pitted against each other visually with magnitude representing the relative strength of a factor. The analysis can help a team overcome barriers to necessary change. The 5 key steps to FFA include:

- Pre-determined goal statement prepared by project team
- Brainstorming session to capture the driving and resisting forces to the goal
- Document all driving forces that help reach the goal, as well as the resisting forces that inhibit the goal
- Assign scores or arrow magnitudes to each force to represent prioritization and influence, respectively
- Develop strategies to weaken the resisting forces and strengthen the driving forces towards change

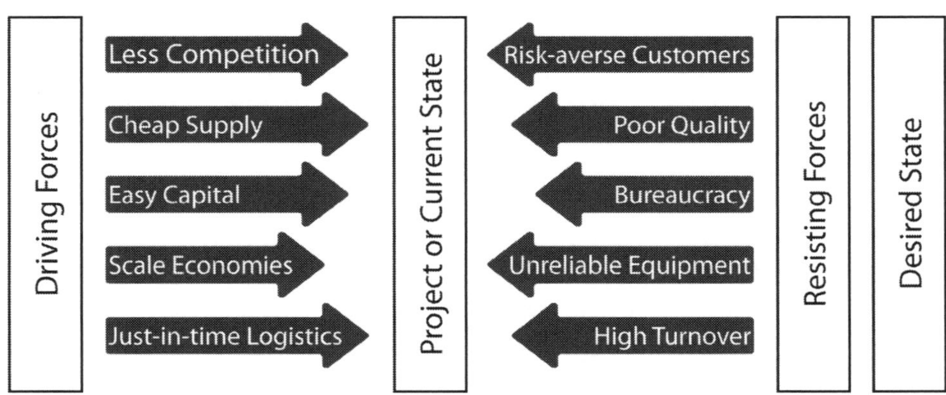

EFFORT/IMPACT ANALYSIS

The effort/impact analysis is a simple matrix that categorizes potential actions by their degree of impact to the goals of the organization and by their degree of work and resources needed to complete. The simple matrix is a quick and effective prioritization tool for starting improvement tasks. Clarity is needed among stakeholders regarding the subjective levels of impact and effort for the actions considered. The tool is very similar to a Johari window.

	Effort (resources needed)	
IMPACT (towards goals)	**Small**	**Large**
Large	Complete these actions first. Most benefit for the least resources.	Longer-term planning needed to achieve these actions.
Small	Easy to complete. Complete between highest priority actions.	Avoid these costly and low-impact actions until all other priorities are done.

BRAINSTORMING PROCESS

Brainstorming is an ideation and innovation process where teams generate uninhibited ideas related to a certain subject. Brainstorming is often used in the analyze phase of DMAIC to generate testable improvement ideas and new lines of thinking about solving old problems. A critical element to effective brainstorming is uninhibited and non-judgmental sharing and collaboration of ideas. Ground rules should include no positive or negative feedback on ideas. Post-brainstorming analysis and feasibility of ideas will occur. Creative brainstorming is not effective if team members are critical and evaluative of each other. Even the most mundane ideas can spark creativity and new thinking in others.

Brainstorming Process and Caveats

Step	Caveat
Set brainstorming rules for the whole team	Provide helpful material to document ideas. Reinforce openness, creativity, and non-critique of ideas until later.
Frame and discuss the issue at hand.	Offer additional perspective to help members make exploratory ideas. Frame the idea generation but do not bias the ideas to fit preconceived direction by its leaders.
Give individuals time to think	Balance thinking time with creative ideation time.
All ideas are spoken aloud and recorded	Encourage expansion of past ideas, encourage wild ideas. No idea is unfit to be documented. Everyone should participate.

TEAM PROBLEM AREAS

JUMPING TO SOLUTIONS

Teams are represented by many types of personalities. Some are very enthusiastic about solving the problem and moving on to the next effort. Such individuals, and the teams they work on, can fall victim to the problem of jumping to solutions. Jumping to solutions refers to individuals or the group determining a solution before measurement, analysis, and validation are able to confirm that a solution will effectively eliminate the problem. Individuals are often pressured to make an accomplishment, be quick to solve the problem, or are reluctant to spend resources in testing ideas for valid solutions. Black belts must be skilled at pacing the project effectively, keeping individuals from jumping too quickly without effective analysis, and know when to have impatient stakeholders contribute to the improvement process at effective steps in the project.

Negatives

Many workers looking to solve workplace problems with other colleagues have encountered negative attitudes towards continuous improvement and innovation. The classic response from negative persons include, "We tried that and it failed," "That will never work," or "That's not the way we do it here." These responses are often intended to undermine the improvement effort and maintain the status quo. Sometimes, the comments are the result of frustration over previous improvements that were ineffective. A skilled black belt can recognize the stakeholders and team members that assume this role and to shield the motivation of the remaining team from these emotions. Keeping dedicated time for constructive criticism and counter-arguments can help balance participation from positive and negative individuals. Motivating the negative persons to lead analysis efforts so that those persons help objectively validate or reject improvement ideas can help change negative attitudes into optimistic ones. Coaching negative players or replacing such influences with better contributors can be a last resort.

Dominating and/or Overbearing Member

A dominating and/or overbearing team member is someone that exerts detrimental and disproportionate influence over the group. These persons are often self-proclaimed experts or persons with role power over the other team members. These persons dominate the conversations and tend to subvert the team process in order to achieve their own objectives. Black belts can lessen the influence and disruption these members exert by controlling discussions, facilitating meetings effectively, encourage broad participation from other members, and coach the overbearing person to be a better participant. Effective team selection, stakeholder analysis, and project chartering can lessen the influence of such persons.

A3 Report

The A3 report was popularized by Toyota as a means to consolidate a full lean Six Sigma project report into one A3 size paper (11 inch by 17 inch) to simplify the communication of the project results. Several variants of the A3 style can be used based on the purpose of a report and the DMAIC phase represented. Key elements include simple and succinct word choices, visuals for communicating results, and limited bullet points. All content has meaning. A3 variants include:

Variant	DMAIC phase used	Description
Proposal	Define	Define the evidence for improving current problems
Problem solving	Analyze improve	Explain how analyzed data led to execution of improvements
Status update	All	Updating current state of the project to stakeholders
Sustaining	Control	Summarize the project to preserve organizational knowledge

Management and Planning Tools

The commonly known management tools for quality include activity network diagrams, affinity diagrams, interrelationship diagraphs, tree diagrams, matrix diagrams, priority matrices, and the process decision program chart (PDPC). These tools collectively are heavy with project management features and allow the improvement leader to be effective with planning quality and lean Six Sigma projects. The tools support the determination of interrelationships, schedules, and ideas that make up project components. All are designed to take complex data and make project decision-making and execution easier for the leader and team.

Maslow's Hierarchy of Needs

Maslow categorized a hierarchy based on how human needs are satisfied by priority. Lower-order needs must be met first before higher-order needs can be fulfilled. Maslow also theorized that persons' desire to continue moving higher on the hierarchy fuels motivation for meeting their own needs. To Maslow, unsatisfied needs motivate one's behavior. Different persons, team-members, stakeholders, and employees have different needs based on many contributing factors. The hierarchy is useful when team or project leaders must create and sustain performance; they must be aware of the individual needs of stakeholders.

Hawthorne and Herzberg Studies

The studies performed at the Hawthorne factory were designed to determine the working conditions that optimized worker productivity. The study focused on variables such as lighting intensity, duration of breaks, and length of the workday. Results indicated that employees were more productive when lighting was increased or decreased. The study concluded that workers were more productive when attention was paid to them, as in the study. The Hawthorne effect began what is known as human relations theory.

The Herzberg studies popularized satisfiers and dissatisfiers in management theory. As the names imply, satisfiers were factors of employment that were generally pleasing to workers. Satisfiers included recognition, advancement, responsibility, and achievement. Dissatisfiers, also called hygiene factors, were factors that, if not well addressed, would create dissatisfaction among workers. Dissatisfiers include salary, benefits, working conditions, and worker-manager relationship.

DMAIC PROCESS

The DMAIC acronym is used in Six Sigma to represent the 5 phases of statistical improvement: define, measure, analyze, improve, and control. The define phase identifies the process, the problem, and the quality expectations. The measure phase seeks to establish correct and accurate measurement systems to drive analysis. The analysis phase generates hypotheses and tests those hypotheses with valid data to draw improvement conclusions. Implement phases execute on the statistically validated improvement approaches. Control ensures that improvements are sustained long after the project ends.

Phase	Example Tools Used
Define	SIPOC, project charter, critical-to-quality, benchmarking, project management, house of quality
Measure	MSA, data collection plans, sampling, capability, yield, descriptive statistics and distributions
Analyze	Pareto, hypothesis testing, regression, ANOVA, FMEA, non-parametric tests
Improve	Kaizen, DOE, lean
Control	Statistical process control, auditing, work instructions, SOPs, check sheets

Internal Customers

Internal customers to the Six Sigma team may be at the micro level or the macro level. Micro level internal customers may be the next piece of equipment down the production line that receives high DPMO parts from the machine in the scope of a project. A micro level internal customer may also be another department operating within the factory that depends on effective work from others internally. In contrast, the macro level internal customers can include other divisions such as sales and marketing that benefit from quality and customer satisfaction improvements. Macro level internal customers also include executives and project champions.

Generally, these internal customers expect different levels of quality between each other but can all agree that quality must meet or exceed expectations. For example, downstream line workers might expect WIP parts to be within tolerances. Sales colleagues may expect that customer needs are anticipated and product performance adapts to those changing needs.

External Customers

External customers are stakeholders that are not directly employed by the organization. Most traditionally, external customers are those that purchase a firm's products or services and have the most significant stake in product quality in return for revenue. External customers may also be partnering firms that do business with an organization and have a stake in the success of the primary organization. Examples include service vendors, legal firms, consultants, and outsourcing firms. Traditional external customers consider basic economic principles when deciding how to spend their money. Where substitute or competitive products or services exist, many factors such as quality will influence how customers spend their limit resources. The voice of the customer drives quality requirements. External customer analyses must focus on quality expectations. Voice of the customer, house of quality, and quality function deployment are all common tools for translating quality expectations into practice.

Customer Data Collection Methods

Customer data collection is a critical element to the define phase of DMAIC and to affirm what is considered not value added in a lean initiative. Customer surveys are question banks, often done online, where qualitative and quantitative data on experience, satisfaction, service, and quality can be obtained. Surveys often have dichotomies, where questions beget various follow-up questions based on response. Focus groups bring together participants from target demographics and an individual or panel of researchers seek perspectives, opinions, and behaviors from the targets. Interviews generally have fewer participants or are one-on-one. Customers are individually interviewed to gain their preferences and input. Observations are generally passive and focus on witnessing customer behavior in random or mock settings. To have richer information, market and customer research often combines multiple customer data collection approaches.

Effective Data Collection Design and Challenges of Validity and Reliability of Customer Data

Well-designed customer data collection programs begin with several essential elements. Collection methods must be non-subjective and reliable, regardless of collection approach. Consistency and objectivity ensure that data integrity and the resulting analyses using the data are reliable. Collection must be relevant to the analyses intended. Approaches to how data is collected must be focused enough so that relevant data is gathered. Third, capturing data from a variety of sources aids in robustness of the data set as a whole. Finally, validated, unbiased, and independent data sources are ideal in order to get real-world data integrity for further analysis.

Data validity refers to the collection of correct and useful data. Data validation is important so that analyses will contain minimal erroneous data points that reduce the effectiveness of the analysis itself. An example of validation is designing a database to only accept a certain format of temperature data in defined units of measure. Data reliability involves how well a collection plan is reproducible, meaning how well the same collection method would generate similar results if used on two separate sample sets.

Customer Expectations and Needs

Customers often seek to impose quality expectations upon their suppliers or vendors. These expectations can be explicitly described in product specifications or implicitly discussed in product development or failure claims settings. Both internal and external customers have defined expectations for the goods they purchase. Expectations can range from generalities (500 parts delivered by Tuesday) to highly detailed (wafer thickness tolerance of 2.0mm ±0.01mm and capability of >1.33). Customer expectations or needs may or may not be quantifiable. Quality tools include critical to X and CTQ flow-down diagrams.

Critical to X

Critical to X (CTX) is a process that identifies critical quality expectations and needs from customers. The CTX process supports the transition of such critical factors into a quality function deployment and buildout of internal quality programs to meet customer expectations.

X serves as a placeholder for a variety of important factors to customers. Common X variables include critical to quality (CTQ), critical to process (CTP) and critical to cost (CTC). The factors may be documented qualitatively or in the form of customer specifications. CTQ focuses on the customer impact of quality. CTP focuses on the independent input variables that make an effective process used to create customer goods. CTC aims to meet customer requirements surrounding product or service cost.

Critical to Quality Tree and a CTQ Flow-Down Diagram

A critical to quality tree diagram provides a team with a visual breakdown of the critical customer quality requirements and often includes known or likely tolerance information. The level of detail increases as the tree continues to branch out. CTQ trees offer a mind map of quality and are a strong precursor to quality function deployment. A critical to quality flow-down is a mapping process that joins organizational strategy to the CTQs and their relevant specifications. The flow-down diagram begins with strategic initiatives or KPIs listed, with following layers of the diagram indicating subordinate objectives. Those subordinate objectives are linked to CTQs (or other CTX elements). CTQs bear characteristics known as constituents, or elemental data streams that may create the

CTQ. Finally, measurement systems are the most granular element of the diagram. CTQ flow-downs are very effective in the define phase of DMAIC and DFSS.

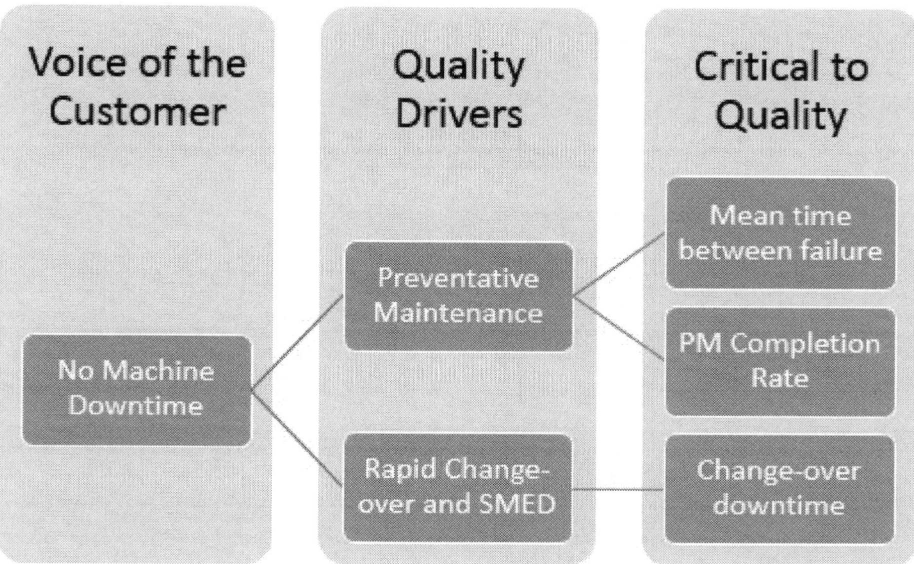

Quality Function Deployment

Quality function deployment (QFD) is a tool used in the define phase of DMAIC to systematically translate customer-defined critical to quality (CTQ) elements into technical requirements and engineering specifications. The tool uses four combined matrices to create a summary of relationships between customer requirements and resulting process parameters to create goods or services that meet those requirements. QFD also translates the customer voice into salesforce language and further into engineering and operations understanding. Cross-functional teams from the organization are important for creating a QFD successfully. To further strengthen the analysis of customer voice, the QFD matrix often includes competitive data, co-relationships of requirements, and weighted scores for communicating significance to requirements. QFD deployment in product development can significantly reduce post-launch quality costs, especially when used in development with designed experiments.

Components to the Houses of Quality

The quality function deployment (QFD) tool includes eight distinct features that build the house of quality. Customer requirements are the first element. These are derived from voice of the customer studies and are often categorized. The technical requirements that determine how to meet the customer requirements are next listed perpendicular across the top of an L-matrix. The relationship matrix plot is created for eventual symbol and scoring of relationships. These relationships are scored by strength and weakness in positive or negative direction of impact. Fourth, two additional sides of the matrix are added for documenting competitive comparisons against technical and customer requirements. Those competitive comparisons are ranked by internal strength. Action plans based on the competitive analysis are then included in the matrix. Target values for the technical requirements and weighted scores for each customer requirement are then added. Weights are calculated from customer requirement importance scores and matrix relationship values. Lastly, co-relationships are plotted as the roof of the house to show positive or negative relationships between technical requirements.

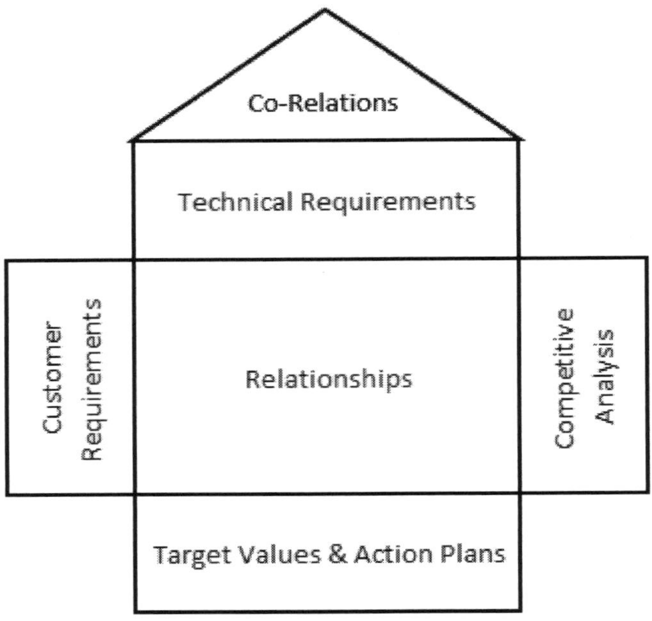

TRANSLATION OF CUSTOMER INPUTS AND REQUIREMENTS INTO PROCESS AND PRODUCT PARAMETERS

The results of the initial house of quality exercise that directly translates customer requirements into engineering characteristics can and should be reanalyzed in follow-up house matrices. This ensures that customer-validated engineering specifications are baked into the manufacturing process. The quality house matrix and method can translate engineering specs into parts specification plans. Parts plans can be translated into operating process planning. Finally, the operating plans can be translated into production planning requirements. End-to-end linkage using the house matrix is unambiguous, validated, and quantitative. Translating customer needs to processing parameters is minimally subjective using multi-level house of quality analyses.

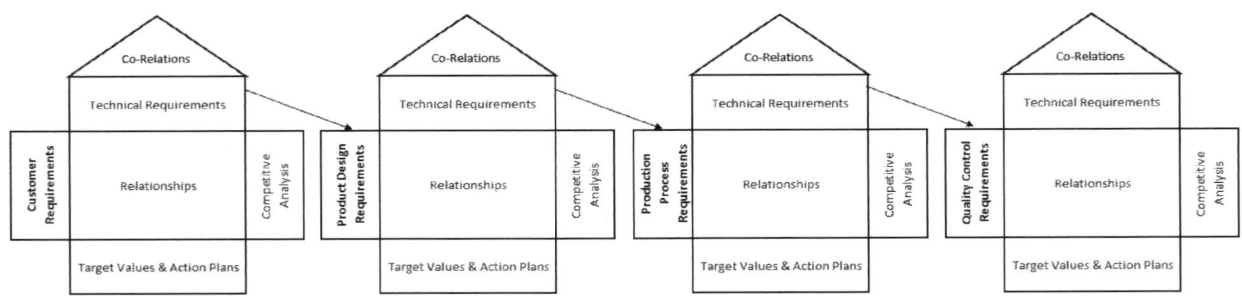

SIPOC MAP

The acronym SIPOC stands for suppliers, inputs, processes, outputs, and customers. SIPOC maps outline the value chain of a process and are commonly used in the define phase of DMAIC in order to present the scope of the stakeholders, raw elements, expectations, and processes bearing the problem(s). The map helps provide a higher-level perspective of the key elements to a process. The map begins with listing all relevant processes under consideration. Inputs and outputs, often in the form of specifications which are relevant to the process, are then listed, followed by the upstream suppliers and downstream customers. Additional data is often included to define the measurement tools used or needed to assess the inputs and outputs. SIPOC diagrams help improvement teams and their stakeholders agree on the process to be fixed.

Suppliers	Inputs	Process	Outputs	Customers
Acme Sliced Pepper Company Mom's Bulk Cheese Company Homestyle Breading Company	2-inch sliced jalapeño peppers in brine 1-inch sliced jalapeño peppers in brine 55-gallon liquid cheddar cheese Fine crumb whole wheat breadcrumbs	[1] Rinse peppers [2] Pump cheese to dispensers [3] Fill peppers [4] Double pass breading [5] Freeze [6] Package	34 count/pound breaded stuffed peppers 52 count/pound breaded stuffed peppers	Big Box Retail Center Happy's Restaurant Chain Pacific Prison System

Kano Model

Noriaki Kano's customer satisfaction model describes the relationship between three customer factors: dissatisfiers (must-be), satisfiers (more is good), and delighters. Customer awareness through these factors can help an organization obtain or sustain competitive advantage in a market. Dissatisfiers are factors that must be present in the final product, service, or experience else the customer is immediately dissatisfied with the purchase. Examples include basic safety and essential function. Satisfiers are factors that can increase the overall satisfaction of a customer when more are experienced by that customer. Examples include long-term reliability of a car and seeing several exciting innings of a baseball game. Delighters are factors that the customer does not expect but takes exceptional satisfaction in receiving. An example would be winning a special customer loyalty prize while shopping at your favorite store. As competition grows and evolves, features in one category may shift to another. What used to delight may become a dissatisfier if not included as a feature.

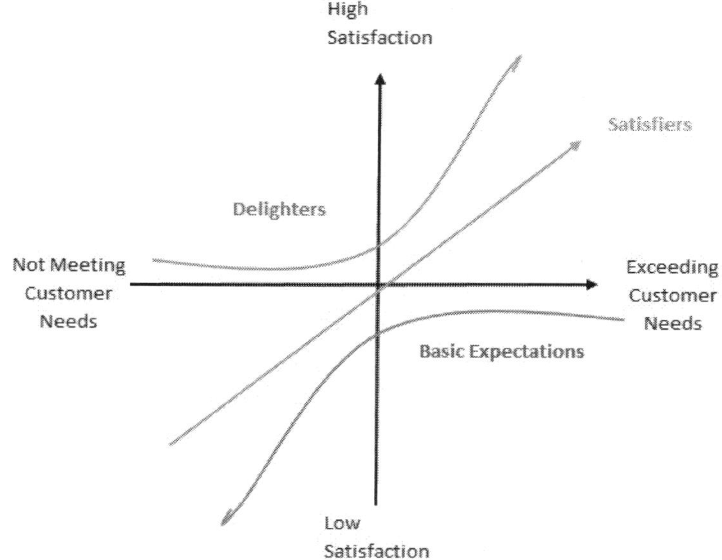

Sources of Data and Information Useful in Defining Process or Product Problems

Clear, concise, and appropriate problem statements help to ensure the project is executed with the right objectives in mind and to keep all participants with a consistent understanding of the challenge. Objectivity is essential to a problem statement. Subjective opinions in a problem statement do not provide any valid problem. Data sources are necessary for making a good problem statement. Common sources can include financial data; cost accounting data; Pareto charts of defects, complaints or issues; SPC charting results, fishbone (cause and effect) diagrams, matrix diagrams, and operations and productivity reports. The colleagues or stakeholders that compile and tend to these sources can be key experts in interpreting the data into rational information that benefits the project team.

Project Scope

The project scope sets the boundaries around the processes that will be impacted and those that will not be impacted by the project. Scope must be clear and concise before being finalized. An unclear and far-reaching project scope will not allow the team to focus on the matter at hand. An excessively succinct and constricted scope may not result in valuable contributions to the organization. Two valuable methods are used to create project scopes; the methods differ on how technically quantitative or casually qualitative they present the scope.

The functional method is also known as the Y = f(x) process. This process creates a dichotomy that drills down the contributing functionality between process quantitative inputs and outputs. Consider it similar to a 5why analysis but looking at process cause and effect relationships. Drill-downs can then be translated into appropriate project scope. The dimensional method assesses the situation to be improved by using eight types of qualitative dimensions of perspective.

- Customer (e.g., individual or brand-based)
- Demographics
- Geographical
- Organizational (divisions in the company)
- Process (input through to output)
- Relationships (vertical and horizontal to organization)
- Systems
- Combinations of the above dimensions

Connection of Key Process Outputs of a Project to Business Performance Measures

Project charters include the communication of project goals or objectives. The business case for initiating the project must be adequate else the project would not be well justified. These project goals or objectives may be in terms of improved quality, lower operating expense, improved efficiency, lower cost of poor quality, or other similar measures. Each of these examples can be tied back into financial and customer-oriented business performance metrics. Tollgate reviews can serve as an ongoing check by executives that a project continues to align with business performance measures.

Project Charter

Components and Benefits

Project charters are an essential part of the define phase of a DMAIC Six Sigma effort. Charters provide an assembled team and relevant stakeholders with an overview of all key elements of the project and its expected results. Charters are communication tools regarding what is within and outside of the scope of the project.

KEY ELEMENTS

Key elements of a charter include:

Charter Element	Description
Project name and location	Names the project for reference and the site or business unit(s) involved.
Team leader and champion	Defines the project leader (often a black belt or master black belt) and the executive champion.
Project mission	Describes what the team and project is expected to complete.
Problem statement	Defines the problem at hand and in terms of the customer. Objective and numerical data is expected. The problem statement must draw premature conclusions.
Business case	Define why this project is worth undertaking compared to something else.
Deliverables/goals/ metrics	List out the improvements to be delivered by the project, the goals of each deliverable, and related metrics that provide objectivity to achievement.
Scope	Setting boundaries of the processes that will be impacted and that will not be impacted.
Stakeholders and their expectations	Defining stakeholders and expectations keeps these interests relevant to the project team.
Hard and soft costs, savings estimates, ROI	Financial expectations are important to many stakeholders to LSS projects.
Team members and expected resource needs	Defines the team and what other resources the project may need.

PROBLEM STATEMENT

A problem statement in a charter must be clearly defined and unambiguous in content. The statement should not be judgmental, accusing, or based on opinion. Key elements to a well-worded statement include a historical timeframe of the issue, the impacted measures in the organization, the business impact in terms familiar to management, and how has performance lagged from expectations. A well-worded and objective problem statement helps make the team consistent in understanding the scope and definition of the problem at hand.

Example: In-patient recordkeeping since 2014 has performed 55% below target defect levels with 40% of defects occurring at the insurance billing sections of records.

PROJECT MILESTONES AND DELIVERABLES

Project milestones are helpful to a project charter as a means to break the endeavor into smaller, manageable sections. Multiple subsequent short duration phases to the overall project allows teams to focus on the immediate tasks at hand rather than those occurring much later. Milestones can also provide leadership and champions with the opportunity to give positive recognition or helpful feedback at intervals. Milestones can thus help strengthen and align performance. Deliverables are self-evident. They are the tangible results that will be created as a result of the project work. Examples include metric improvements, financial results, new equipment, new procedures or processes, and specific reductions in variation or waste. Deliverables demonstrate to stakeholders the observable progress that the project will make towards solving the problem. Deliverables are not fixed when developing the charter in the early phase of the project. Discoveries and setbacks may lead to revisions of the deliverables and milestones lists.

Project Management

Documentation and Archiving

Documentation serves to capture the actual history of processes, projects, and operations. Documentation can serve as a regulatory compliance role as well as an internal organizational learning and analysis tool. In many ways, if an activity did not get documented, it did not happen. Documentation also serves as evidence and communication among colleagues and hierarchy within an organization. Progress towards a project completion can be evaluated and communicated with strong documentation of completed work. Archiving serves to preserve improvement and process evidence for future needs or learning. Maintaining a document and record archive also serves as a regulatory compliance element and can also allow for historical empirical research during DMAIC phases. Good documentation and archiving can support A3 reporting and organizational learning on a continuous improvement journey.

Gantt Charts

A Gantt chart is a project management tool that adds focus and time boundaries to project execution. It is visually illustrated as a horizontal bar graph that allows project tasks and milestones to be planned out sequentially over the duration of the project. Tasks can be supplemented with cost and critical path data to help the project team better execute to budget and time expectations. Building the chart begins with vertically listing all necessary tasks and milestones in the project, each with a start date, time needed for completion, and responsible team member name. Sorting the list in descending order by start date helps the team achieve each milestone—and ultimately complete the project—by knowing who does what by when. Advanced project management features in Gantt charts can include precursor steps and percent completion values for each task.

Tollgate Reviews

Tollgate reviews are checkpoints along the DMAIC process where each subsequent phase cannot begin without passing a review. Tollgate reviews are typically performed by master black belts or champions to a project and serve to ensure ongoing supervisory awareness, continued alignment with strategy, and valid conclusions from tools used. The reviewer often uses standardized investigative questions to determine progress and provides a "proceed" or "reassess" decision to the team leader. The review verifies that the team is ready to move on to the next DMAIC phase.

Example questions used in tollgate reviews	
Define	Do the project goals align with organization objectives and strategy? Are sufficient resources available?
Measure	Are validated measurement systems established? Is customer voice sufficiently represented?
Analyze	Is the project drifting from its organizational goals? Are statistical conclusions appropriate?
Implement	Are appropriate resources available to execute? Are stakeholders engaged for implementation?
Control	Are sustaining actions sufficient and valid? Is the control plan well defined?

Work Breakdown Structure

Work breakdown structures (WBS) divide a project into smaller manageable pieces in order to make sense of the steps necessary to complete the project. WBS can provide the team with the actions necessary to enact the vision and deliverables in the project within schedule and budget. The defined goals or objectives are important parts of the WBS; all tasks and subtasks are derived from the goals. WBS plans create a hierarchy of the project by creating layers, including work packages, tasks, and subtasks. Details such as precursory and subsequent tasks, costs, and performance expectations are all included in each level of the WBS. The full WBS acts as a project organizational chart to control the process and guide the team to completion.

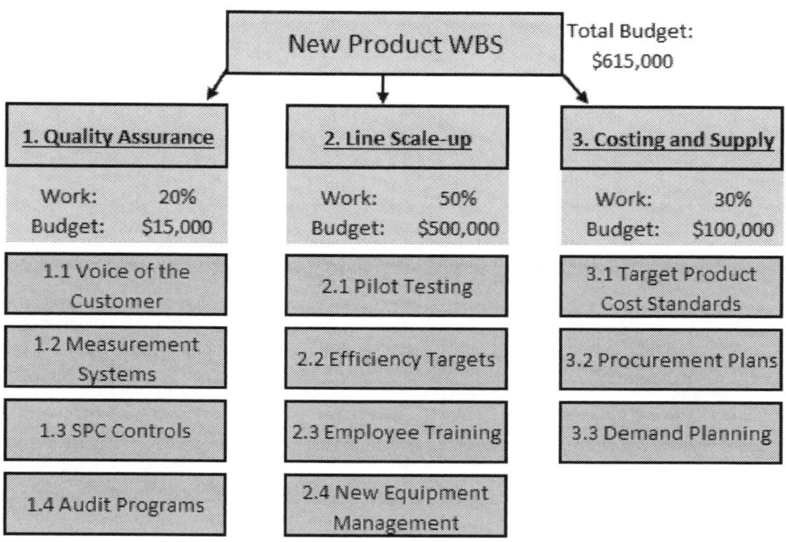

RACI Matrix

RACI stands for responsible, accountable, consulted, and informed. Key stakeholders and team members of an improvement effort are listed horizontally in a matrix. Tasks, milestones, or functions of the improvement initiative are listed vertically in the matrix. For each task, a stakeholder or team member is assigned R, A, C, or I depending on their role in the project. Responsible is defined as expected to complete the immediate task or function. Accountable is defined as assuring that tasks or functions are performed, often by other persons. Consulted represents persons that hold valuable knowledge that will help achieve a task or function. Inform represents persons that must receive communication regarding certain parts of the project.

Tasks	Amanda	Bryan	Regina	Scott
Survey customer base for updated quality expectations	*R*	*A*	*C, I*	*C*
Compile a critical to quality program with new data	*C*	*R*	*I*	*A*
Translate CTQ process into revised specifications	*I*	*I, A*	*R*	*C*
Train operations staff to new specifications	*C*	*A*	*R*	*I*

Affinity Diagrams

Affinity diagrams are used to cluster similar, related elements or ideas into groupings in order to better understand the broader themes of the ideas themselves. The team or persons building the affinity diagram conclude the affinity themes that exist and where each idea or element fits in the affinity categories. Affinity diagrams are commonly used in the define and analyze phases of DMAIC, often in brainstorming or root cause analysis events. The fishbone diagram is an example of factors grouped by affinity (material, method, measurement, etc.). The affinity diagram is one of the seven planning and management quality tools.

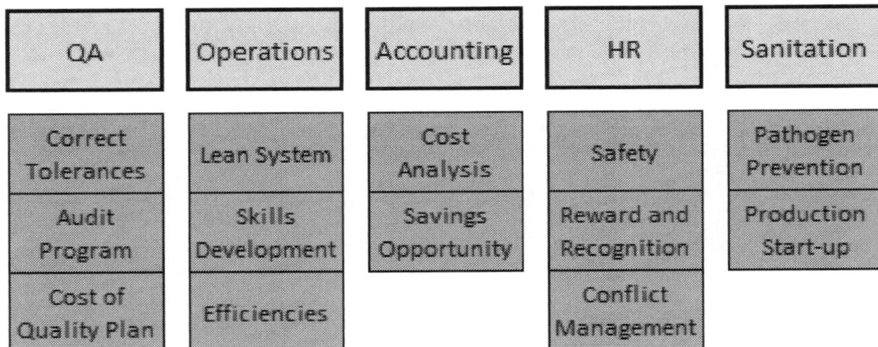

Tree Diagrams

Tree diagrams represent another type of the seven planning and management quality tools. Tree diagrams show a dichotomous breakdown of a goal or objective into its tasks and subtasks. An example of a tree diagram is in a work breakdown structure (WBS) graph. A team or individual begins a tree diagram by understanding the goal or objective to be assessed. Underlying subtasks are grouped according to parent task category. Parent categories are created if not previously determined. The diagram is most commonly used in the define phase but can be a stepping stone to creating implementation plans and detailing control measures in DMAIC.

Variations of Matrix Diagrams

Matrix diagrams are two-dimensional charts that permit us to compare different datasets in order to investigate relationships between those datasets. The number of variables is a key element in choosing between different types. Matrix diagrams often use common symbols to distinguish relationships and weight of different elements. Hoshin-Kanri X diagrams show step-wise strategic plans and are built in a clockwise pattern with four variables and with a characteristic X in the center. C matrix diagrams provide a three-dimensional perspective on a dataset. L matrix diagrams assess two variables and are the most commonly used. T diagrams show relations between three variables and look like an L-matrix divided horizontally. Y diagrams represent three variables and are like X diagrams with one less variable element included. Roof diagrams are unique in plotting the relationship between one variable relating to itself. Roof diagrams are common in voice of the customer projects.

Prioritization Matrix

Prioritization matrices are generally two-dimensional matrices that compare alternative choices against selection criteria. The criteria in the L-shaped matrix is weighted, allowing for ranked choices to be prioritized based on weighted importance or relevance. The alternatives are then scored and narrowed down to the one or few highest priority choices. The general steps needed to create an effective prioritization matrix include:

- Define the goal and the alternatives to analyze
- Define the selection criteria used
- Define the weighted importance of each criteria

- Construct the L-matrix with alternatives listed vertically and weighted criteria listed horizontally.
- Rank each alternative based on the criteria, multiply ranks by weights, and select top priorities.

Cause-and-Effect Matrix

The cause-and-effect (C&E) matrix is used in simplified voice of the customer projects to provide a weighted score and ranking of the relationship between key process output variables (KPOVs) and key process input variables (KPIVs). KPOVs are determined for an objective or goal. Each output is weighted. KPIVs are then brainstormed and listed perpendicular to the output variables. Each input is given a score, and that score is then multiplied by each output weight. The sum of each weighted score represents the relative importance of that input to the output(s) that affect the achievement of the objective at hand. The total scores for each input are sorted and highest-scoring inputs are evaluated and improved first. The results of the C&E matrix are often used to support implement and control phase work in DMAIC.

OUTPUT REQUIREMENTS / Causes	Importance Rating	INPUTS: HR Hiring and Scheduling	INPUTS: Compensation and Benefits to Cooks	INPUTS: Standard Work Expectations
Accurate Meals to Diners	High	+++	+++	++
Proper Temperature	Med	+	+++	++
Safe to Eat	Low	+++	+++	++
Luxury Presentation	Med	++	++	+
Accurate Flavors	High	+++	+	+++
Minimal Waste	Low	+	++	++

Customer Service and Strategies for Customer Retention

Customer service is defined as the set of interactions and relationships maintained by the firm in order to gain new customers and maintain existing customers for the sake of generating revenue. Customer service is a role that various internal stakeholders fulfill within an organization. Quality professionals often provide customer-directed service by supporting complaint resolution, compliance assurance, adherence to quality specifications, and integrating the voice of the customer into internal processes. Sales, marketing, quality, and customer service representatives are the most common customer service-oriented roles in an organization. Customer service professionals can play a valuable role in the define and measure phases of DMAIC, especially where voice of the customer and house of quality initiatives are implemented.

Perceptual Mapping as a Simplified Voice of the Customer Tool

The perceptual map tool is a simple plot of customer data to validate perceptions of what product or service features are most important and satisfying to customers. Additionally, the same validation can be done on customer perceptions towards the most important and satisfying problem resolutions. Features or problems are identified by internal stakeholders, given perceived rankings of importance, and posed within unbiased customer surveys to a sample set of customers. The plotted results identify customer feedback against internal rankings. The method can be thought of as a simple calibration of internal customer perception to real customer perception.

Customer Perceptual Map

Importance to Customer	1	2	3	4	5	6	7
7							
6		B				F	
5				I			G
4		D				C	
3							
2	H	E		A			
1							

Importance to Customer: Low to High; Customer Satisfaction: Low to High

Perceived Product Features	
A	Stainless Steel
B	Multicolored
C	Light weight
D	Waterproof
E	Long battery life
F	High capacity
G	Clear Audio
H	Low Price
I	Expandable Features

PERT

A program evaluation and review technique (PERT) is used to provide short, long, and best estimates of duration to tasks. The method is often used when a project team is not certain of the likely duration of a task. PERT allows for the testing of project timing and scheduling scenarios based on the three estimates. Advantages to PERT include accounting for risks, calculating probabilities of various plan alternatives, and agile resource shifting. Disadvantages to PERT include complexity and general limitation to time analysis of success. PERT diagrams are often joined with critical path method and slack time data to outline the project schedule and be a precursor to better defined schedules in Gantt charting.

Critical Path Method

The critical path of a project is the longest total time necessary to complete the project when other tasks are performed in parallel to the set of tasks along that critical path. The critical path is the primary constraint throughout the project and is also the length of the longest single chain of activities linked together. The critical path is determined after the activity nodes are all laid out in a PERT or AND diagram. The longest necessary chain of events allows the project manager to set a discrete or approximate project end date. Cost data is also included in the diagram. A caveat to the method is that the path is based on time assumptions for each step. Those assumptions may be strongly or weakly supported by past experience.

Calculation of Slack Time

Slack time refers to the flexibility of delaying a project task without causing delay to the overall project. It may also be referred to as float or path float. Individual steps or non-critical paths in a PERT or AND chart can include permitted tolerances on early or late start or stop timeframes. As projects become more frequent by an organization, confidence in anticipated early or late timeframes becomes stronger. Expert opinion and mathematical calculation can also derive step durations and lag times. In AND processes, slack equals the difference between the latest start timeframe and earliest starting timeframe. Timeframes are often indicated by sequential days of the project. In a PERT diagram, the difference between the critical path and non-critical paths represents available slack time for the tasks exclusive to those non-critical chains.

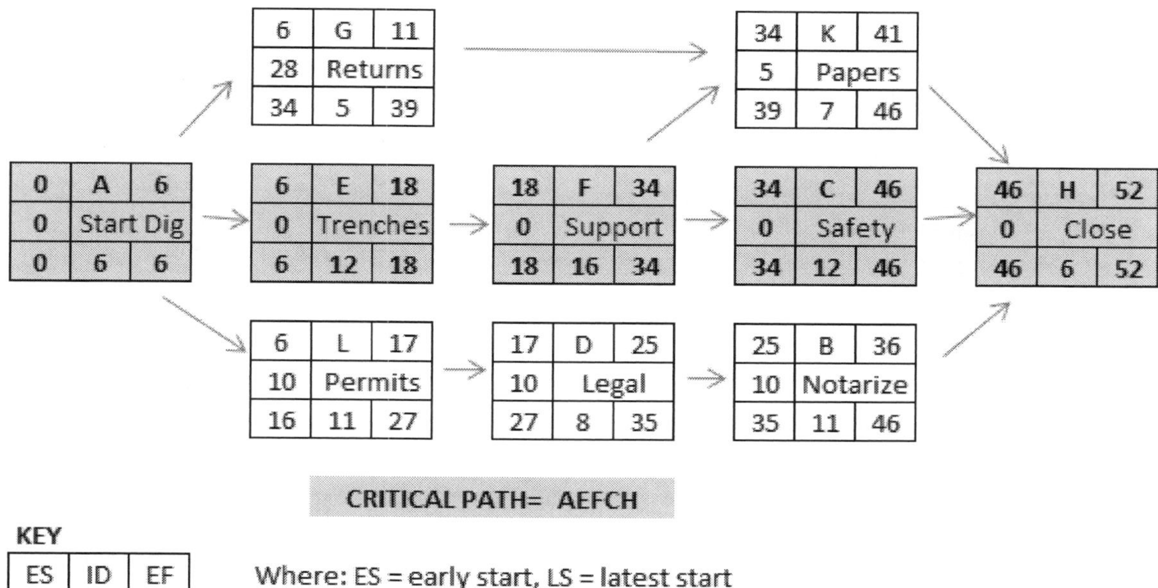

KEY

ES	ID	EF
SL	Descript	
LS	Dur	LF

Where: ES = early start, LS = latest start
EF = early finish, LF= latest finish
Dur = Duration, SL = Slack Time

Measure

WIP, WIQ, and Touch Time

Work in process (WIP) is the collective set of materials that have entered a process but are not yet considered final output of that process. WIP can be derived from any point along the steps of a process or from inventory. WIP is not typically included in calculations of yield. Work in queue (WIQ) materials are those that are in buffer points awaiting immediate processing and transformation into output. Monitoring of WIQ and any WIP material removed from a process due to flow constraints are indicators of process constraints. Touch time is defined as the time used in a process or step where value-added transformation is occurring on the input material. Touch time is a useful measure in value stream mapping and constraint mitigation. All listed measures are applicable to material goods manufacture and processing, as well as in service-oriented processes.

Cycle Time and Takt Time

Cycle time is a quantitative measurement of how long it takes to complete one run or step of a process from start to finish, transforming input materials into one unit of output or WIP. Cycle time is often calculated from the number of units produced over a defined period of time. Knowing the cycle time of a process at baseline can help validate improvements in their ability to reduce cycle time. Takt time represents the ratio of total available process time to customer demand. The ratio can provide a team with a benchmark or cadence for process flow and output rate needed to fulfill customer needs within an allotted timeframe.

$$\text{Cycle time} = \frac{\text{Number of units produced}}{\text{Defined period of time}}$$

$$\text{Takt time} = \frac{\text{Total available process time}}{\text{Customer demand}}$$

Takt time can also be used to measure throughput of component steps of a process. The ratio of time available to output capacity (in place of customer demand) can give a throughput performance value to each step. In other words, takt time is the inverse of throughput. Knowing throughput capabilities of process steps helps identify constraints or bottlenecks in a process. A simple assessment of ability to meet demand is to ensure cycle time is less than takt time.

Hidden Factories and Process Flow Impact

The euphemism of hidden factories represents unseen and unaccounted waste in a process or operation. Despite management involvement in coordinating the overall operation, individuals, informal groups, and workplace, cultural norms may create unwritten and undocumented actions that result in waste and inefficiencies. Hidden factory activities often include wastes in labor and inefficiencies, a lacking standard of work procedures, rework, excess material costs, and excess WIP. The seven deadly wastes of lean are commonly implicated as causes of the hidden factory externalities. Compounded effects can occur when multiple deadly wastes are perpetuated within a process as hidden factory activities. Compounding effects of hidden wastes will reduce process throughput and yield while increasing cycle time and cost of poor quality. Process flow becomes volatile when inefficiencies hamper setups, process rates, and meeting demand. Rooting out and eliminating hidden wastes is essential to effective flow and throughput.

VALUE STREAM MAPS

Value stream mapping (VSM) provides a visual depiction of the design, creation, and movement of information, inputs, works-in-progress, and outputs of a process. VSM is performed as a precursor to process improvement work. Mapping helps individual contributors and improvement agents understand the steps and larger process and how those parts work as a system. VSM is commonly used in lean to identify value and non-value (waste). Points of customer value in a production or service process are essential to lean while waste is to be eliminated. VSM processes often include data such as cycle time, takt time, wait times, lead times, and throughput. Non-value-added activities are those where direct customer value is not added into a good or service to satisfy the customer. Examples include storage time, time as WIP, raw material lead time, and transportation to customer. Inversely, value-added activities are those that are directly meaningful to the customer.

Example of a value stream map:

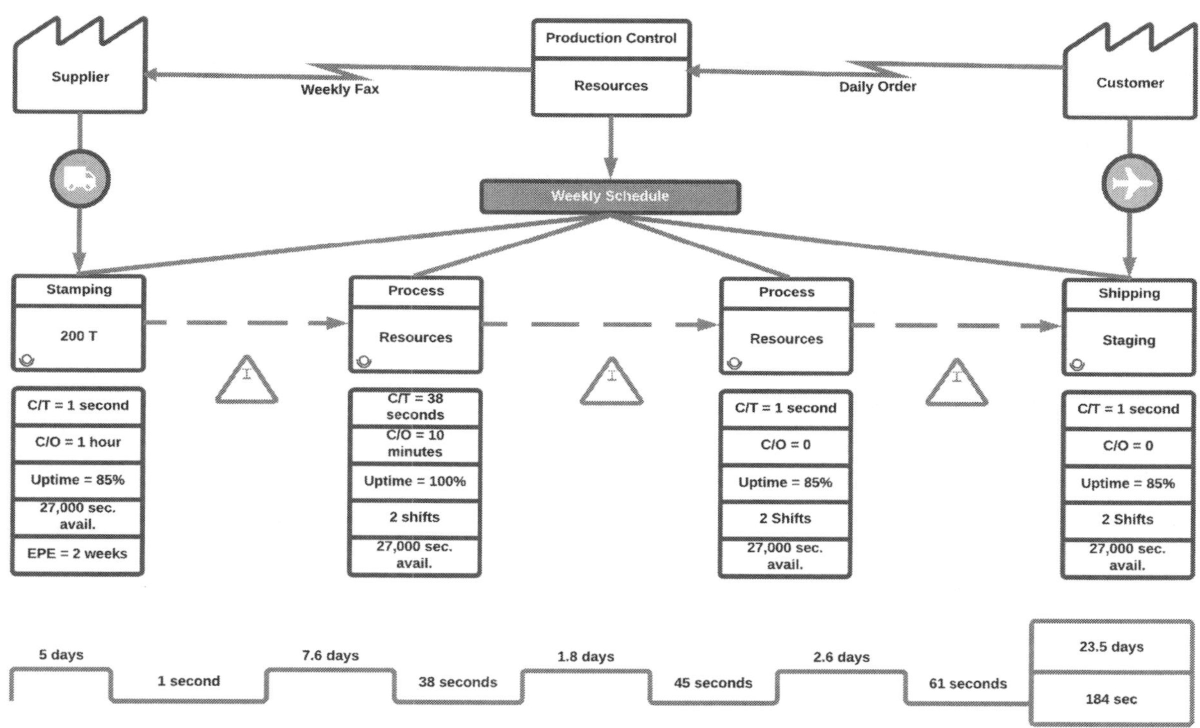

REDUCING PROCESS WASTE

Value-stream mapping (VSM) is a lean tool to visually separate customer value from waste in a process with the goal of reducing or eliminating the latter. Consider a simple process where a factory adds an embroidered set of letters on men's dress shirts. Procurement of shirts, storage of raw materials, unfolding, sewing letters, refolding, temporary storage during quality inspections, warehousing, packaging orders, and shipment are the general steps. Each step may be necessary for the factory's method of business, but none are necessarily value-added to the customer. Wait or storage times between steps is often a primary example of non-value-added waste. From the example, there is a distinction between what creates value for the customer (folding, sewing, refolding) and what does not (waiting, storage, quality inspection, shipping). The total lead time from customer order to receipt may be 14 days, but the value-added time is 30 minutes. The difference represents wasted time and an opportunity for lean improvement through projects like Kaizen Blitz and just-in-time.

Flow Charts and Swimming Lane Maps

Flow charts provide a visual layout of a process and can help teams understand the interrelationships between process steps. Flow charts are often used to verify that all process steps are considered when performing an FMEA or process improvement initiative. Hypothesis decision trees are designed with flow charts. Swimming lane maps are a richer form of flow charting. Swim maps trace a process or work flow and also show how steps, information, or materials move through departments or stakeholders from start to finish. Swim maps can help a team understand wastes to analyze and stakeholders to involve in process improvement. Both tools are commonly used in the define and analyze steps of DMAIC.

Flow Chart Used in a DMAIC Project

Example of a flow chart used in a DMAIC project:

Flow Diagram: Export Inspection of Goods

Swimming Lane Map Used in a DMAIC Project

Example of a swimming lane map used in a DMAIC project:

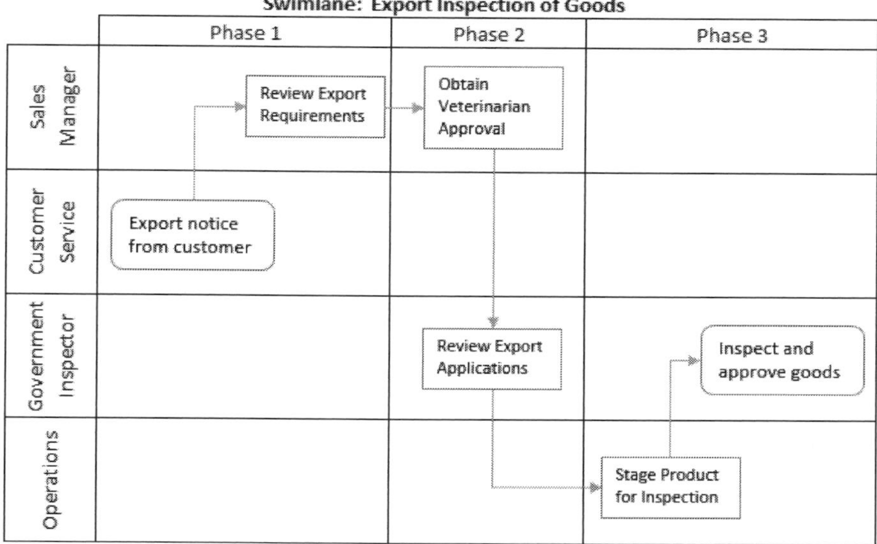

Work Instructions

Work instructions are comprehensive guides that detail the steps, resources, and quality parameters necessary to complete a job or task in a process. Work instructions tend to be more straightforward than standard operating procedures, more succinct than training programs, and richer than signage. Work instructions often include listings of relevant tools, safety precautions, quality parameters, raw materials, and equipment necessary to perform a step in a process. The listing of steps on the work instruction are clear yet detailed and often provide images for further clarity. Work instructions are often controlled documents and may be commonly used in measurement systems, lean standardized work, and in the control phase of DMAIC.

Spaghetti and Circle Diagrams

Spaghetti diagrams are performed in lean improvements to map the comprehensive set of motions used during a period of time. The full set is analyzed to determine wasted personal motions and material movement in a process. Process maps, for example of an office setting or a manufacturing line, are used as a template upon which the movement is traced. One continuous drawing of the movement resembles long strands of spaghetti when finished. Circle diagrams show the relationships between parts of a flow or process. All steps or components of a process are listed on points evenly spaced on a circle. Relationships and the material or information flow are shown using directional arrows. Both diagrams can identify constraints, wastes, and relationships between parts of a process

Circle Diagram

Example of a circle diagram:

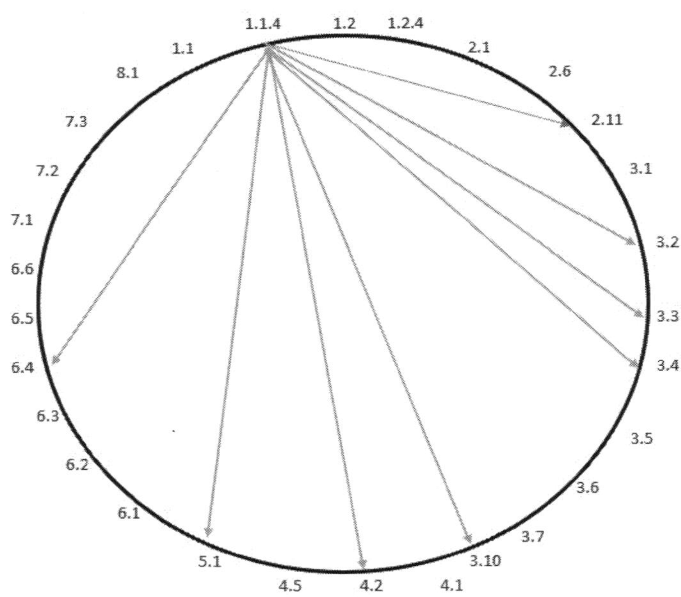

Circle Diagram: Quality System Clauses Relevant to Annual Quality Objectives

Spaghetti Diagram

Example of a spaghetti diagram:

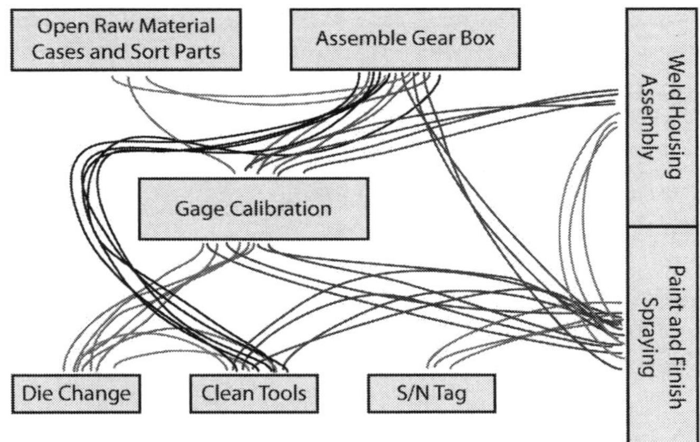

Gemba Walks

"Gemba" is the Japanese word for "where to find the truth." Gemba walks refer to the necessity of management to walk a process in order to understand it. Gemba walks are effective techniques for many phases of DMAIC, including in voice of the customer projects, control auditing, and root cause analysis. It is also widely considered a lean tool for evaluating the flow and waste in a process. Learning about a process and its strengths and weaknesses is often poorly understood from an office alone. Gemba walks are successful if they are focused, relevant, observational, non-punitive, and have management commitment. Gemba walks can also be used to validate a process flow chart or swim map before moving ahead with improvement. Walks can be by individual leaders, stakeholders, or performed by a larger improvement team.

Qualitative and Quantitative Data

Qualitative data is descriptive in nature. Examples of qualitative data include attributes, color scales, and non-numerical properties of observed objects. Qualitative data is commonly used in grading agricultural products, determining a crisis threat level, customer feedback interviews, and defining product or process defects. Quantitative data is numerical in form, such as temperature, diameter, mass, and pressure. Qualitative data is subjective while quantitative data is objective. Quantitative data is exceptionally well analyzed with statistics, while most but not all forms of qualitative data can be analyzed with statistical tools.

Continuous and Discrete Data

Continuous and discrete data are both forms of quantitative data. The types differ in the degree to which they can be divided in the act of data measurement. Discrete data fall into a defined and fixed set of possible results. An example of discrete data would be a temperature scale consisting of positive and negative whole-number integers. Continuous data may be more finely divided in terms of the possible measurements that can be obtained. Continuous data also provides more accuracy in the measurement and is considered variable. Statistical process control, for example, has higher sensitivity to process change when using continuous data. An example of continuous data would be a temperature scale measured to thousandths decimal places.

Nominal, Ordinal, Interval, and Ratio Measurement Scales

The four scales differ by the numerical presence and degree of division used for scaling. Nominal measurement scales are defined as scales with categorical terms, non-numerical and unordered. Ordinal scales add order and bearing to non-numerical categories. Some ordinal scales may include numbers, but they are generally categorical. Interval scales implement numerical divisions in continuous style. No absolute null point is present in interval scales. Ratio scales are defined by their numerical divisions and their use of an absolute beginning point, often zero. Ratio scales allow for fractional and multiplicative comparisons across the scale.

Scale	Example
Nominal	Quality defect categories; teams in a sports division; divisions in a company
Ordinal	Months of the calendar year; "red, yellow, or green" on a scorecard
Interval	Hours and minutes on a clock; Kelvin or Celsius temperature scale
Ratio	Calipers measuring silicon wafer thickness; survey responses on a scale from 1 to 10

Representative Sampling and Homogeneity

Representative sampling is defined as a sample set having consistent characteristics to that of the larger population that the sample is intended to depict. Representative sampling can approach an ideal state, but is not likely performed perfectly unless statistical randomness is involved for sample selection. A random sample for representation must have a similar distribution as the population in order to be used for making inferences. Validating sample distribution to that of the population can be achieved through Z-tests, K-S tests, or chi-squared tests. Homogeneity is defined as how well a certain characteristic is consistent within the population to be sampled and analyzed. Stratification sampling of a population into divisions based on a certain parameter is an example of separation by homogeneity.

Sampling Bias

Sampling bias is defined as intentional added errors in sample collection practices that favor certain segments of a population over a random sampling in order to influence the statistical outcomes of the test. Sampling bias can occur if project or test leaders have an interest in achieving a defined outcome that is beneficial to themselves or to close beneficiaries. Sampling bias is prevented through effective sampling calculations and pre-defined sampling schemes. Several types of bias sources exist for sampling, the most common of which is sampling bias by refusal. This occurs when subjects or data points refuse to participate in the analysis. Other types include ease of accessibility, seasonality, availability of data, and of willingness to participate. Strong representative data sampling minimizes statistical bias.

Accuracy and Precision

Think of archery and a target. Accuracy represents how close data points are to the expected result or target. In other words, how close each arrow came to hitting the bullseye. Precision represents how dispersed the data points are as a group upon the expected target. In other words, how tightly clustered were the collection of fired arrows on the target. Both precision and accuracy are better determined as data sample sets increase. From a graphical distribution perspective, precision is analogous to the spread (or variation) of a data set while the accuracy is analogous to how centered a dataset lies between control limits. Both accuracy and precision against a target can be assessed using CpK or PpK process capability systems and represented in continuous qualitative terms.

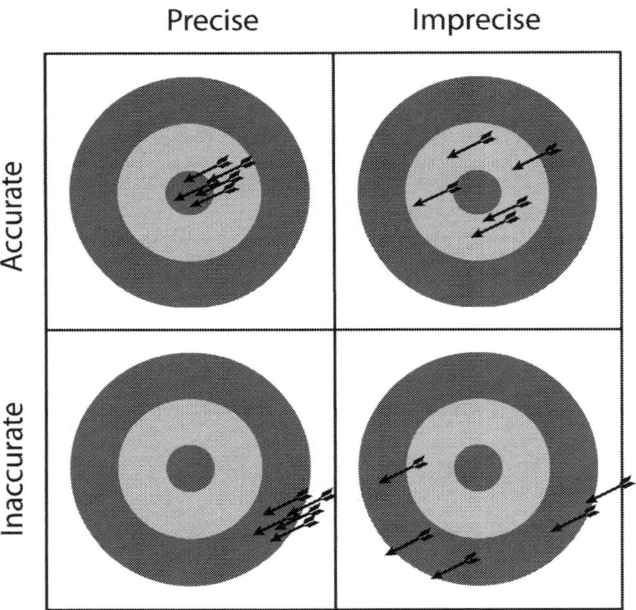

Common Approaches to Sampling

Random sampling represents the equal likelihood that representative samples in a population are chosen for testing. Random sampling in acceptance sampling prevents bias in the resulting data. Stratification is a method where a population is divided into strata (layers or blocks of units) from which individual samples can be selected for analysis. Though this does not necessarily ensure randomized sampling, the sample group is considered representative of the whole. Systematic (or interval) sampling is defined as selecting a sample at consistent intervals across the flow of an ordered population. Examples of systematic sampling include collecting in-process defect testing every 30 minutes or every 100 units of output.

Subgroup sampling, also known as rational subgrouping, is used commonly in control charting. For example, taking five subgroups of 10 tortellini every hour from a production line and measuring piece weights to calculate mean and variance as piece weight control. Block sampling, commonly used in auditing, involves a random unit chosen from a defined block of population. The selected unit and all other units within the chosen block are also sampled.

Strategies for Determining the Appropriate Sampling Method

Sampling methods should have minimal bias and standard error. Bias from the data collector must also be minimized. It is also ideal to choose a method that maximizes the efficiency and minimizes the cost, all while resulting in effective collection. Sample randomness and representation are essential to ensure inferential analyses reflect the population studied and are valid. The proper grasp and use of statistical analyses ensure that valid results are derived from data. Lastly, an effective sample size is selected so that representative and valid results are achieved.

Developing a Data Collection Plan

Effective data collection planning leads to valuable data that can be analyzed for reliable information and decision-making. Data collection plans provide an improvement team with uniformity, reliability, and effective analysis for improvement. A collection plan must first ensure relevance to the project goals and hypotheses themselves. Next, the plan might detail all responsible persons and the collection process each is responsible for. Collection plans ideally have upper and lower control limits set so that corrective actions can be made if observations are outside of expectations. Controls must be built into the collection plan so that data is reliable, accurate, and of high integrity when analyzed. Advanced collection methods such as computer databases or automatic data capture can prevent data errors. Training and measurement system analyses approaches will also work to ensure errors are minimized. Check sheets are an example that can be modified and adjusted based on the desired outcome of the data collection process.

Data Collection Table

Who	How	What	Where	How often
Quality technician	Calibrated precision gage	Measure seam thickness	High speed production line #3	10 samples every 15 minutes
Machine operator	Calibrated mass balance	Measure product net weight control using SPC	At can filling station	5 samples every 10 minutes

Data Coding and Common Data Collection Points and Techniques

Data coding is defined as a transformation of measured data from the original form (often in a long or complex form) to a coded and more simplistic format for ease of recording and verification. Data coding is helpful when measurements can appear confusing to operators or analysts needing to quickly assess the values against specifications or control limits. Deeper analysis on the true encoded values can be done separately where greater analysis time is available. Examples of coding can include the use of only the last digits in a long decimal or algebraic functions. Common data collection points in a process include between workstations within a process, at the raw material point at the start of a process, at the end of the process, at diverging or converging points in the process flow, and where different organizational functions transfer WIP material to continue production. Common data collection techniques include design of experiments, process capability, sampling in hypothesis testing, statistical process control subgrouping, and measurement systems analysis.

MSA

Measurement system analysis (MSA) is a process used commonly in measure phase of DMAIC. The intent of MSA is to make means of data measurement uniform among available instruments, persons, and techniques. Uniformity builds confidence in the validity of the measurement system data and supports effective analysis and improvement. A measurement systems capability analysis (often called a gage repeatability and reproducibility study) is a key part of performing tollgate reviews of the measure phase of DMAIC. MSA seeks to understand the sources of variation in measurement activities, isolate and minimize such variation, and confirm if the gages used are suitable for the measurement job. A variety of statistical tools are used in MSA to quantify capability, including ANOVA, process capability, and testing of variances.

Application of Measurement Systems Across an Organization

Measurement systems effectively work to compile and analyze key organizational data for the benefit of decision-making. Operations and manufacturing are a common source of measurement systems. Other functions within an organization can benefit from effective data collection and measurements. Logistics and supply chain functions can benefit from tracking inventories, transportation costs, and error rates in product selection accuracy and supplier quality systems. Employee performance appraisals and calibrated appraisals can make human resources functions more effective. Data measurement and analysis are essential parts of voice of the customer studies. Therefore, marketing and sales divisions commonly use measurement systems to stay aware of customer needs. Lastly, finance and accounting are deeply committed to measurement systems for tracking revenues and expenses, among many other types of data. Often, financial experts support Six Sigma black belts in measuring project expense savings and revenue generation.

Calibration and Traceability

Calibration is a set of methods to verify the performance of a measuring device of uncertain accuracy against a known reference standard of known accuracy. Calibration is based on validated frequency and reference standards so that confidence can be obtained in the accuracy of the calibrated device. Calibration should be made with at least two measurement points in order to assure linearity with the reference standard(s). Examples of calibration include calibrating thermometers to two NIST reference thermometers at specific temperature points or calibrating a pH meter to two buffers of different pH.

Traceability refers to the chain of assurance in a calibration process whereby the reference standard to which a device is calibrated to can be traced back to a master reference point. The master reference point is generally an exceptionally accurate scientific standard at a governmental standards agency such as the NIST in the United States.

Standards in Metrology and Methods for Control and Integrity of Measurement Devices

Metrology is the study of measurement and the precision and accuracy of measuring devices. Processes, especially manufacturing where physical transformation occurs, will impose negative effects upon measuring devices and lead to lower levels of accuracy and precision if action is not taken to calibrate against a known reference standard periodically. Measurement error is a source of variation in a process and is important to a Six Sigma black belt. Calibration, NIST traceability, and measurement system analysis (MSA) are effective ways that black belts ensure measuring devices are not adding variation to a process. Several factors can be root causes of metrology error. For example, vibrations, poor operator training, weak calibration SOPs, and gage instability can all lead to measurement variation.

Mean, Standard Deviation, and Proportion

Mean is represented by the Greek letter mu (μ) while the standard deviation is represented by the Greek sigma (σ). Six Sigma's namesake comes from the standard deviation measure.

The mean is also referred to as the average of a data set. It is a measure of central tendency. The mean is the sum of a numerical dataset divided by the total number of data points of the summation. The standard deviation is the measure of dispersion or spread of the values in a numerical dataset away from the mean. Standard deviation is higher when the data points are more spread out and lower when the data points are more clustered around the mean.

Mean and standard deviation measures are very common in hypothesis tests, process capability, statistical process control, and data analysis. Proportion, related to ratios, is defined as numerical value of a part versus the whole.

Mean	Standard Deviation	Proportion
$\frac{\sum(x_1, x_2, \dots x_n)}{n} = \mu$	$\sigma = \sqrt{\frac{1}{N}\sum_{i=1}^{N}(x_i - \mu)^2}$ Where N = total data points x = sample mean μ = population mean	$\frac{23 \text{ completions}}{45 \text{ passing attempts}} =$ 51.1% pass completion rate

Central Limit Theorem in Inferential Statistics

The central limit theorem is best summarized as the tendency of the mean of a sample to approach a normal distribution and the mean of the whole population as the sample size increases. The theorem is the basis for inferential statistics or the use of sample statistics to infer the behavior of the population as a whole. Samples are representative of the entire population; logically, greater sample sizes become more representative of the population as a whole. Generally, sample sizes of $n \geq 30$ the sample mean distribution will be approximately normal. The central limit theorem is the basis for Z-scores and calculating confidence intervals for statistical analysis in DMAIC. It is also essential for testing hypotheses about improvement ideas and for building statistical process control charts.

Confidence Intervals

A confidence interval is a range of values where a population parameter will exist to a given degree of probability. Observed values in a sample from the population will have a mean and standard deviation and likely follow a normal distribution. Given the mean and standard deviation of the sample, a confidence interval can be calculated to provide an assessment of how likely the population will fall between two values. The probability distribution bounded by upper and lower limits will increase as the desired confidence level increases. The most common confidence intervals used in Six Sigma include 95% and 99%. An analysis may describe an example interval that there is 95% confidence that an individual will measure between X and Y values within the distribution.

DESCRIPTIVE STATISTICAL CONCEPTS OF DISPERSION AND CENTRAL TENDENCY

Dispersion is defined as the degree of scatter or spread of points in a data set across a scale. Dispersion is mathematically represented by standard deviation and variance. Imagine a shotgun blast at a target. The shot will have a mathematical spread of all projectiles as measured on the target itself. Dispersion, for example, is an important factor in many hypothesis tests, x-bar statistical process controls, stem-and-leaf plots, and in histograms. Central tendency is defined as the mathematical proximity of data near a central point, often represented by a mean or average. Other measures of central tendency include mode and median. A box and whisker plot can simultaneously present the spread and central tendency of a data set.

BOX AND WHISKER PLOTS

Box and whisker plots are a visualization of calculated dispersion, central tendency, and outliers. They are also used to show symmetry of data, or lack thereof, by visualizing interquartile (Q) ranges of the data. The key dataset statistics needed to form a box plot include the median, range, maximum, and minimum. Whiskers are added as straight lines extending from quartile 3 (Q3) and quartile 1 (Q1) lines along the y-axis in both directions at a magnitude equal to (Q3-Q1). Data points outside of the whiskers are considered outliers. The mean is commonly added as a point within the box on the plot. Software programs commonly generate the plot. The plots are useful in the amount of descriptive information presented. Box and whisker plots are commonly used in the measure and analyze phases of DMAIC.

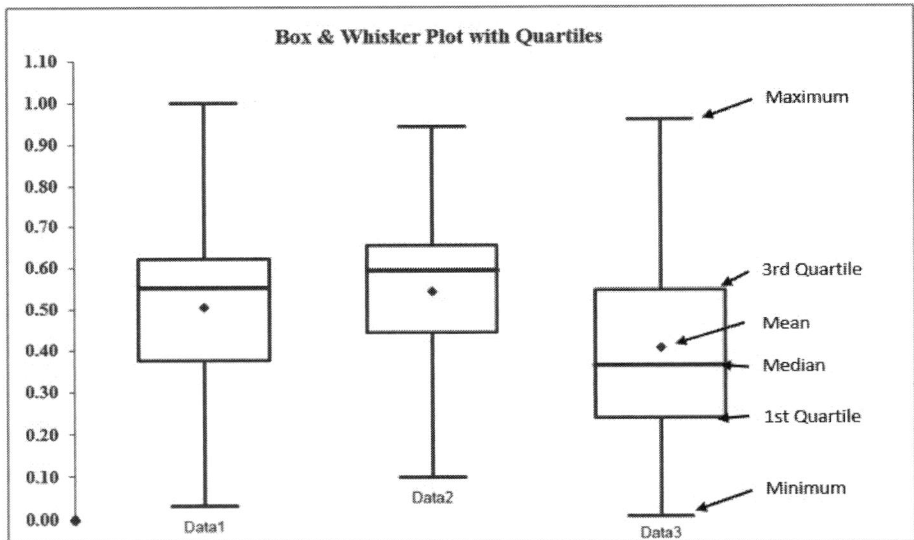

SCATTER DIAGRAMS

Scatter diagrams plot two variables in a dataset within one single graph in order to determine their relationship. Scatter diagrams are part of the seven essential quality tools, sometimes called the magnificent seven. They are useful in assessing the relationship of test data in the analyze phase of DMAIC. Scatter plots are used to support other improvement tools, such as regression modelling and correlation studies. A two-variable dataset is plotted on a two-dimensional plot in order to visualize the scatter of the data. Linear regression and trend lines can be added to determine a level of correlation.

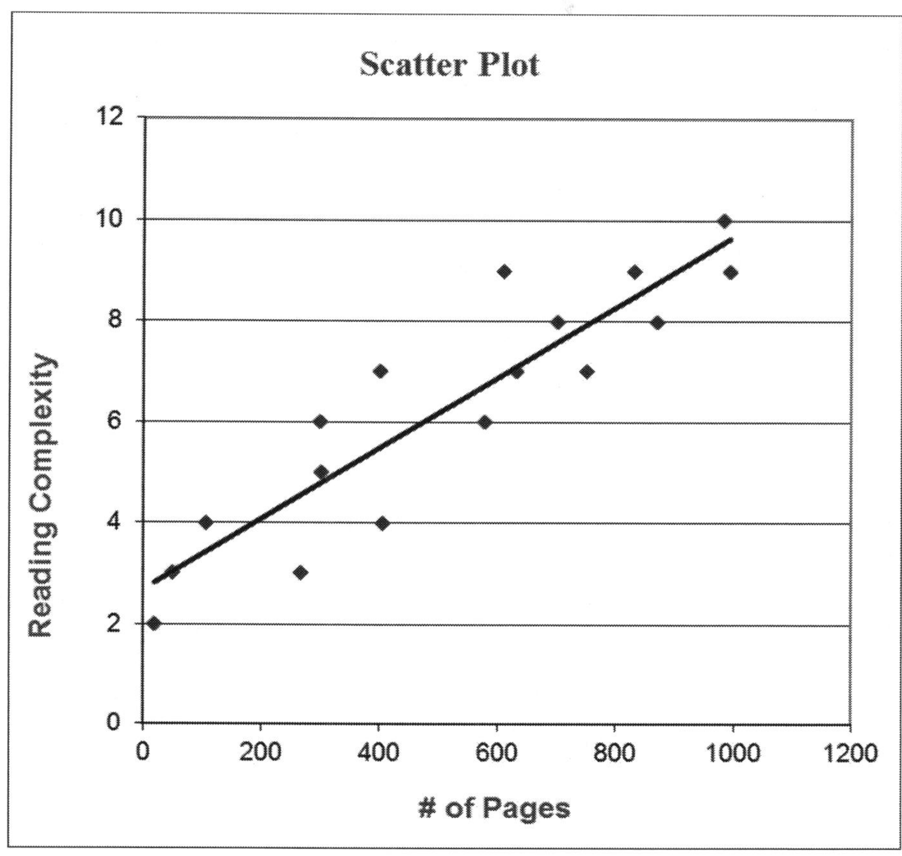

HISTOGRAMS

A histogram is a bar chart depiction data where bars, called bins, communicate a frequency distribution of points within a dataset. Visualization of a dataset can help determine degree of normality or skewedness to either side of the plot. Binary distributions would also be easily visible when plotting a frequency distribution. Present-day histograms are commonly computer generated; histograms are one of the seven basic quality tools. A variety of mathematical methods exist for calculating the number of bins used in the distribution based on sample size and visualization preference. All use the independent variable n and the dependent variable k, representing the number of samples and the desired number of bins, respectively. Examples of bin calculations include Rice's rule, 2^k rule, Sturge's rule, and the commonly used square root rule.

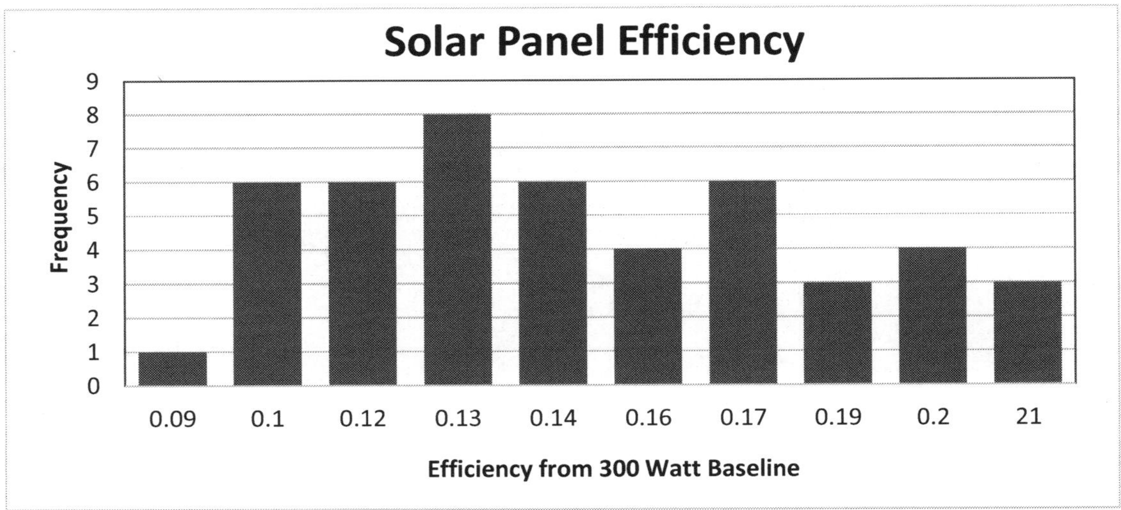

Normal Probability Plots

Normal probability plots are a method of validating that a data set believed to be normally distributed is statistically comparable to a theoretical normal distribution. It can also be used to determine how the data do not fit the normal distribution. The plot can be useful when needing to verify the normality of a dataset before performing statistical analyses, such as process capability. The theoretical target distribution is represented as a straight line on the plot. The test data is plotted as a scatter overlaying the straight line. Calculations are performed to assess how close the dataset falls in a linear pattern against the theoretical.

Skewedness can also be noted when comparing a normal probability plot to a histogram of the same data. The skewedness of the data allows for black belts to determine the type of distribution they are working with. Examples include Weibull, logistic, Laplace, lognormal, beta, and chi-squared.

Frequency Distributions

Frequency distributions provide a cleaner visual organization of large datasets and serve as a precursor to determining the type of distribution a dataset follows. Frequency distributions use classes, frequencies, and boundaries to construct a visual diagram of the distribution. Classes are used like bins to divide up the dataset by select ranges with upper and lower limits. Bounded bins are arranged sequentially when forming the plot to prevent overlap. Frequencies are the count of data points that fall within each class boundary. Classes, boundaries, and frequencies are now generally created using statistical software. An example of a frequency distribution is a histogram.

Cumulative Frequency

Cumulative frequency charts are calculated from histograms. Cumulative frequency charts represent the ongoing cumulative total of data points within each bin in the histogram. This summation continues through all bins on the continuous interval scale on the histogram axis. The increase in bin height between subsequent bins is reflected in the absolute frequency and relative frequency values of the table for select bins. The chart shows the analysis and quantitative features of a histogram plot. Cumulative frequency values are commonly attached visually to descending sorted histograms called Pareto charts.

Bin	Data Points	Absolute frequency	Cumulative absolute frequency	Relative frequency	Cumulative relative frequency
A	1, 1, 1, 2, 2	5	5	0.20	0.20
B	3, 3, 3, 3, 3, 3, 4, 4, 4, 4, 4, 4, 4	13	18	0.52	0.72
C	5, 5, 5, 6, 6, 6, 6	7	25	0.28	1.00

Determining Valid Conclusions from Statistical Results

Valid conclusions are derived from statistical analyses when those analyses and conclusions are supported by mathematical and statistical axioms. Validity of Six Sigma statistical studies is important when seeking validity to hypothesized improvements. Valid conclusions can be drawn from two types of studies: descriptive (enumerative) and analytical (inferential). Inferential studies use a mathematically derived sample set to draw conclusions about the larger population being studied. The proper use of a null and alternative hypothesis, an alpha risk or confidence interval, and test statistic will generally lead to a valid conclusion about the nature of the population. Descriptive studies are more focused on the statistical characteristics of data. Descriptive measures of central tendency and dispersion can be on the sample itself (called statistics) or on the population (called parameters).

Probability Concepts

Independence and Mutual Exclusivity

In probability, independence is defined as two events or variables where the operation of one does not affect the operation of the other. Both events are strictly independent of each other and their probabilities do not affect one another. For example, the roll of one die is independent from the roll of a second die. For reference, dependence occurs in probability when these independence rules are null. Mutually exclusive (or disjointed) events are those that cannot occur simultaneously. For example, when a die is rolled, there can only be one side facing up upon the die coming to rest. Only one side can face up per roll; all other potential values cannot occur.

Mathematical operation	Independent events	Mutually exclusive events
Independence	$P(A\|B) = P(A)$ AND $P(B\|A) = P(B)$	$P(A \cap B) = 0$
Multiplication	$P(A \cap B) = P(A) \times P(B)$	
Addition	$P(A \cup B) = P(A) + P(B)$	

Conditional, Complementary, and Joint Occurrence

Conditional probability implies that one of two conditions is already met before assessing the probability of the other condition. In other words, seeking the probability of event Y when the condition of event X already occurred.

Complementary probability represents an event and its complement. The probability of an event having one of only two possible outcomes is mathematically represented by one minus the complementary probability.

Joint occurrence is defined as the likelihood that two events will occur simultaneously. Probabilities of each event are multiplied to derive the joint probability that both events will occur.

Conditional, Complementary, and Joint Occurrence

Type	Expression	Venn diagram	Example
Conditional	$P(A\|B)=\frac{P(A\cap B)}{P(B)}$; where P(B)>0	A x B Y	Being stuck in a traffic jam while late for work
Complementary	P(X') = 1- P(X) Where X' and X are complements	X X'	Flip of a coin can be heads or tails
Joint	P(A and B) or $P(A \cap B)$	A B A∩B	Two horses with same owner win and place in a race.

Normal Distribution and the Use of Z-Scores

The normal probability distribution, also called a bell curve or Gaussian curve, is the most commonly used distribution in Six Sigma statistics. The distribution follows a specific formula with known mean (μ) and non-zero variance (σ^2). A distinct feature of the normal probability distribution is consistent areas of the distribution that lie at each standard deviation distance from the mean. For example, ±1 standard deviation (σ) from the mean represents 68.26% of the population. Many statistical tests used in Six Sigma require or presume that datasets are normally distributed. Transformation of part of the distribution formula into a simple z-score allows for the estimation of the probability that a sample will fall within a certain range on the distribution.

The normal distribution is commonly represented in explaining the concept of Six Sigma defect levels. A normally distributed model of quality measures centered at a target with spread of $\pm 3\sigma$ would represent 99.73% of output being within the upper and lower specifications. Factoring in Motorola's $\pm 1.5\sigma$ shift about the target expands the model from 3σ to 6σ specification limits and results in 3.4 defective parts per million.

Graphical Representation

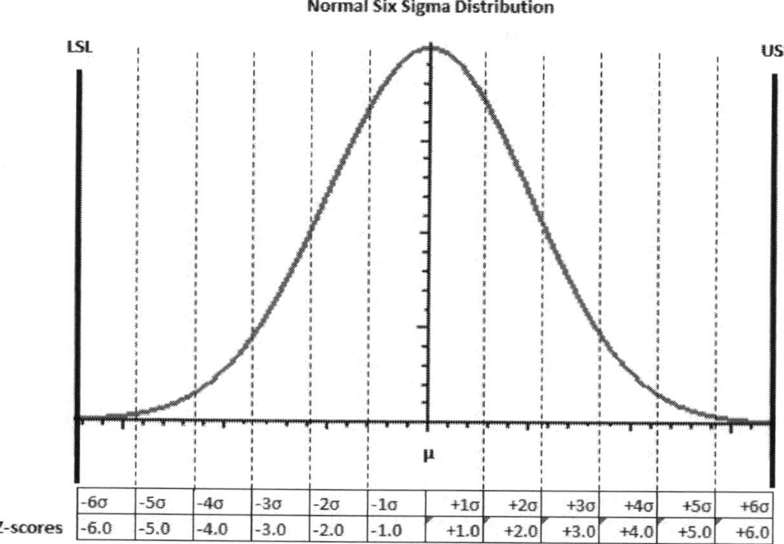

Poisson Distribution

Poisson distributions are used widely in statistical process control calculations when setting control limits on defect attribute charts. In fact, two of the four attribute SPC models are based on the Poisson distribution: the *u* and *c* charts. The Poisson distribution serves as a good approximation for the mean defects (or mean occurrences) per unit. As the observed mean increases, the distribution becomes more normal in shape. Lower mean values in the Poisson distribution create a skewed probability density function offset towards one end of the graph. The distribution function can be used to estimate the probability of observing a number or range of likely defects on a random unit of output. Such a function can be helpful in comparing past defect probability performance to an experimental improvement state.

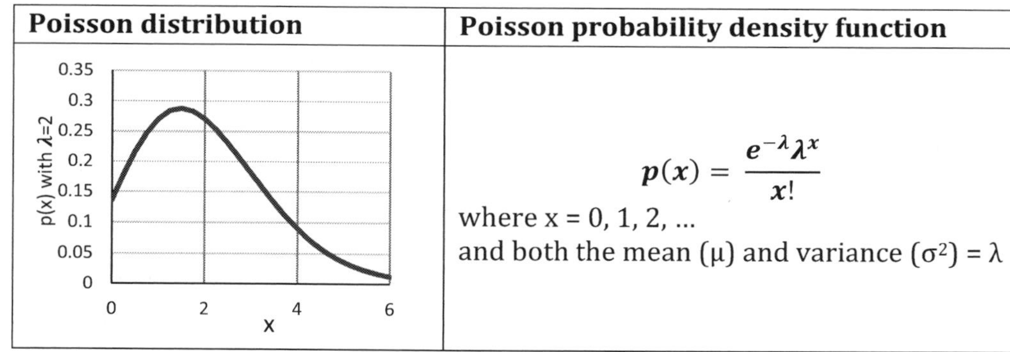

Poisson distribution	Poisson probability density function
	$$p(x) = \frac{e^{-\lambda}\lambda^{x}}{x!}$$ where x = 0, 1, 2, ... and both the mean (μ) and variance (σ^2) = λ

Example data for distribution

Example data for distribution		
x	λ	p(x)
0.5	2	0.135335
1	2	0.270671
2	2	0.270671
3	2	0.180447
4	2	0.090224
5	2	0.036089
6	2	0.01203

BINOMIAL AND BIVARIATE DISTRIBUTIONS

Binomial refers to two, and only two, types of outcomes. Binomial distributions are used to determine the probability of observing a value of an outcome among a sample size. For example, the binomial probability density function would be used to estimate the probability that 2 units of a 10-unit sample were defects when a process is known to produce a defect rate of five percent. The binomial function contains two components: the probability of non-failure in a sample set, and the combinations of how such non-failure can happen in that sample set. Bivariate refers to two random variables. The bivariate distribution represents the joint probability distribution between these variables. The distribution and corresponding probability density function allow for the estimation of the probability that x units in a sample set meet the non-failure criteria for both of two dependent variables. The function and corresponding calculations are often calculated from datasets using statistics software. The graphical representation of binomial distributions is two-dimensional, while the bivariate distribution is three-dimensional. Both graphs indicate probability on the y axis with x axis (and z axis) as the variables.

Binomial and bivariate distributions and their graphical representation and calculation:

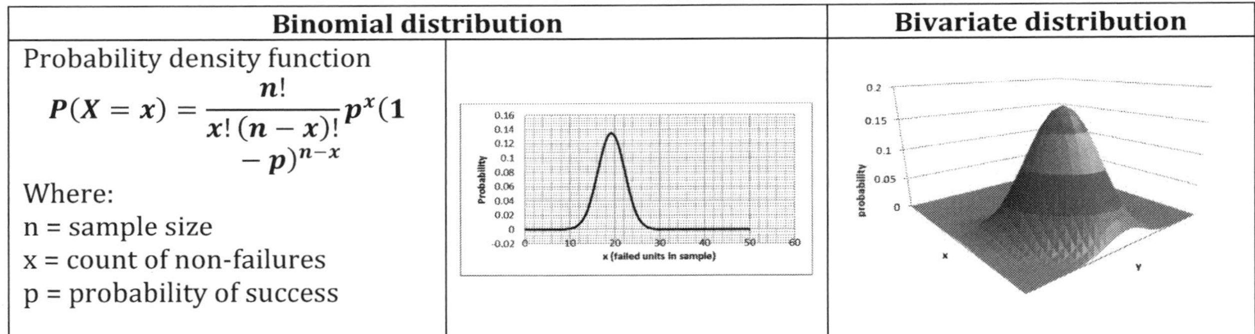

Binomial distribution		Bivariate distribution
Probability density function $P(X = x) = \frac{n!}{x!\,(n-x)!} p^x (1 - p)^{n-x}$ Where: n = sample size x = count of non-failures p = probability of success		

CHI-SQUARED DISTRIBUTION

The chi-squared (χ^2) distributions, commonly called sum of squares, are widely used as sampling distributions in test statistic approximation in Six Sigma. The distribution and its function are useful when estimating the probability that a set of random samples will fall within a certain range. Chi-squared probability density distributions are representations of the normal distribution with a skewedness that decreases (approaching normal) as the degrees of freedom increase. The degrees of freedom used is equal to the distribution mean, as well as twice the variance. The distribution involves the use of standard normal deviates—also known as z-scores—as the amount of variance at any point is away from its population mean.

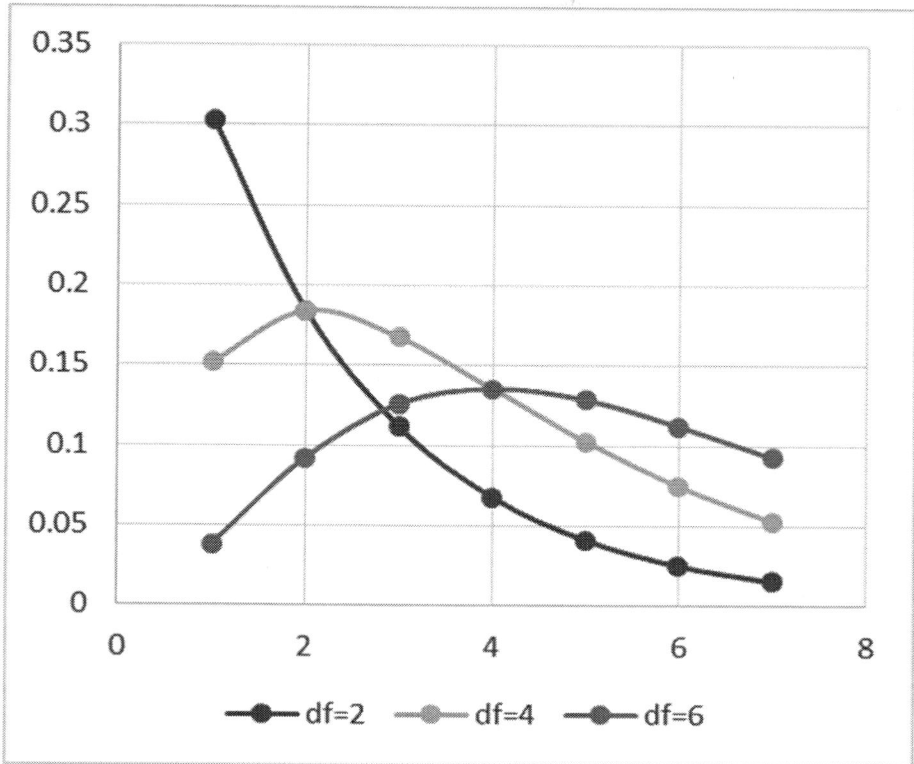

Chi-squared probability density function:

$$\chi^2 = \frac{(n-1)s^2}{\sigma^2}$$

where n = number of samples

degrees of freedom = n-1

s^2 = sample variance

σ^2 = population variance = 2n

Example calculation:

With a sample size of 10

Degrees of freedom = (10-1) = 9

$\sigma^2 = 2*10 = 20$

s^2 = sample variance = 15

$\chi^2 = (9)(15)/20 = 6.75$

Using the distribution function, what will be the probability that a second sample deviation is below 15?

$$p = 0.34 \text{ (34\% chance that sample deviation is} \leq 15)$$

Student's T-Distribution

The student's t-distribution and probability density function are commonly used to assess a population when the variance is unknown and the sample size is small. Incoming material or ingredient testing functions often employ the student's t-test to evaluate a "lot" of goods based on a small sample size. The student's t-test probability density function relies on the degrees of freedom in the denominator to graphically represent convergence or divergence from a normal distribution. As the degrees of freedom increase, the more normal the t-test curve becomes. The student's test is most appropriately used when the sample size is less than 30 and the variance is unknown. The calculated standard deviation, s, is represented in the density function to indicate that the variation must be calculated from the small sample set.

Quartiles

Quartiles divide a data set into four separate sections based on descriptive statistics. Because the median of a dataset divides the set into two equal halves, the first quartile (Q1) represents the midpoint between the median and the lowest data point in the set. The third quartile (Q3) is the midpoint between the median and the largest data point in the set. The interquartile range is the difference between Q3 and Q1 and can be an estimation of variability in the data set. Quartile formulas are based on the ordered sequence of observed data being analyzed. Generally, multiplying the number of observations by the percentile being sought will define which measurement (or between which two measurements) represents Q3 or Q1. Quartile measurements are used in box plots and stem and leaf plots to add visualization to descriptive statistics.

Exponential and Lognormal Distribution

The exponential distribution is used in reliability engineering to model the time between defects in a process or service. This can be valuable as an additional measure of equipment function, productive and predictive maintenance, and capability. The distribution has a probability density function that can be used to calculate the probability that a defect will occur within a defined test timeframe. The lognormal distribution is representative of product lifespan and depreciation over time. Such a model is important in quality attribute analysis on the longevity of a product. The probability density function for the lognormal distribution allows a black belt to predict the probability that a random output unit will have a lifespan beyond a test value. Experimentation and repeated hypothesis testing can be done with both distributions to increase mean time between defects and product lifespan.

Weibull Distribution

The Weibull distribution is used most often by engineers affirming process or equipment reliability. More specifically, the function models time to failure and is useful in equipment mean time to failure (MTTF) analyses. The Weibull distribution holds three parameters: scale (α), shape (β), and location (γ). As the scale parameter increases, the distribution becomes more effective at modeling different types of failure. When scale approaches 3.5, the distribution becomes nearly normal (Gaussian) in appearance. Scale values at 1 and greater are often considered estimations of equipment wear. The related probability density function provides a statistic that estimates the percentage of equipment or parts that will have a lifespan beyond some failure point.

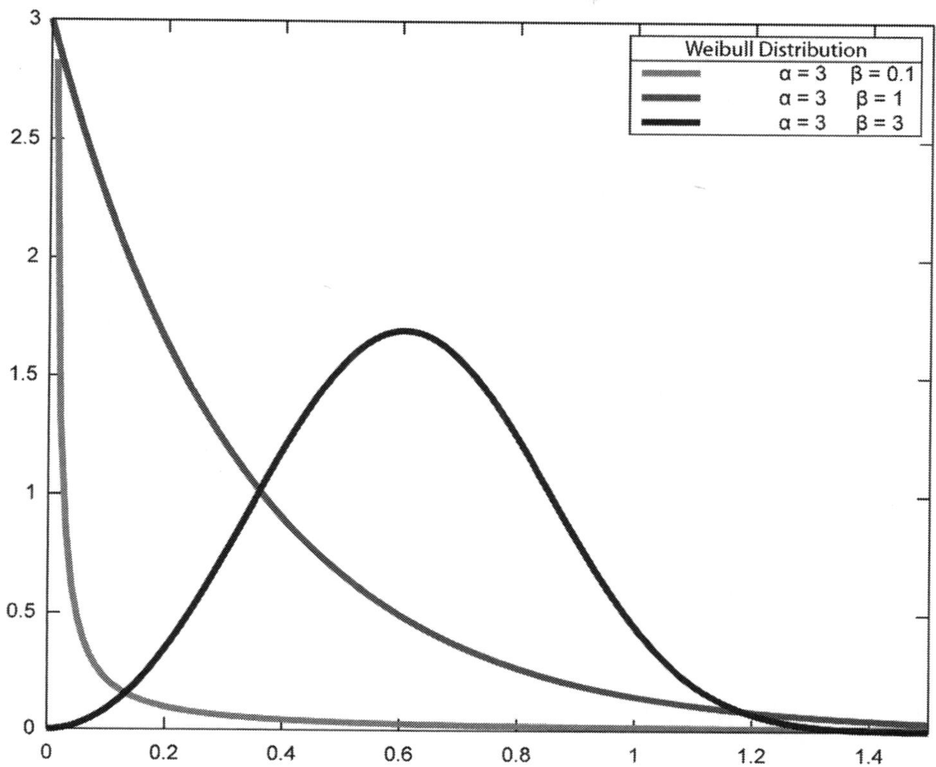

Process Capability Indices Cp and Cpk

Process capability is a tool that allows one to be statistically certain of how likely a process output will be able to meet a given range of values. Think of it as a way to verify precision and accuracy to a target. It assumes the process is under statistical process control and the output is normally distributed. The tool can be used to qualify certain processes or equipment over others, prove the ability of a process can meet specifications, justify capital for machine upgrades, evaluate operators, or differentiate a process as a competitive advantage. The statistical measure is the spread of a specification range divided by the spread of the deviation of a process output. If the mean plus or minus three multiples of the deviation of an output can fit within the specification range, you have a capable process. The lower the deviation and more centered the mean, the better your capability index will be. The unit-less index value of potential capability is represented by Cp. When including how centered the output is on the midpoint of the range, we can determine the actual capability: Cpk. Generally, Cp and Cpk values above 1.0 are considered capable but may need close monitoring. Values above 1.33 are considered excellent.

Process Performance Indices Pp and Ppk

Process capability indices are used when a normally distributed set of process data originates from a process in control. A process deemed to be in control does not have assignable cause variation present. Process performance indices differ in that they are used when a process is not in control. A controlled process allows process capability measures (Cp and Cpk) to predict process behavior. When the process is not in control, there is no predictive ability and therefore the Pp and Ppk values are to be calculated from a sample set. The mean, standard deviation, and indices are all calculated similarly, whether using capability or performance approaches.

Sigma Value of a Process

A process sigma value represents the probability that process output will fall within upper and lower specification levels set at ±6σ from the mean. As the namesake of the discipline of Six Sigma, the metric can represent the likelihood that a process will create a defect, generally expressed as per million or parts per million. For example, a 6σ process will create 3.4 defects per million opportunities when factoring in a ±1.5σ shift about the mean to account for system disorder. Roughly 99.9996% of all units would be defect-free under such a system. The normal distribution is commonly represented in explaining the concept of Six Sigma defect levels. A normally distributed model of quality measures centered at a target with a spread of ±3σ would represent 99.73% of output being within the upper and lower specifications. Factoring in Motorola's ±1.5σ shift about the target expands the model from 3σ to 6σ specification limits and results in 3.4 defective parts per million. Capability measures and defect ratio measures can be converted into a sigma value to express a sigma level for a process.

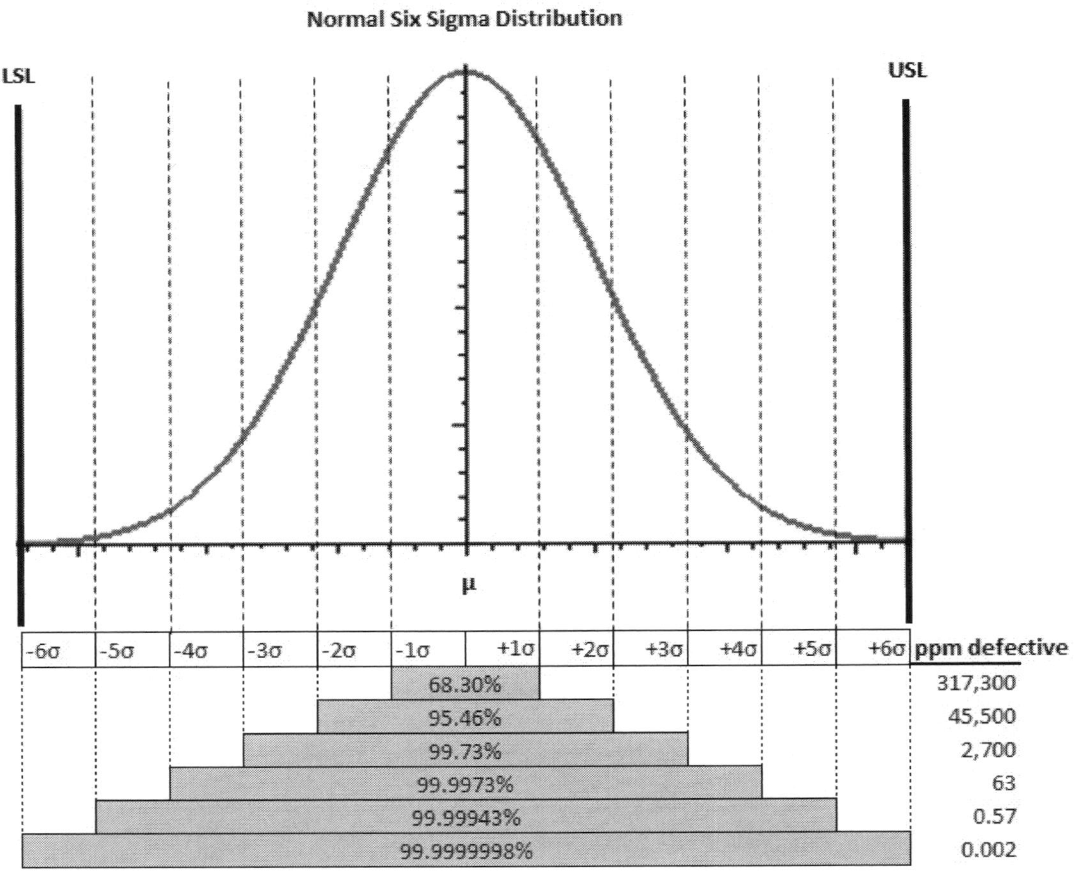

Calculating Process Capability for Attributes Data

Capability measures can be generated from attributes data, either tabular from one-time studies or from ongoing attribute control charting. Attribute measurements are those that are descriptive rather than variable and continuous. Descriptive data—such as conforming, non-conforming, long, short, hot, or cold—can be plotted on control charts and analyzed for capability. The capability measures are derived directly from the respective attribute charts: n, p, u, or c. Averages on the charts provide the capability. The average proportions or count of non-conforming units or non-conformities per unit will express capability though such measures but will not give the richness of information for attributes as available for variables charting. Sigma values can also be used as an approximation for capability when using attribute data such as defects.

	Constant	Varying
Binomial	Np-chart Average number of non-conforming units from system	P-chart Average proportion of non-conforming units per subgroup
Poisson	C-chart Average number of non-conforming units per subgroup	U-chart Average number of non-conformities per unit

Calculating Process Capability for Non-Normal Data

An underlying tenant of process capability is that the distribution analyzed must follow a normal distribution. In reality, not all process outputs that require capability studies also follow a normal distribution. The dilemma is resolved by transforming the non-normal data into a normal pattern. Transformation can come in several ways. One approach is to test a non-normal dataset in statistical transformation software against common distributions like chi-squared and Weibull. Alternatively, transformation using a Box-Cox method will add a variable to the dataset and make the normalized output appear more normal.

Percent Defective and Parts-Per-Million

Processes can result in non-conformities or defects. Measures of percent defective or parts per million defective are used when performance is based on the fraction of non-conforming output. Percent defective is represented by the ratio of defective units to acceptable units multiplied by 100. Parts per million occur on a larger scale or are extrapolated to represent results on the scale of one million assumed output units. Multiply the ratio of defective units to acceptable units by 1 million to derive the PPM. Six Sigma is often expressed as 3.4ppm defects assuming a 1.5σ shift.

Percent defective	Defective parts per million (PPM)
$\% \text{ defective} = \frac{\text{Number of defective parts}}{\text{Total parts}} \times 100$	$\text{PPM} = \frac{\text{Number of defective parts}}{\text{Total parts}} \times 1{,}000{,}000$

DPMO and DPU

When process outputs have multiple features that, if not produced correctly, may be considered a defect, the DPU measurement is used. DPU is absolute and does not account for how multifaceted the quality profile of the output unit may be. The DPMO measurement normalizes the DPU value by extrapolating the tallied defects to show how many defects are likely to occur given one million chances in output. Larger sample sizes result in more reliable ratios. Consistency in the definition of a defect and the identification of defects is important in using both measures. Measurement system analysis is commonly used to ensure defect evaluations are performed uniformly. DPMO can be converted into a sigma value for scorecard reporting.

Defects per unit (DPU)	Defects per million opportunities (DPMO)
$DPU = \frac{\text{Total number of defects}}{\text{Total number of units}}$	$DPMO = \frac{\text{Total number of defects}}{\text{Number of units} \times \text{number of opportunities}} \times 1{,}000{,}000$
EXAMPLE: 14 defects observed in 760 units DPU = 14/760 = 0.018	EXAMPLE: 14 defects observed in 760 units. Each unit has 7 defect opportunities. DPMO = 14/(760 x 7) x 1,000,000 = 2,631

Yield and Rolled Throughput Yield

Throughput yield (TY) is a calculated percentage of units of output that will pass through a certain step in a process without a defect. Rolled throughput yield (RTY) represents the multiplicative percentage that one unit will pass through the entire process without a defect. All TY values are multiplied to derive the RTY. As individual steps decrease in TY, the cumulative effect they have on the RTY increases and thus decreases the overall RTY for the process. RTY has an advantage in that it represents a first pass quality measure and accounts for the costly steps of rework and scrap from the concept of throughput.

Short-Term and Long-Term Capability

Process capability indices of Cp and Cpk are considered short term indicators and used when controlled processes deliver normally distributed results. Cp and Cpk and their respective mean and intra subgroup variance calculations are often derived from statistical process control charts. Process performance indices of Pp and Ppk are considered long-term indicators and are reserved for uncontrolled processes. Pp and Ppk include both inter subgroup and intra subgroup spread. A major difference between both sets of indices is the source of the calculated variance. Short term process capability relies on short sample sets from Xbar R, Xbar S, or moving averages control charts. Long term variance is often considered to represent the sum of the short-term capability $\pm 1.5\sigma$ shift, as defined by Motorola.

Analyze

Correlation and Causation

Correlation is defined as two or more variables having a patterned relationship with each other. A correlation is positive when the directional change of one variable is identical to the direction of the other correlated variables. A negative correlation would imply that change in variable value would lead to the opposite direction for related variables. Linear statistical plots are often used between two variables to show degree of correlation, expressed as a correlation coefficient (r).

Causation is defined as the direct influence of one variable upon the value of another dependent variable. This influential relationship must be derived, often in Six Sigma projects through designed experiments. The two concepts may be exclusive of one another. Two correlated variables might have a dependent relationship, or may have an outside cause for their correlated movement. Correlated variables may be completely unrelated but follow a similar pattern when plotted on a graph. Six Sigma teams and their leaders must be careful when interpreting correlating data sets.

Linear Regression Analysis

Linear regression analysis is a tool that reveals the linear relationship between a dependent response variable (often Y), and an independent predictive variable (often X). The independent variable is used to predict the behavior of the dependent variable along some diagonal line. A linear equation in the general form of Y = β0 + β1X+ ε is generated, where β1 is a regression coefficient, ε is the random error, and β0 is the graphical Y axis intercept.

$$Y = \beta_0 + \beta_1 X + \varepsilon$$

The model is created using the least squares method. The least squares method helps create the best fit linear line reflecting the variables. That best fit line represents an equation where both Y-intercept and regression coefficient are derived by the sum of squared discrepancy values between expected and experimental responses. The coefficient preceding the predictor variable represents the amount of response from Y that occurs when the predictor variable shifts.

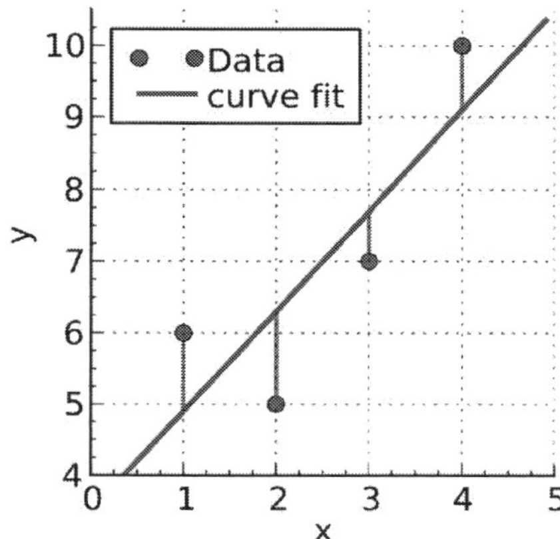

Multiple Linear Regression

Multiple linear regression models are those that have more than one independent predictor variables (x) that influence the resulting dependent response variable (Y). Linear regression coefficients (denoted by β) and random error (denoted by ε) complete the model. When all other independent predictors and coefficients are held constant, each β coefficient reflects the change in dependent response per unit change of its corresponding predictor (x). First-order, second-order, and multiple-order response surface graphs can be generated using the algebraic models. From there, the predictive models describe how several variables elicit dependent response.

Multiple linear regression example	$Y = \beta_0 + \beta_1 x_1 + \beta_2 x_2 + \ldots \beta_k x_k + \varepsilon$ Y = dependent response variable X = independent predictor variable (regressors) β = regression coefficient ε = random error (of a normal distribution)

Estimation and Prediction Using Regression Analysis

Regression analysis is the evaluation of the relationship and response of one dependent variable (Y) relative to multiple independent variables (X). The dependent variable can be considered an output while the independent variables may represent inputs or input transformations in a process. Regression analysis is performed when evaluating a linear regression model built by the method of least squares. A least squares regression line is the sum of the squared residuals, or differences between each data point on the plot and the best fit line. The linear regression equation is represented with linear coefficients, the independent and dependent variables, and a random error. Confidence intervals and prediction intervals about a mean can be calculated using independent variables. Hypothesis tests for linear regression models are commonly used to validate the relationship between the X and Y variables based on the regression line slope not being zero.

Regression analysis is the evaluation of the relationship and response of one dependent variable (Y) relative to multiple independent variables (X). The dependent variable can be considered an output while the independent variables may represent inputs or input transformations in a process. Regression analysis is performed when evaluating a linear regression model built by the method of least squares. A least squares regression line is the sum of the squared residuals, or differences between each data point on the plot and the best fit line. The linear regression equation is represented with linear coefficients, the independent and dependent variables, and a random error. Confidence intervals and prediction intervals about a mean can be calculated using independent variables. Hypothesis tests for linear regression models are commonly used to validate the relationship between the X and Y variables based on the regression line slope not being zero.

Multivariate Factor Analysis

Factor analysis is a statistical tool that serves to reduce the number of observable factors in a multivariate study or experiment down to common or correlated subsets that can explain the majority of the observed response variance. The technique is useful in narrowing factors to a more manageable set for analysis based on association of factors among themselves. This reduction focuses on the common elements that are most attributable to the observed variance, leaving the most important to further analysis. Many statistical software tools have factor analysis calculations available for black belts. Correlation coefficients are analyzed in the factor analysis.

Multivariate Discriminant Analysis

Discriminant analysis is a multivariate tool that puts multiple observed variables into two or more subgroups in order to more easily discern between the two groups. Variables that differ between the two groups can be analyzed and reduced to a single pair of discriminant factors and a mathematical function that can help predict how observed measurements indicate either of the two groups. For example, several characteristics may determine if water is potable or not. Reducing these variables to two discriminant functions allows observed data to be analyzed and a probability derived showing how likely the observation fits into potable or non-potable discriminants.

MANOVA

The multiple analysis of variance (MANOVA) analysis is similar to ANOVA, but it contains more than one dependent variable (Y) influenced by multiple independent variables (X). The MANOVA tests for statistically significant mean differences between groups of dependent variables (Y). MANOVA is used commonly in both balanced and unbalanced designed experiments and, unlike one-way ANOVAs, it does not adversely affect the group error rate (alpha). Rather than a sum of squares for treatments, MANOVA uses a cross-product matrix approach to analyze multiple dependent variables without increasing risk.

Statistical Significance (P) and Power in Hypothesis Testing

P-value and power are related to alpha (α) and beta (β) risks respectively and are helpful in determining type I or type II errors. The p-value in a hypothesis test is a level of significance at or below which represents an opportunity to accept the alternative hypothesis and reject the null. The p-value is compared to the chosen alpha risk value (α) for the test. A p-value lower than the alpha risk indicates statistical significance and the rejection of the null hypothesis. Power ($1-\beta$) is defined as the probability that we will accurately accept the alternative hypothesis and reject the null. Increasing power is comparable to decreasing the likelihood of a type II error.

Type I and II Errors in Statistical Tests

A type I error occurs when the null hypothesis is rejected when it should not be, while a type II error occurs when the null hypothesis is not rejected when it should be. A type I error may be an operating loss and a moderate cost of poor quality. A type II error impacts the consumer and can be a much higher cost of poor quality.

The alpha risk represents the probability of a type I error while the beta risk represents the probability of a type II error. These are often considered in hypothesis testing and various statistical tools. Alpha also plays an important role as the significance level in hypothesis testing. Alpha risk is the probability that many repeated runs of the test will result in a type I error. Alpha subtracted from 1 allows the risk to be expressed inversely as a level of confidence in the hypothesis. Commonly used confidence levels include 0.99, 0.95, and 0.90 (also called 99%, 95%, and 90% confidence).

Hypothesis test true result	**Team accepted the null hypothesis (Ho)**	**Team rejected the null hypothesis (Ho)**
Null hypothesis (Ho) is true	Correct decision	Type 1 error committed
Null hypothesis (Ho) is false	Type II error committed	Correct decision

Statistical and Practical Significance

Statistical significance is defined as the probability at which the interaction between variables is due to cause rather than by random chance. In hypothesis testing, the results of a statistical test are said to be statistically significant, and thus ideally reliable, if the resulting p-value is below a certain threshold, often $P<0.05$. Through statistical testing of a hypothesis, one of two alternatives tested may show a statistically significant benefit over the other option. However, both options may meet or exceed customer expectations and the significant option may be highly resource prohibitive for the organization to implement. Though one option is more statistically significant, that option may not be practically significant. Statistical tests can be used within the business realm of strategic decision making, stakeholder analysis, and the allocation of scarce resources.

Calculating Sample Size for the Equality of Means and Equality of Proportions

When performing statistical tests comparing means and proportions, meaningful results can only be achieved when a sufficient sample size is analyzed. Adequate sample size provides assurance of the results of the statistical test. Essential components of such sample size formulas include the confidence level (α), a one- or two-sided hypothesis, β-values, and relevant descriptive statistics. Sample size calculations for equalities also use z-scores; relevant Z tables would be valuable for ease of calculation. The formulas can alternate between one-sided or two-sided alternative hypotheses simply by the interchangeable use of $Z_{\alpha/2}$ and Z_{α}, respectively. Both values can be found in Z tables. When fractional sample sizes result from the calculations, it is proper to round up to the nearest integer.

Unbiased and Efficient Point Estimates

An unbiased point estimate is a statistical equivalence where the expected value of the estimate becomes the parameter itself. The estimate is performed with statistical calculations, but does not take into account how the estimate mirrors the actual population. The mathematical notation in estimate functions differ from those that include the population; such notation is a way to know that a point estimate is being used. An English letter with a caret (^) indicates use of a point estimate. The estimator is unbiased if the parameter being evaluated is the expected value. Confidence intervals are used to supplement point estimates and allow the analyst to have a representation against the population. For example, the sample variance s^2 is an unbiased estimator of the population variance σ^2.

Efficiency can be calculated for estimators of parameters. As efficiency approaches 1 for all values of the parameter, the estimate approaches maximum efficiency.

Tolerance Prediction Intervals

Tolerance intervals are estimations that provide confidence that a sampled proportion of a population fit within such boundaries. Tolerance intervals can be two-sided or one-sided. Two-sided tolerance intervals seek to know the range of values where a proportion of the population will occur. One-sided intervals focus on the proportion of population that will be above or below some limit. Tolerance prediction interval calculations use normal distribution-derived K factors to derive an upper tolerance limit and a lower tolerance limit. Tolerance factor values must be derived using the same sidedness as the confidence interval being used in the evaluation.

$$\text{Lower tolerance limit (LTL)} = \overline{X} - \text{Ks}$$

$$\text{Upper tolerance limit (= UTL)} = \overline{X} + \text{Ks}$$

Where $\overline{X}$ is the sample mean, K is the tolerance coefficient, and s is the sample deviation.

Alpha (α) confidence level and sample size are necessary for K lookup in reference tables where:

$$P = (1 - \alpha)$$

Use of Hypothesis Tests for Mean, Variance, and Proportions

Hypothesis testing is a critical part to the analyze phase of DMAIC and essential to validating that improvement concepts will work. Descriptive statistics calculated from process data is necessary for running such hypothesis tests. Mean, standard deviation (variance), and proportion are available measures and useful in validating a process improvement. Such hypothesis tests used in Six Sigma are categorized based on the descriptive statistic used, the statistical measures that are known or unknown, the distribution of the data (e.g., normal), and the sample size. The tests include defined null and alternative hypotheses approaches and the relevant test statistic used to accept or reject the null hypothesis. Mean tests include several types of z-tests and t-tests. Variance tests include chi-squared and F-test statistics. Proportion tests include z-tests. For example, the z-test for a population mean has a known variance and is normally distributed. Using the test statistic and defined null and alternative hypotheses, a black belt can use observed data from the improvement to validate the change.

Z-Tests for Means and Relationship to Central Limit Theorem

The central limit theorem holds that as the sample size increases to or above a sufficiently large count (>30), the nature of the distribution of sample means approaches a normal distribution. The central limit theorem is a linchpin for the discipline of inferential statistics, where sample analysis is used to make inference for the population as a whole. The population is generally notated in Greek letters such as μ for mean and σ for the variance. The sample statistics are in Roman, such as $\bar{x}$ for the sample mean and s for the sample deviation. Z-scores are used as a method to transform mean and standard deviation values of a distribution into a standard scale. Z-scores help estimate the proportion of the distribution falling above, below, or between various points within the distribution. Transformation into the z-scale is a very common approach in confidence intervals and statistical tests within the analyze phase of DMAIC. Simple hypothesis tests regarding the sample means can be achieved using the z-scores.

Statistical Unpaired T-Tests for Means

The unpaired t-test is an analysis of a sample mean ($\bar{x}$) compared to a known hypothesized mean that is expected (μ). The test is useful for comparing the mean of a sample set to a known standard mean that is considered to be representative of the population. For example, a hospital may use a t-test to determine if an incident rate of infectious disease patients is statistically different from the population's incident rate. The t-test is a parametric test, having a known variance, and uses common elements of other tests in the analyze phase of DMAIC, including alpha risk, null and alternative hypotheses, and degrees of freedom.

Paired T-Test for Means

The paired t-test of means is an analysis tool to determine if two paired datasets are statistically different from each other. Paired t-tests focus on the differences between the normally distributed datasets. The difference of each data pair (d) in the total dataset is the primary element in the hypothesis test in this analysis. The mean of d is calculated from all pair differences and used, along with the degrees of freedom and the standard error, in the t-test statistic and compared against 0 to resolve the hypotheses. The hypothesis tests can be two-tailed or one-tailed depending on the nature of the process analyzed.

Chi-Squared Test for Variances

The chi-squared test for variances compares the variance of an observed process to a known reference variance. Often the reference variance is the existing state of a process and the observed variance is the result of a process improvement. The test relies on the sample originating from a normally distributed population. The chi-squared tests can measure a sample variance or a population variance against a known variance. For example, the test can be used to give statistical confidence in a process improvement to reduce output variance compared to the pre-improvement state. The central determinant of the test in accepting or rejecting the null hypothesis lies in the test statistic calculation itself. As the ratio of the sample deviation to the known deviation increases or decreases from 1.0, the more likely it becomes that a significant difference will be verified.

F-Test of Variances

The F-test of variance is a comparative data analysis calculation that determines if a significant difference exists between the variances of two populations, often comparing a pre-improvement state to a post-improvement. It is useful in validating a reduction in process variation in Six Sigma projects. To demonstrate analytical relevance, the F-test begins with a null hypothesis of equivalent variances and an alternate hypothesis where the original process variance is greater than the variance after improvement implementation. The variance of each population is calculated. The F statistic is a ratio of the larger variance to the smaller variance. The calculated F statistic is compared to a known table of critical F-values using the degrees of freedom from both the larger variance and the smaller variance as well as the level of risk, α. The degrees of freedom equal the sample size minus one. Where the calculated F-statistic is greater than the critical F table value, the null hypothesis is rejected and the improvement is a valid reduction in variance. In a two tailed F-test, the risk is doubled and the alternative hypothesis becomes $\sigma_1^2 \neq \sigma_2^2$.

F-test for variance (one tailed)	Example
H_o: $\sigma_1^2 = \sigma_2^2$ H_a: $\sigma_1^2 > \sigma_2^2$ Where σ_1 is the initial variance and σ_2 is the improved variance; $F_{calc} = (s_1^2)/(s_2^2)$ $F_{calc} > F_{critical}$: reject H_o	Population [1]: standard deviation (s) = 0.55 Variance (s_1^2) = 0.3025, Sample size (n) = 14 Population [2] standard deviation (s) = 0.26 Variance (s_2^2) = 0.0676, Sample size (n) = 14 P = (1-α) = 0.95 F_{calc} = (0.3025/0.0676) = 4.47 $F_{critical}$ = 2.58 < F_{calc}; reject null hypothesis H_o

One-Way ANOVA Test

A one-way analysis of variance (ANOVA) test is a statistical comparison of several population means that resulted from different treatments in the same single factor experiment. The basic null hypothesis being tested is that all population means are equal. Using the F-test, the ANOVA process transforms sum of squares and degrees of freedom data points into an assessment of how much the variation between treatment and the inherent error in the experiment itself. After defining the null and alternative hypotheses, the alpha risk and the rejection criteria are defined. Critical F-values are found in pre-defined reference tables, represent the inherent error, and are the basis upon which to compare the test statistic when resolving the hypothesis test. The F-test statistic is calculated from the treatment data and compared to the critical F-value to conclude whether to accept or reject the null hypothesis. A test statistic greater than the critical F-value (greater than the experimental error) indicates at the alpha risk level that there is a statistically significant difference between the means.

Two-Way ANOVA Test

The two-way analysis of variance (ANOVA) test expands upon the one-way ANOVA to include the effect of each of two tested factors as well as the effect of the interaction between the two factors. A two-way ANOVA also uses the F-test, but has an expanded ANOVA data table. After defining the null and alternative hypotheses, the alpha risk and the rejection criteria are defined. Critical F-values are found in pre-defined reference tables, represent the inherent error, and are the basis upon which to compare the test statistic when resolving the hypothesis test. The F-test statistics are calculated from the treatment data and compared to the critical F-values to conclude whether to accept or reject the null hypothesis. A test statistic greater than the critical F-value (greater than the experimental error) indicates that, at the alpha risk level, there is a statistically significant difference between the means as a result of either treatment or the combination of both treatments.

Chi-Squared Goodness of Fit Tests

The chi-squared goodness of fit test allows a black belt team to analyze an expected distribution of outcomes against an experimental distribution, seeking to know if the experiment fits well with the expected performance. The tool can be used to assess an improvement's ability to meet a desired state of distribution or determine if an improvement made a change compared to the original expected state.

The ratio of the squared difference between observed and expected frequencies to the total expected frequencies is summed for all class intervals assessed (k). This total frequency is compared to a chi-squared reference table to accept or reject a null hypothesis that the experimental data follow the expected distribution. The chi-squared critical value within the reference table is identified using the alpha risk of the test and the value of k-p-1. K-p-1 represents the difference between the class intervals and the number of parameters assessed minus one.

Contingency Tables

Contingency tables allow the black belt to separate and define the probability of occurrence of select characteristics or attributes within a population. The tables depict combinations of attributes and the frequency of observation for each of those combinations within the data set. When each attribute is summed, the full table can be queried and analyzed for likelihood that any given sample will meet the queried attribute(s). The rules of probability, including additive and intersections, apply to a query. Contingency tables are also used to test statistical significance of the interaction of two attributes. By affixing null and alternative hypotheses and using a chi-squared test statistic, the contingency table becomes a stronger test for attribute independence. The test statistic relies on summing a ratio of the squared difference between observed and expected attribute frequencies to the expected alone. The statistic compared to the α level will prompt the null hypothesis to be accepted or rejected.

Form Size	English	Spanish	French	Total
A	16	7	23	46
B	13	10	18	41
C	14	11	20	45
TOTAL	43	28	61	132

P(French) = 61/132 = 0.46

P(Spanish and Form C) = 11/132 = 0.08

P(English or Form A) = P(English)+P(Form A) - P(English and Form A)

= [(43)+(46)-(16)]/132 = 0.55

Non-Parametric Kruskal-Wallis Test

Non-parametric tests are used as alternative though less influential statistical tests when the underlying distribution of the test data is unknown. The Kruskal-Wallis non-parametric test works analogously to the one-way ANOVA in evaluating the equivalence of more than two test means derived from sources with unequal sample sizes. The null hypothesis used in Kruskal-Wallis tests is that all means are equal; the alternative hypothesis is often that one, several, or all of the pairs of means are not equal. A key difference in calculating the test statistic compared to ANOVA is the ranking of populations. The rank of each population is factored into the overall test statistic before comparing the test statistic against the critical chi-squared value. Similar to a goodness-of-fit test, the number of populations (k) and the alpha risk are used to derive the critical value from the chi-squared critical table. The result will conclude whether the means of unequal sample size are equivalent or significantly different.

Non-Parametric Mann-Whitney Test

Non-parametric tests are those that do not have known data distributions. A Mann-Whitney non-parametric test determines if there is a statistically significant difference between two means of dissimilar (often random) sample sizes. The alternative hypotheses commonly used include proposals that the two means are not equal, greater than, or less than each other. These decisions will determine if a one- (greater-than or less-than) or two-tailed (not equal) test will be performed. Similar to the Kruskal-Wallis non-parametric test, the Mann-Whitney test uses ranking of sample sets in the test statistic calculation, with calculated ranks and average ranks for each sample. The critical value is derived using the scope of the hypothesis test, the alpha risk, and the sample size within each of the two populations. The test statistic and initial hypothesis test wording will determine if we conclude that the means are equal or significantly different.

FMEA

Failure mode and effect analysis (FMEA) is used to add failure and defect prevention to an existing process or to design quality and prevention into a new process. It is often documented in a chart format and routinely updated or reassessed by a team as changes occur to the process or to influential inputs. FMEA is predicated on having a knowledgeable project team verifying the steps of the process being evaluated. Once verified, the team gathers all possible types of failures that are likely to occur at each process step. The effect of each failure and likely cause is also listed. After assessing the risk of each mode, the team determines the most effective controls to implement in descending order of risk so that biggest risks are addressed first. Design FMEA (DFMEA) is performed to control for failures in the design and specifications of a product or service. A process FMEA (PFMEA) focuses on removing failure from the method of creating a product or service.

Calculation of Risk Priority Number

Ranking of failure modes is done by applying valid or estimated levels of severity, likelihood, and detectability to each mode. These are often supported with challenge studies, peer-reviewed experiments, or accepted standards. Typically, each component of RPN is scored 1 to 10, with 1 being lowest and 10 being highest. The product of these measures for a failure mode gives the risk priority number (RPN) for each. After successful actions to eliminate the most critical modes, the process should provide overall lower RPN values when next addressed. The process of eliminating risks by RPN continues.

Common Strategic Approaches

Failure mode and effect analysis (FMEA) is applicable to several types of business and improvement activities. Design for Six Sigma (DFSS) projects find valuable use of FMEA studies when designing quality and customer value into a product. The design FMEA approach focuses on assembly equipment used for manufacturing and begins with a broad assessment of failure risk. More granular analyses are performed specific to the process being developed. FMEA is most commonly used to assess the failure modes and risks in a system or process. The FMEA tool is also highly applicable to service organizations delivering a non-tangible product. Services have execution processes and potential failures in those processes.

Gap Analysis in Analyzing Approaches for Improvement

Gap analyses are performed as an audit between a set of standards and the current state of an organization or process. A gap analysis can also be performed on a production operation compared to the ideal state. The tool is commonly used in define and analyze phases of DMAIC. The gaps identified by the improvement effort are then analyzed in various lean or DMAIC tools such as fishbone diagraming, affinity mapping, multi-voting, or hypothesis testing. Gap analyses are commonly used as a precursor to performing a certification or audit program such as ISO. Gap audits allow for expert review of an organization's strengths and weaknesses against the standard that they intend to subject themselves to at a later date.

5 Whys in Root Cause Analysis

A 5 Why tool begins with the problem at hand and asks sequential "Why did this occur?" questions until the bottom-line root cause is identified. Generally, 5 Whys are needed to reach the root cause but less or more may be necessary given the problem at hand. 5 Why root cause analyses are performed on critical or moderately complex types of problems. Due to time constraints that often face organizations, 5 Why is not typically a tool for non-critical or simple problems. The tool is followed by determination of the corrective and preventative actions to prevent the issue and root cause from recurring. Follow-up verification of sustained improvements is often performed 30-90 days later. The process is fully documented on a 5 Why analysis worksheet.

Whys	Responses
Why did the recall occur?	The recall occurred due to foreign material in packaging.
Why did foreign material get inside the packaging?	Foreign material was glass fragments from a shattered gage dial.
Why did the gage shatter?	Gage material was not shatter-proofed.
Why was gage not shatter proof?	Procurement criteria do not define hazard controls.
Why did procurement not have defined controls?	No quality representative supporting the procurement team, no defined specifications from quality department.

Fishbone Diagram (Ishikawa Diagram)

Ishikawa developed the fishbone diagram as a cause-and-effect tool to initiate root cause analysis and process improvement. The fishbone diagram begins with the failure to be analyzed. That failure can also be a process output, an effect, or a problem statement. The tool then diverges into 6 common groupings of root causes: man (human), machine, method, measurement, materials, and environment. The six groupings for service industry fishbone diagrams are typically people, material, policies, measurement, environment, and equipment.

Root causes are identified through team analysis or brainstorming and added to each grouping based on the best fit. More specific causes can be added as supplementary information to each root cause. The diagram provides improvement teams with a visual way to separate all possible causes to an effect and begin testing each potential root cause for validity.

A fishbone diagram (Ishikawa diagram):

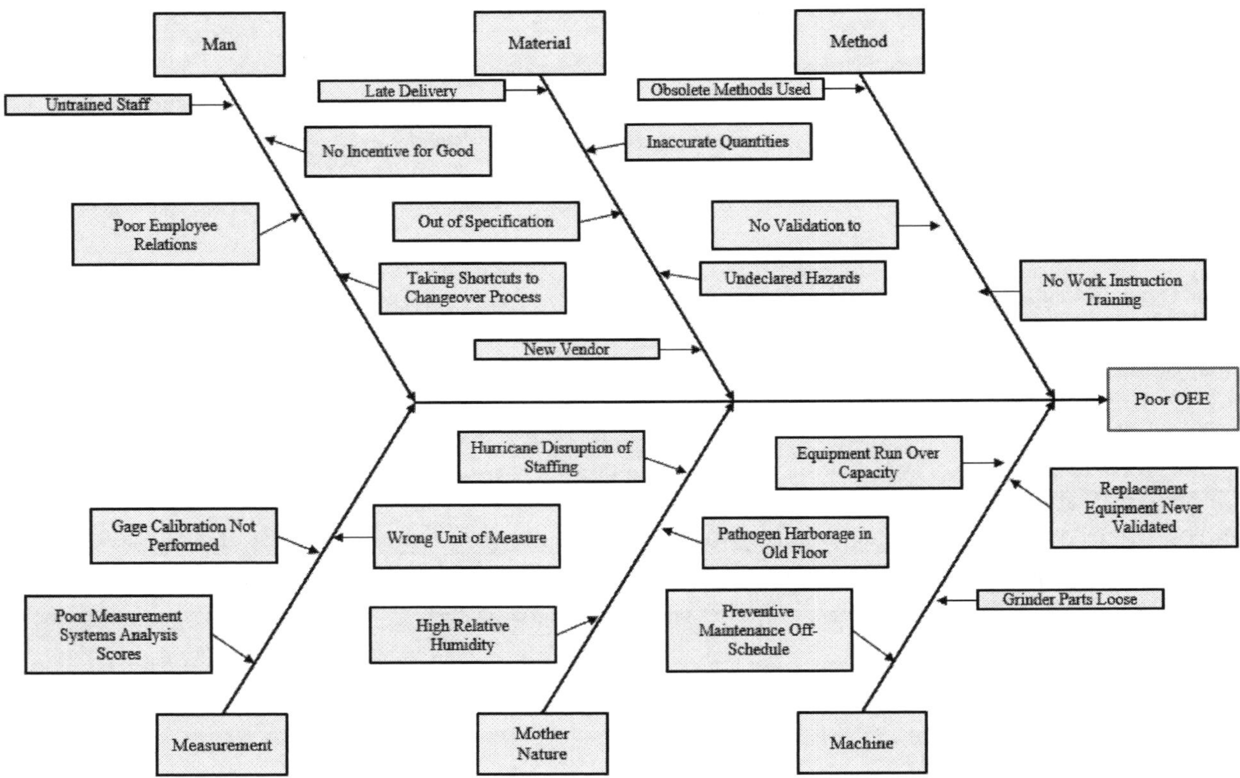

Pareto Chart

Developed by Vilfredo Pareto, the quality tool identifies the vital few within a dataset. The chart is a frequency distribution graph that aids in prioritizing the most significant issues first to achieve the most effective improvement swiftly. Each failure reason is charted on the x-axis while the count of each failure in the dataset is represented in the y-axis. Vertical bar graphs of the total frequency of each failure are sorted with the most frequent starting on the left and descending towards the right of the graph. Cumulative percentage of all failure is also charted. Pareto also established a principle whereby approximately 80% of the failures are due to approximately 20% of the probable reasons.

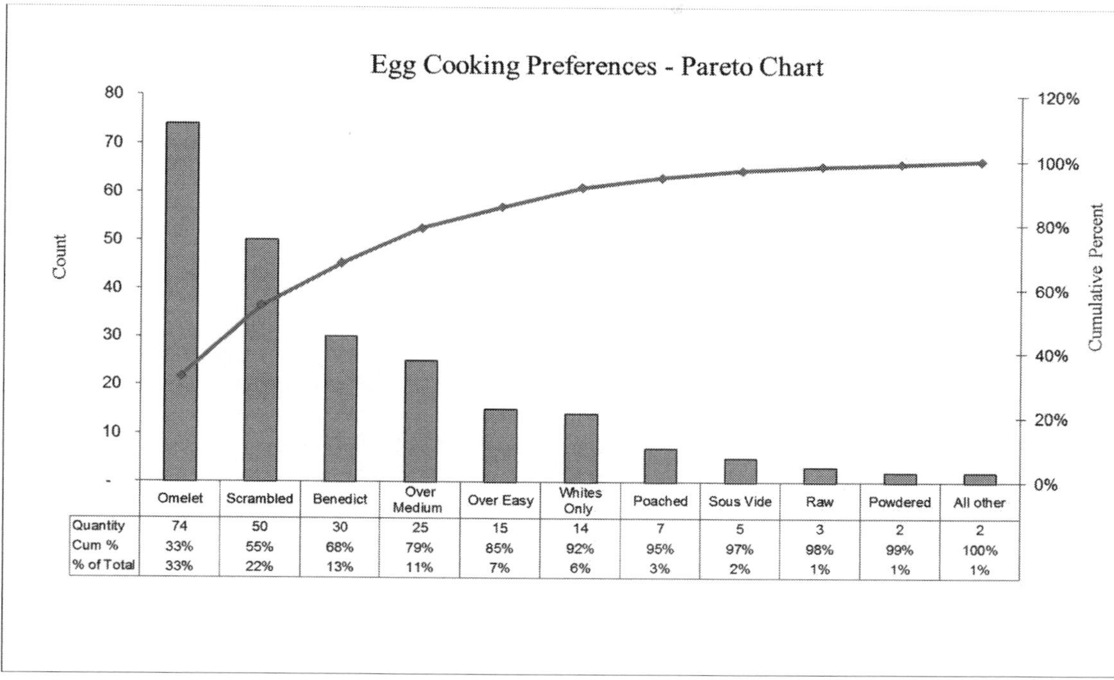

	Omelet	Scrambled	Benedict	Over Medium	Over Easy	Whites Only	Poached	Sous Vide	Raw	Powdered	All other
Quantity	74	50	30	25	15	14	7	5	3	2	2
Cum %	33%	55%	68%	79%	85%	92%	95%	97%	98%	99%	100%
% of Total	33%	22%	13%	11%	7%	6%	3%	2%	1%	1%	1%

FTA

A fault tree analysis (FTA) is a systematic tool for identifying the parts to a process that would lead to overall failure. Both single and multiple causes are addressed. The tool combines probability calculations and flow diagramming to express the system's failure points and likelihood. Ideal uses of FTA include product design planning, reliability engineering, and root cause analysis. FTA is preferred over FMEA when a full functional evaluation is needed and process functionality is highly complex among multiple parts and steps. Diagrams consist of events and logic gate symbols.

Diagrams start with top-level fault events, continue to basic events, and display the resulting fault. Gate symbols are inserted to note parallel or series types of faults at each point.

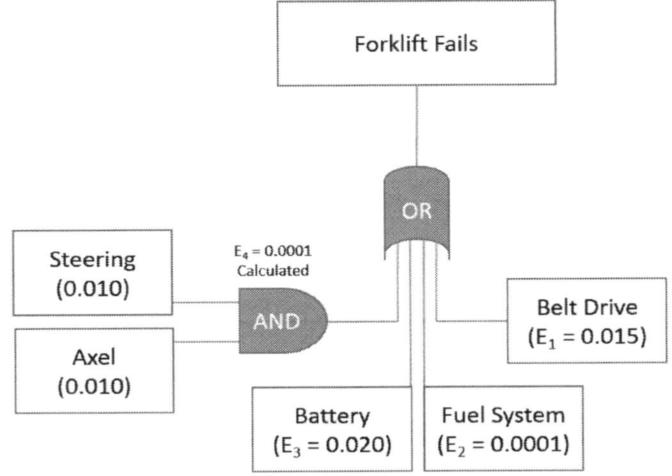

$$\mu_{system} = 1 - (1 - E_1)(1 - E_2)(1 - E_3)(1 - E_4)$$
$$\mu_{system} = 1 - (1 - 0.015)(1 - 0.0001)(1 - 0.020)(1 - 0.0001)$$
$$\mu_{system} = 3.49\% \text{ probability of failure}$$

Waste Analysis

Reducing or eliminating waste is the primary axiom in lean systems. Waste, called "muda" by Toyota, is considered non-value added to the customer. Waste can come in many forms depending on whether an operation is in manufacturing or service. The eight types of waste form the acronym TIMMWOOD and can be analyzed in a process through basic quality tools like check sheets, time studies, value stream mapping, defect monitoring, and financial results. Using thorough measurement methods, all eight wastes can be analyzed for methods to reduce or eliminate them from the process.

T	**Transportation**	Movement of material or finished goods to non-value-added locations
I	**Inventory**	Extra storage of materials and finished goods plus tied up cash
M	**Movement**	Walking and body movements not adding value to customer
M	**Managerial**	Clerical and supervisory personnel needed to manage waste points
W	**Waiting**	Any operator or specialist idle time waiting
O	**Overproduction**	Producing more output than what customer desires
O	**Over-processing**	Extra effort and materials used for preparing customer goods
D	**Defectives**	Wasted effort to create and sort out defectives, warranty costs

Gage R&R

Gage repeatability and reproducibility is a measurement process that provides statistical confidence in how reproducible and repeatable a measuring device performs in a process. Gages are typically those that measure continuous process data, but may also include discrete data and might even include human observation. Repeatability is defined as how well the outputs of consecutive measurements agree given the same inputs and operating conditions. Reproducibility takes into account that different human operators perform a gage process differently. Reproducibility is defined as how well the outputs of repeated measurement processes agree given the same inputs and process over time. The R&R results can be analyzed using three common statistical methods. The range method assesses the combined R&R of the whole system, while the average and range method allows for separation of reproducibility and repeatability. The ideal analysis method is ANOVA, allowing to determine the variation and response between the units measured and the persons or gages performing the measurement.

Improve

Factor in Design of Experiments

A factor in a designed experiment is defined as an independent variable that, at varying levels, will yield predictable changes in a dependent response variable. Factors are relevant to the dependent variable being analyzed and behave in a predictable manner. Noise factors are those that do not behave in a predictable manner and, if included in an experiment, would yield invalid and/or weak results without meaning. Commonly, two or three factor-designed experiments are analyzed for dependent response. The term "full factorial" means that all relevant factors and levels of such factors are run through a designed experiment seeking variable relationships.

Experimental Design and Observed Value in Design of Experiments

Experimental design is defined as the roadmap to building the factors, levels, treatments, and blocking that generates valid experimental results for predicting dependent variable behavior due to the studied factors and levels. The experimental design summary can be considered a cheat sheet of the critical elements and settings used to run the experiment. The observed value is the measured response of the dependent variable that results from each experimental run. Observed values are tallied in a data collection sheet alongside all factors and levels defined for each run of the experiment.

Application of Repetition and Replication in Design of Experiments

Repetition in design of experiments (DOE) refers to the successive repeats of response measurement in an experiment under identical or nearly identical conditions. Such repetition allows the experimenter to observe the common cause variation or measurement variation that exists within the measurement system. Repetitions are common in groups of three. Replication in DOE is a stronger assessment of the experimental effects than just response repetition. Replication repeats the entire collection of experimental variables. Greater confidence and lower error are gained by replication.

Blocking and Balance in Design of Experiments

In the design of experiments (DOE), blocking is a technique where the experimenter wishes to remove the influence of certain assignable causes or factors on the experimental results. Blocking involves making subdivisions, called blocks, of the experimental trials with the targeted cause or factor nullified of its influence. Randomization of the trials by the factor under blocking will help eliminate its influence. Blocking creates a more homogeneous trial set.

Balance is defined as a design where equivalent numbers of trials are performed for each factor at all indicated levels. Balance is intended to provide each combination of factor and level to contribute to the overall analysis.

Confounding, Order, and Randomization in Design of Experiments

In the fractional factorial design of experiments (DOE), confounding when the effects of two factors cannot be distinguished or separated from each other. In design visualizations, the confounded factors are linked by arrows to indicate that they are confounded. For positive-negative response indications, these confounded alias factors are depicted with like or opposite signs as well as the confounding indicator arrow.

Order in DOE is defined in two ways. Run order is the order of experimental trials when randomized. Standard order, also called Yates order, reciprocates the experimental levels of each factor in a distinct pattern. Trials are performed sequentially in descending order. Trials are not randomized but rather deliberately planned. Randomization allows test units or subjects to have an equal opportunity to be given a particular trial in the experiment.

Yates Order Table (3 Factor Full Factorial)

Factor 1 Level	Factor 2 Level	Factor 3 Level
+	+	+
-	+	+
+	-	+
+	+	-
-	-	+
-	+	-
+	-	-
-	-	-

Interaction, Resolution, and Efficiency in Design of Experiments

Interaction in designed experiments (DOE) is defined as the patterns of how levels of experimental factors influence each other relative to the response variable. When imagining that levels of each factor in an experiment can be (+) or (-), the interactions of each level are multiplicative and can predict the main effect given the input factors and levels used. Resolution in DOE is consistent with its general meaning. The level of factor confounding determines the resolution on a scale of I through VII. Lower resolution experiments (resolutions I and II) are weak in allowing the experimenter to discern between relevant effects and noise; main effects may be confounded. Ideal resolutions are III, IV, and V, where no confounding exists on the main effects, but may exist on the interactions. Higher resolutions of VI and VII often have too great of runs to be of value. Efficiency is measured as a percentage among estimators in a DOE where higher efficiency is given to lower variance values.

Planning and Evaluating a Design for Experiments

DOE are used to determine causality and statistically valid conclusions from intentionally designed experimentation and data collection. The objectivity of DOE in deriving statistical conclusions of process behavior makes it a very valuable tool to improve and plan quality performance into a system. DOE allows a black belt to understand the relationship between independent and dependent variables in a process for the purposes of adjusting and fine-tuning the process for improvement. Knowing the questions seeking answers is the first step in planning the experiment. The DOE is often planned in statistical software to account for the experimenter's desired factors, effects, levels, and runs of the experiment. The layout of the designed experiment can also be represented in a table and response values to each treatment are tabulated and the results again analyzed in software to derive the optimal performing factor levels for highest quality.

Random One-Factor Experiments and Randomized Block One-Factor Experiments

Random one-factor experiments are a one-way type of ANOVA-designed experiment where blocking is not used. A randomized complete block design allows for the experimenter to prevent the negative impact of conditions that cannot be controlled, such as time constraints and environmental factors. Randomized blocks are planned groups where the measurement of each treatment is obtained per block. Randomized blocking allows the experiment to be flexible with the real-world constraints that the experiment may encounter when evaluating the DOE.

Latin Squares One-Factor Experiments

Latin squares-designed experiments are a more straightforward type of one-factor fractional factorial experiment. In Latin squares, the response of an output factor is measured using one input factor blocked of nuisances. The design is mapped out in a matrix where the number of rows and columns are equal. An experimental treatment is applied and a controlled number of tests are performed based on the matrix. It is important to be aware of potential interactions between the input and experimental factors; interactions will have an impact on the sensitivity of the design. In the example 3x3 matrix, three baseball players will use any of three types of wood bat and face the indicated pitcher (A, B, or C). In this example, the experiment is testing bat performance in hit distance.

	BASEBALL BAT TYPE		
PLAYER	**OAK**	**ASH**	**MAPLE**
JONES	A	B	C
SMITH	B	C	A
WILLIAMS	C	A	B

Where pitchers are

A	STEVENS
B	JOHNSON
C	RAMIREZ

Two-Level Fractional Factorial Experiments

Factorial design refers to the evaluation of all combinations of k levels for two factors that are tested within the trials or the repetitions performed in the experiment. The two-level fractional factorial will resolve the specific input factors that have the most important effect on optimizing the output. Several input factors may be evaluated. Prior knowledge of the output results and surveying the test subjects on the actual level of each input factor will allow the experiment to determine the critical factors and the insignificant factors. Positive or negative signage is used to represent which level was observed in each test/factor combination. The signage linked to an output continuous variable data point can allow the experimenter to resolve a quantitative degree of impact for each treatment on the outcomes.

Lean Philosophy to Continuous Improvement

Lean is an improvement discipline focused on eliminating all waste and wasteful practices from a process that do not add value to the customer. Lean is also focused on pulling the customer-desired amount of output through a process at the customer's command and at the optimal flow. Just as in DMAIC Six Sigma, lean begins with defining customer value. Only after defining value can the lean initiative begin measuring the value stream and enhance flow through the process. The lean journey repeats due to the fifth step of perfection in the improvement process.

Pull Systems for Waste Elimination

Pull systems are means to signal upstream in a process when more activity or raw material is needed by the customer or downstream demand source. Pull systems are the opposite of push systems, where raw materials and activity are forced through a process under the assumption that buyers will have a strong desire for them. By controlling needed WIP inventory at various stages in the process, pull will reduce or eliminate sources of excess finished goods that tie up capital awaiting sale. Pull systems rely on Kanban systems as indicators of when more raw material needs to be ordered from upstream. Pull systems only consume the amount required at the time by the customer. Excess inventories are minimized under a functioning pull system.

KANBAN

Kanban is a visual control program used to notify or signal when parts or WIP material need to be replenished. As parts are needed by customers or by other stakeholders to a process, material is pulled by these persons as needed. This prompts replenishment and leaves only the immediate demand available in Kanban inventory. Kanban systems must be carefully planned to not underestimate or overestimate the needed amount of available pull supply.

A factory parts department can be an example of a Kanban. Parts may be stored and sorted with like products. When specific parts are needed, they are pulled from inventory by a mechanic and an existing stock supply remains available for another to use. The pull of the initial stock unit prompted the department to replenish the used item.

PHASES OF 5S

The Japanese concept of 5S is an acronym used to describe a process for creating a visually controlled and standardized workplace that minimizes wastes and errors. The tool is commonly used at manufacturing work stations as a way to support consistency of operation between shifts and over time. The five terms, all beginning with "s," include:

Phase #	Japanese	English
1	Seiri	Sort
2	Seiton	Set in Order
3	Seiso	Shine
4	Seiketsu	Standardize
5	Shitsuke	Sustain

The sort phase begins with the project team separating out the desired parts and tools used at the work station. The undesired materials are red tagged for eventual disposal or yellow tagged for repair. Set in order continues with the team determining how the needed parts and tools should be set up at the work station for maximum effectiveness. The shine phase is intended to return all parts, tools, and work stations to their original and intended conditions. Cleaning, maintenance, painting, and ergonomics can all be parts of this phase. Standardization includes the commitment of all persons involved in the workstation to keeping the same standards and cleanliness at the improved area. Standard work instructions and visual controls are implemented. Finally, the sustain step usually involves auditing the improvement to ensure it remains in place.

STANDARD WORK

Standard work is defined as workstation design that eliminates waste and suboptimal personnel motion through the use of standard working conditions and steps. This includes the workstation, the equipment and materials available to the worker, and the physical movements made. All elements are identical, regardless of the employee scheduled to perform at the work station. The goal of standard work is to have personnel work habits contribute to high levels of product or service consistency and thus increase quality. Documented work instructions support the continuation of knowledge of the standardized practices. As slight incremental improvements are made to the standards, instructions are updated. Standard work programs also document key flow and pace measures such as takt time, cycle time, Kanban inventories at the station, and sequence of tasks. Standard work is an excellent follow-up tool after a SMED or rapid change-over project.

Poka-Yoke

Poka-yoke is a lean tool meaning "error-proofing." Teams use poka-yoke to better prevent or detect errors in a process so that waste and poor quality are avoided. The tool is common in lean projects but also has utility in Six Sigma projects aimed at variation reduction. Mistake-proofing to avoid inadvertent errors can take many forms. For example, a team may create a color-coding system for different documents such that the flow of paperwork within an office process is performed correctly. As another example, a part in an automobile assembly line may be designed so that it fits into the larger assembly process in only one orientation.

Calculating Cycle Time and Work Balancing

Cycle time is defined as the amount of time needed to complete one (or a series) of tasks within a process. A process cycle time is the sum of the cycle times for each step of a process. Calculating work balancing first requires knowledge of the takt time. The ratio of takt time to cycle time for a process (or step) derives the number of work cells or headcount needed to keep pace with customer needs. The goal of cycle time reduction is to optimize customer satisfaction through improved ability to meet demand. Alternative goals to cycle time reduction include better productivity and reinforcing level production.

Example of cycle time and work balancing:

Process: [1] Melt (4sec) [2] Fill (10sec) [3] Form (8 sec) [4] Cure (7 sec) [5] Polish (4 sec) [6] Pack (10 sec)			
Demand and availability	**Takt time**	**Cycle time**	**Balance**
10,000 units demanded. 2 shifts available for a total of 900 minutes.	$\frac{900 \text{ minutes}}{10{,}000 \text{ units}} = \frac{5.4\text{s}}{\text{unit}}$	$\sum(4, 10, 8, 7, 4, 10$ $= 43\text{sec}$	$\frac{43 \text{ sec}}{5.4\text{sec/unit}}$ $= 8$ work cells needed
Customer needs and available workforce.	Time allotted per unit of demand.	How long it takes to create one unit.	How many work cells or employees needed to meet demand and time requirements?

CFM

Continuous-flow manufacturing (CFM) is also referred to as single-piece flow; the method results in one unit being transferred at a time, from step to step in a process. CFM processes are typically high volume, low cost outputs that maximize economies of scale to produce output. High degrees of product uniformity and minimal downtime support these output goals.

SMED and RCO

SMED stands for single-minute exchange of dies. A SMED project may enlist several other lean tools with the overall goal of having a change-over process reduced to single-digit minutes in duration (less than 10 minutes). This is a common improvement tool where many smaller custom jobs are performed and parts such as dies differ between jobs. Rapid changeover (RCO) is a process improvement tool that aims to drastically reduce the time spent transitioning an operation between two separate products. There is no set minimum target change time in RCO. Effective execution of these tools includes a cross-functional team well aware of the process to be analyzed. Other necessary actions include Gemba walking the process, mapping and timing the current and future states of the process, and sustaining the improvements.

Heijunka in Lean Programs

Heijunka is a stabilizing force for production operations experiencing fluctuation in customer (pull) demand. The tool is used to provide predictable customer supply in the face of demand volatility while creating a stable and predictable work environment. Leveling actions take into account strong patterns of demand, flexibility in production tooling, rapid changeover plans, subjugating constraints, and holding finished goods inventory. Heijunka is often preferred over batching and large-scale production runs if such actions are not effectively responsive to customer demand and mix. Highly effective customer communication and demand forecast data are essential to the effectiveness of Heijunka exercises.

Kaizen

Kaizen is defined as "improvement" or, in other words, change for the better. Kaizen was popularized by Toyota in Japan after World War II. Kaizen is a continuous improvement strategy that uses short, planned improvement sessions to make incremental improvements throughout an organization over time. The sum of the incremental improvements is considered transformative to the organization. Kaizen events are commonly executed over the course of several weeks and use the PDCA (or PDSA) cycle to drive ongoing change for the better. Kaizen is commonly used on the factory floor but is also very useful in service and office work.

Kaizen Blitz

A Kaizen Blitz improvement event is a shortened version of the Kaizen project. While Kaizen typically lasts for weeks, Kaizen Blitz projects last less than one week, generally 3 to 5 days. The blitz has a narrow focus within the operation, generally a piece of equipment or a step in a process that warrants improvement efforts. Quick and inexpensive improvements are sought and implemented by the blitz team within the 3- to 5-day timeframe. This work often involves the team directly observing the process, brainstorming improvement ideas, and testing improvements where feasible before fully implementing. Checklists, audits, or statistical process control are common ways to sustain these quick improvements. The blitz can be an effective customer complaint response tool such that major customer claims and issues can be prevented by focusing a team on the opportunities for significant preventative quality programs.

Goldratt's Theory of Constraints

The theory of constraints (TOC) is best summarized as a method to identify the weakest flow point of material through a process and implement strategies to stabilize or strengthen the throughput through the weakest point. The weakest point is called the bottleneck or constraint in the process. Increasing the throughput for the evaluated process can only occur if the rate increases through the bottleneck. TOC uses five essential steps to find and attack the bottleneck. Identification of the constraint begins the process, and knowing the rate and throughput of each individual step in the process provides this answer. Next, the TOC team must exploit the constraint and never let it stop producing. Strategies to exploit include Six Sigma defect levels for input parts, Kanban systems for WIP materials, SMED/RCO initiatives to shorten changeover times, overflow WIP areas, and highly effective planned maintenance. Subordination of other steps in the process to meet the rate of the constraint and elevation through adding more capacity to the constraint are follow-up actions. Finally, when the bottleneck moves in the process, it is repeated on the new constraint.

Bottlenecks

A bottleneck is defined as the point where the demand for a product or service exceeds the ability to provide that product or service. The bottleneck in a process, using consistent units of measure, will be the point at which the amount of maximum throughput is the smallest relative to the rest of the process steps. The rate of the full system can only go as fast as its slowest component. When we measure the throughput rate at each step under consistent units of measurement, we can identify the smallest value and begin planning ways to weaken the bottleneck. The theory of constraints provides five key steps to weakening a process bottleneck. Identification, exploitation, subordination, elevation, and repetition are steps followed to weaken the bottleneck.

OEE

Overall equipment effectiveness (OEE) is an operations measurement of effective performance. The product of rate, yield, and utilization derive OEE. Each component is a vital indicator of effectiveness. Rate is defined as the ratio of the actual number of output units produced per minute to the planned output per minute. The objective of rate is to operate as fast as possible without sacrificing quality, safety, and reliability. Yield is defined as the ratio of actual units of output in a period of time to the number of units that were started during that same time. The goal with yield is to minimize errors that lead to product loss. Utilization is defined as the duration of actual production runtime versus planned runtime. The goal with utilization is to minimize downtime. Profit maximization is supported with effective measurement and awareness of OEE.

Rate	Yield	Utilization	OEE
$\dfrac{\frac{\text{Actual output}}{\text{minute}}}{\frac{\text{Planned output}}{\text{minute}}}$	$\dfrac{\text{Actual output units}}{\text{Total units started}}$	$\dfrac{\text{Actual runtime}}{\text{Planned runtime}}$	Rate% x Yield% x Utilization% = OEE%
In 60 minutes: $\dfrac{\text{10,000 units}}{\text{14,000 units planned}}$ = 71%	$\dfrac{\text{10,000 units}}{\text{11,000 started}}$ = 91%	$\dfrac{\text{53 minutes}}{\text{60 minutes planned}}$ = 88%	(0.71)(0.91)(0.88) = 57% OEE

Pilot Tests, Models, Prototypes, and Simulations

Numerous methods of physical experimentation and scaled operation exist to support, analyze, and implement phases in DMAIC as well as design processes in DFSS. Pilot testing occurs when a limited production of output is performed on a small time or quantity scale using identical or similar equipment intended for use in full production. Pilot operations provide real-world output and feedback on how the design will perform when scaled up. Models are typically non-functioning representations—either physical or computer-generated—that provide a visual or special concept of the end result. Prototypes take modeling one step further. Prototypes are often limited functioning trial versions of the intended final product without some later value-added design features. Prototypes are useful in giving proof of concept and performing hypothesis testing to validate full scale operations. Simulations are computer-based virtual spaces where the design and features of the improvement can be modeled, challenged, and tested with no harm or risk of failure. Simulations can teach the improvement team about how the inputs, process, and outputs interrelate in the studied process.

Noise Factor and Levels in Design of Experiments

Levels in a designed experiment refer to different settings or classifications that exist for factors in a design. A qualitative example of levels would be high and low, while a quantitative example of levels would be 0, 50, and 100. Level count is indicated in DOE calculation and software with an "L." A noise factor in designed experiments is defined as an interfering yet uncontrollable factor that impacts the experiment. Often, noise factors are too burdensome to control in the experiment, but their impact on the experimental results must be accounted for.

Importance of Throughput, Inventory, and Operating Expenses in the TOC

The indicators of throughput, inventory, and operating expense all serve to verify that constraint strategies are having a positive effect on the business systems (often manufacturing) that benefit from the use of the theory. Throughput is defined in TOC as the desired number of good units to be produced over a defined period of time. Inventory is considered to be any finished goods, work-in-progress, or raw materials that have been purchased but have not yet realized revenue. Inventory is a burden and a cost in accounting perspective; minimizing irrational inventory costs is considered. Operating expenses are those that are directly spent on creating the process or product for sale. It can more easily be defined as the cost to transform inventory into throughput. The validation results expected from good constraint management include lowered inventory and operating expenses while increasing throughput through the bottleneck and process.

Treatment, Experimental Unit, and Experimental Run in Design of Experiments

Treatment is defined as the individual or set of factor values used for each experiment unit. For example, if four factors are used in the experiment, the tested levels set for each factor for an experimental unit would represent a treatment. The experimental unit can be considered the individual item or point that receives the experimental treatments and results in the expression of a measurable dependent variable. For example, if a ceramic part received an experimental bake at a certain temperature, the part is the experimental unit.

The number of runs in an experimental design depends on the number of factors and levels to be evaluated. Runs are calculated by $\text{Levels}^{\text{Factors}}$. For example, if an experiment involved three factors of length, height, and density, with each factor tested at two levels (high and low), then the number of experimental runs to derive the response variable would be

$$2^3 = 8.$$

Design Space and Experimental Error in Design of Experiments

Design space in DOE represents the body of treatments tested in combination across several dimensions. Design space is often depicted as a three-dimensional plot of multiple factors and the levels tested in the experiment. Experimental error in designed experiments is comparable to random variation in a studied process. Experimental error can also be a form of inherent noise in the experimental system without a defined cause. This type of error excludes any error attributable to factors and design features.

Nested Design in Design of Experiments

Nested designs are used where multiple factors are in a hierarchical relationship and subsamples of certain factors are to be tested in the experiment. A nested DOE is commonly used to compare multiple suppliers of similar materials for better adherence to quality expectations. The relative comparison of supplier variability can be assessed using the nested model. Vendor qualification, material preference, and performance benchmarking can be derived using nested designs. For example, three suppliers of hardwood doors each operate two barn door hinge assembly stations. Each station produces batches of doors as output. Factor A is the supplier, factor B is the assembly station, and factor C represents the batches of output to be sampled. A three-factor nested experiment can be created to test the relative variation of door batches between these three vendors.

DOE and Benefits to Six Sigma

Design of experiments (DOE) is a statistical tool that analyzes the dependent response derived from various combinations of independent factors and parameter levels tested in a process. The designed factor-level combinations yield a valid prediction tool that helps a process meet or exceed quality requirements. DOE is a strong design for Six Sigma (DFSS) tool that allows operations to design quality into a process and product before launch as a cost of prevention. Designed experiments are commonly generated and modeled in statistics software. The experiments are performed in the true process to be improved. The resulting data is further analyzed by software to determine the optimal settings for the best outcome.

Effect and Response Variable in Design of Experiments

An **effect** in a designed experiment is the relationship of the response variable when factors (at various levels) are analyzed in a run of the experiment. The **main effect** is most commonly analyzed and is calculated from the mean response values at the high and low levels analyzed for that factor. The **interaction effect** derives the relationship of one factor on the dependent variable when the levels of another factor are adjusted. For example, the dependent response of dough elasticity has an experimental factor of flour bulk density. An interacting effect of the levels of flour particle size have a relationship with the bulk density factor. The **response variable** is also known as the dependent variable. The factors analyzed represent significant variables that have an impact on how the level of the dependent variable behaves. In analogous terms, imagine Y as the response variable and f(x) as the simplified designed independent factors being tweaked in the designed runs.

Drum-Buffer-Rope Concept

The drum-buffer-rope concept is a key element in the theory of constraints. Goldratt and Cox described the concept with an analogous reference to a scouting hike. The drum is analogous to the line's constraint or slowest hiker. The drummer creates the tempo that is followed by all other hikers in the line. Similarly, all process steps perform at the same pace (or rate) as the constraint. The drum schedule must be based on the required finished goods shipping schedule. The rope concept is intended to keep all components tied to the pace of the constraint. The analogy in a process is that the rope controls material released to the constraint by tying the first process step to that constraint. The length of the rope in the analogy is equivalent to the size of the buffer. The buffer concept is added to ensure that constraints are never starved of WIP materials to process. Process steps that have higher levels of output generally have a larger buffer. Buffers allow for uninterrupted process when breakdowns at individual process steps occur.

Control

Sources of Variation Within a Process

Several sources of process variation are attributed to measurable factors found in a fishbone diagram. Assignable cause variation from man, material, method, and machine are sources that can be identified and eliminated or reduced using SPC charting. Random cause variation is also discernible in SPC charting, but action is not taken on random causes. More specific sources of assignable cause variation start with overall **process variation**, where long-term variation is analyzed using large amounts of charting data. The sources then become more granular in nature; think of the functional elements working in a process being analyzed by SPC. Production runs have measurable variation between each other, termed **lot-to-lot** variation. **Stream variation** exists where different product formulations, production lines, processing equipment, or operators may contribute to output variation in measurable ways if controls are not established. At the smallest level, measurement variation may exist from **piece-to-piece** between subgroup individuals themselves, or variation can exist between the measurement locations on each subgroup piece—termed **within piece** variation. When all such sources are eliminated, the random cause variation remains.

Statistical Process Control

Statistical process control (SPC) is a statistical analysis tool, first championed by W. A. Shewhart, used to monitor and validate that a process output is behaving as expected. SPC uses control charts to graphically represent the output statistics and their level of performance against expectations. Any process is subject to variation and the expense of quality; SPC and control charting allow two types of variation to be distinguished. Random cause variation can be considered equivalent to noise in that it is always present to some degree in a process output. Assignable cause variation has a certain root cause that can be corrected and thus eliminated as a source of variation. Control charting works in DMAIC to sustain process improvements; charting can also be used to validate capability, predict when output quality is approaching unacceptable levels, test hypotheses, and achieve Six Sigma defect levels. SPC and control charting is applicable to attribute and variables data.

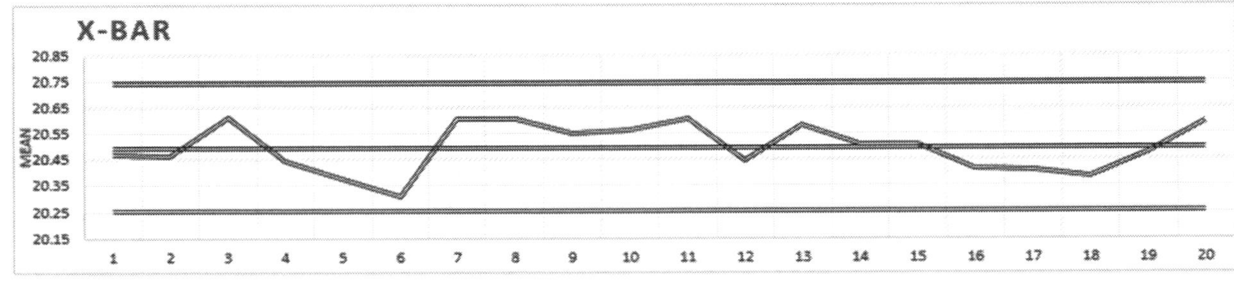

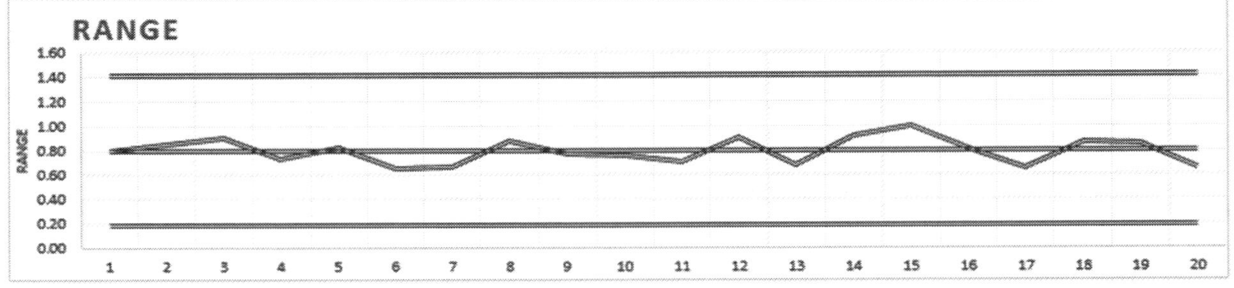

Sample#

Period	1	2	3	4	5	6	7	8	9	10	11	12	13	14	15	16	17	18	19	20
1	20.55	20.34	20.79	20.83	20.88	20.07	20.88	20.49	20.76	20.37	20.90	20.33	20.34	20.77	20.50	20.08	20.56	20.21	20.90	20.74
2	20.01	20.33	20.60	20.72	20.10	20.29	20.32	20.29	20.57	20.70	20.80	20.12	20.52	20.64	20.83	20.85	20.18	20.87	20.25	20.22
3	20.29	20.85	20.53	20.53	20.71	20.49	20.78	20.11	20.70	20.21	20.39	20.64	20.52	20.47	20.05	20.89	20.53	20.27	20.54	20.39
4	20.32	20.76	20.78	20.16	20.06	20.03	20.41	20.95	20.68	20.15	20.54	20.95	20.50	20.46	20.70	20.15	20.45	20.06	20.29	20.70
5	20.75	20.62	20.92	20.11	20.23	20.10	20.98	20.33	20.13	20.84	20.99	20.05	20.84	20.06	20.00	20.32	20.72	20.01	20.48	20.87
6	20.54	20.30	20.62	20.46	20.12	20.57	20.66	20.75	20.79	20.77	20.30	20.62	20.33	20.54	21.00	20.73	20.23	20.37	20.67	20.60
7	20.81	20.33	20.42	20.30	20.79	20.68	20.80	20.95	20.61	20.27	20.99	20.72	20.88	20.41	20.90	20.09	20.32	20.48	20.24	20.87
8	20.12	20.87	20.83	20.42	20.26	20.17	20.38	20.98	20.02	20.63	20.41	20.40	20.20	20.24	20.52	20.27	20.62	20.66	20.13	20.36
9	20.70	20.02	20.64	20.63	20.21	20.44	20.49	20.33	20.79	20.90	20.38	20.35	20.83	20.98	20.53	20.58	20.07	20.26	20.28	20.57
10	20.58	20.22	20.01	20.29	20.40	20.25	20.36	20.88	20.48	20.79	20.37	20.26	20.86	20.51	20.05	20.19	20.42	20.66	20.98	20.64
Total	204.67	204.63	206.14	204.44	203.76	203.08	206.06	206.07	205.52	205.64	206.05	204.44	205.82	205.09	205.09	204.14	204.10	203.84	204.77	205.97
$\bar{X}$	20.47	20.46	20.61	20.44	20.38	20.31	20.61	20.61	20.55	20.56	20.61	20.44	20.58	20.51	20.51	20.41	20.41	20.38	20.48	20.60
R	0.79	0.85	0.91	0.73	0.82	0.65	0.67	0.87	0.77	0.75	0.70	0.90	0.68	0.92	1.00	0.81	0.65	0.86	0.85	0.65

Selecting Critical Process Characteristics

Teams may be tempted to apply SPC control charting to all process variables. This is counter intuitive and can add more cost and wasted effort to a process. Identifying key input variables and key output variables for a process will lead a team to decide which few variables are most important to meeting target outputs. Key inputs can be confirmed using designed experiments or other hypothesis testing approaches; those selected input variables should receive SPC control charting. Process capability can be monitored using control charting on the key output variables. All processes are unique, but many common themes exist when deciding process characteristics to control. Inputs or output variables directly related to customer complaints, process variables, regulatory compliance variables, key customer requirements, and difficult processes are prime characteristics. Continuous improvement processes like DMAIC, DFSS and PDCA cycles are all venues for effective selection of such characteristics.

Rational Subgrouping

Rational subgrouping in control charting is defined as the selection of a homogenous sample size and sampling frequency so that the chronological analysis of the process can be analyzed with minimal variation between homogenous samples and maximum variation between subgroups. In more general terms, rational subgrouping is deciding how often to sample a process and how many units are part of that sample. For example, SPC used to monitor net weight control of retail food bags may have a sample size of five units collected from each bagging machine every 15 minutes to verify declared net weights are within regulations and are not leading to excess product give-away to consumers. A subgroup size of five units, chosen sequentially from a process, is often used so that the chance of introducing variation within the subgroup is minimized. Another example provides a full output analysis using a random sample across the entire output duration. The latter example is often used when making acceptance decisions on a production lot.

XBAR R CHART FOR VARIABLES DATA

Xbar R charting is a very common approach to statistical process control. "Xbar" refers to the mean response among each subgroup and is graphically plotted over time. "R" refers to mathematical range and is also plotted over time on the same chart as Xbar as an indicator of variation within subgroups. The subgroup range is the smallest value subtracted from the largest value. The "X doublebar" (or grand average) and "Rbar" represent the total mean and range of the entire run and can be plotted as a center line within each graph. Upper and lower control limits bind both the Xbar and R charts and represent 99.73% of the expected population. An Xbar R chart can be created using a known subgroup size, sampling frequency, and calculated Xbar and R data across the whole run. Factors A and D are cross-referenced in tables to calculate control limits. Under normal conditions, such boundaries and sample sizes may be used ongoing for future production runs; the chart should also include any upper and lower specification limits applicable to stakeholders. Assignable cause variation can be observed against the control limits.

Xbar R chart for variables data:

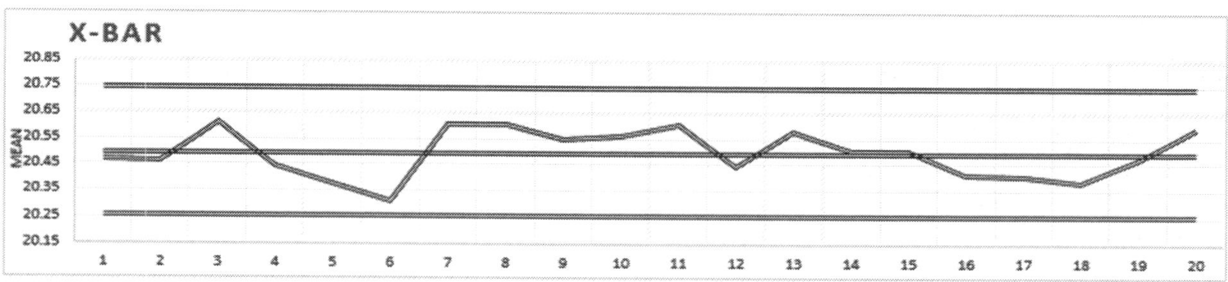

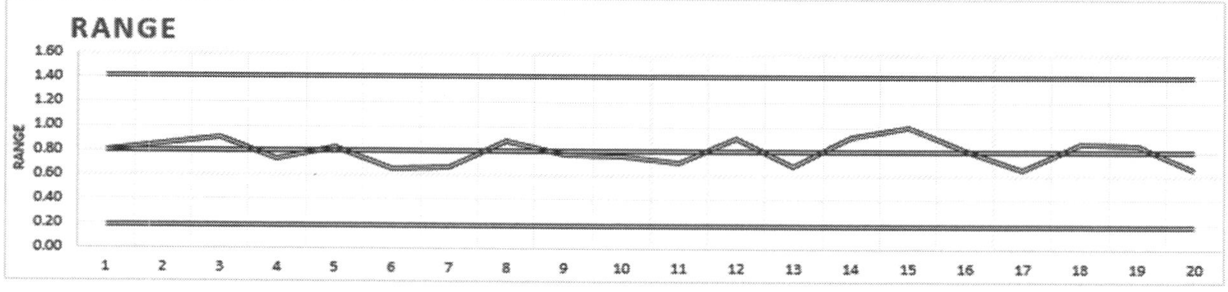

Sample#

Period	1	2	3	4	5	6	7	8	9	10	11	12	13	14	15	16	17	18	19	20
1	20.55	20.34	20.79	20.83	20.88	20.07	20.88	20.49	20.76	20.37	20.90	20.33	20.34	20.77	20.50	20.08	20.56	20.21	20.90	20.74
2	20.01	20.33	20.60	20.72	20.10	20.29	20.32	20.29	20.57	20.70	20.80	20.12	20.52	20.64	20.83	20.85	20.18	20.87	20.25	20.22
3	20.29	20.85	20.53	20.53	20.71	20.49	20.78	20.11	20.70	20.21	20.39	20.64	20.52	20.47	20.05	20.89	20.53	20.27	20.54	20.39
4	20.32	20.76	20.78	20.16	20.06	20.03	20.41	20.95	20.68	20.15	20.54	20.95	20.50	20.46	20.70	20.15	20.45	20.06	20.29	20.70
5	20.75	20.62	20.92	20.11	20.23	20.10	20.98	20.33	20.13	20.84	20.99	20.05	20.84	20.06	20.00	20.32	20.72	20.01	20.48	20.87
6	20.54	20.30	20.62	20.46	20.12	20.57	20.66	20.75	20.79	20.77	20.30	20.62	20.33	20.54	21.00	20.73	20.23	20.37	20.67	20.60
7	20.81	20.33	20.42	20.30	20.79	20.68	20.80	20.95	20.61	20.27	20.99	20.72	20.88	20.41	20.90	20.09	20.32	20.48	20.24	20.87
8	20.12	20.87	20.83	20.42	20.26	20.17	20.38	20.98	20.02	20.63	20.41	20.40	20.20	20.24	20.52	20.27	20.62	20.66	20.13	20.36
9	20.70	20.02	20.64	20.63	20.21	20.44	20.49	20.33	20.79	20.90	20.38	20.35	20.83	20.98	20.53	20.58	20.07	20.26	20.28	20.57
10	20.58	20.22	20.01	20.29	20.40	20.25	20.36	20.88	20.48	20.79	20.37	20.26	20.86	20.51	20.05	20.19	20.42	20.66	20.98	20.64
Total	204.67	204.63	206.14	204.44	203.76	203.08	206.06	206.07	205.52	205.64	206.05	204.44	205.82	205.09	205.09	204.14	204.10	203.84	204.77	205.97
$\bar{X}$	20.47	20.46	20.61	20.44	20.38	20.31	20.61	20.61	20.55	20.56	20.61	20.44	20.58	20.51	20.51	20.41	20.41	20.38	20.48	20.60
R	0.79	0.85	0.91	0.73	0.82	0.65	0.67	0.87	0.77	0.75	0.70	0.90	0.68	0.92	1.00	0.81	0.65	0.86	0.85	0.65

XBAR SIGMA CHART FOR VARIABLES DATA

An Xbar Sigma chart is very similar to an XbarR chart with exception to calculating the standard deviation for each subgroup rather than the subgroup range. Using the deviation provides a more sensitive analysis of the control on the process variation. Upper and lower control limits on the Xbar Sigma chart are calculated in a very similar manner as in XbarR but must use the calculated standard deviation as well as the grand average. Assuming that the output is normally distributed, an advantage of Xbar Sigma charting is that the process capability can be continuously measured using the chart data and a conversion factor, c_4, that is based on the size of the subgroups.

IMR CHART FOR VARIABLES DATA

Individuals and moving range (ImR) control charts are used in the control phase of DMAIC on variables data when sampling in quantities greater than 1 is highly prohibitive. The charting includes a plot of the individual sample means and a separate plot of the moving range of the successive observations. The moving range chart lags behind the individual chart because the moving range is calculated at each observation using the difference between the last measurement and the most prior measurement. Lower and upper control limits for the ImR chart have corresponding formulas and can be constructed using reference coefficients such as D_3 and D_4.

MOVING AVERAGE CHART AND THE MOVING RANGE CHART FOR VARIABLES DATA

The moving average chart represents a control chart plot of individual observations where the ongoing intermittent frequency of measurements over time forces older data to be replaced with new data added. Moving control charts are advantageous for early detection of loss of process control. Weighting provides even more sensitivity to process shifts. An ever-changing mean and variance is calculated each time new data is added. The chart centerline is the target mean; upper and lower control limits are calculated around this centerline given the variance observed. The moving range chart is similarly constructed using the calculated moving range where n=2. Moving charts are ideal where rational subgrouping is not feasible.

P-CHART FOR ATTRIBUTE DATA

Attribute charting is used to plot and analyze control on key features of the output being evaluated. Features have discrete and tabulated data. Often, defects and defectives are analyzed with attribute SPC charting. Defectives follow a binomial distribution, while defects often follow a Poisson distribution. Just like variable SPC charting, attribute charting can identify assignable cause variation and monitor process change. P-charts are highly sensitive and focus on the fraction of individuals defective within varying sequential subgroup sizes over time. The concept of defective must be defined and held consistent by all persons taking p-chart measurements in a process. P-charts often have subgroups greater than 50 units. Remember, p-charts look at fraction defective" and can be expressed as a fraction or percentage on the plot. Upper and lower control limits are calculated from mean defectives and sample size.

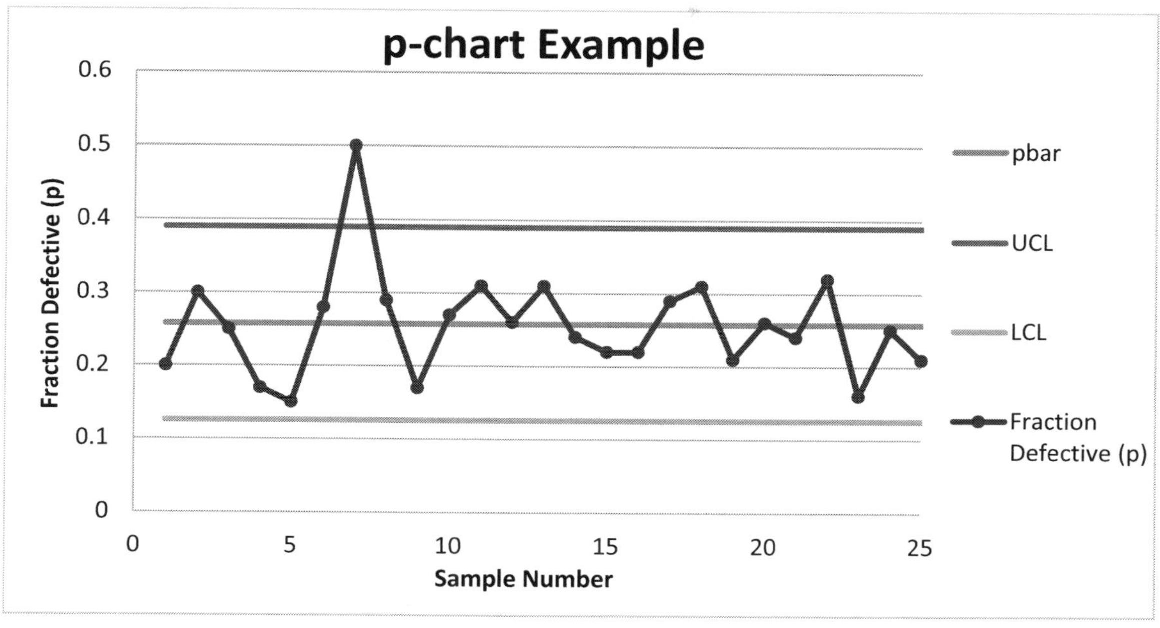

Np-Chart for Attribute Data

Np-charts follow a binomial distribution for defectives like p-charts. Np-charts differ in that they factor in the number of defectives within a constant subgroup size. Though the sensitivity of the chart diminishes compared to p-charts, where constant subgrouping size is essential to a process, these charts are most valuable. The np-chart calculation for control limits includes the number of samples as well as the product of subgroup size and defectives measured. Np-charts are plotted in a similar way to other attribute charts.

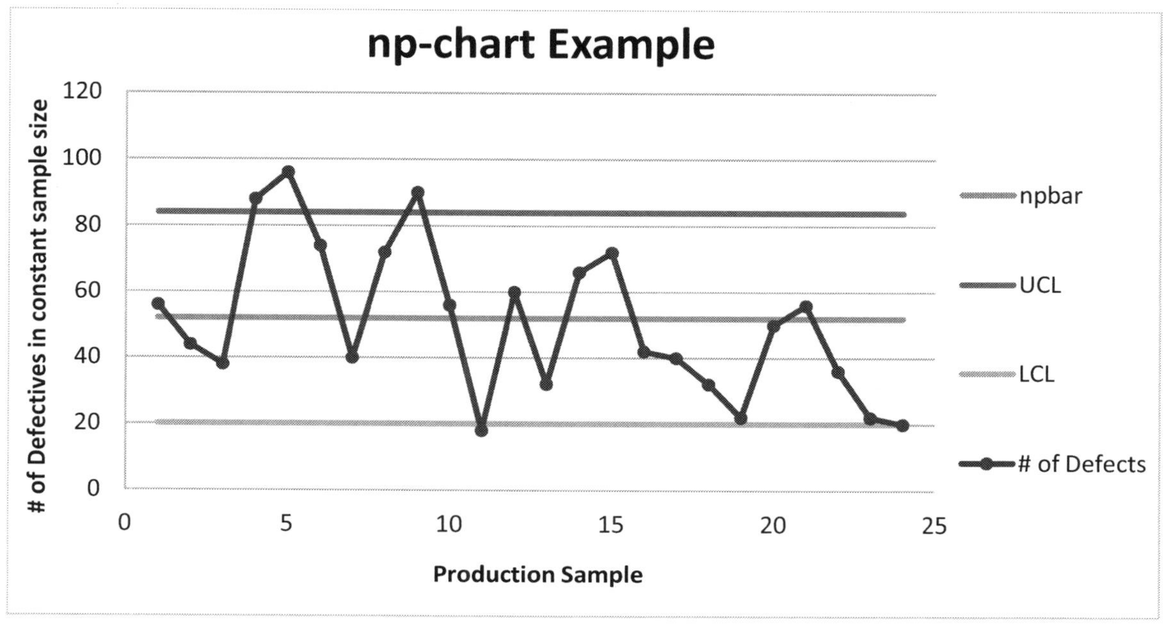

C-Chart for Attribute Data

The c-chart follows a Poisson distribution and reflects the number of defects within a subgroup of constant size. It is important to distinguish that c-charting looks at the number of defects, while p- and np-charting both look at defectives. A part in a subgroup may have one defect or 10 defects, but both situations imply that the part is a defective. The Cbar value within c-chart subgroups is calculated from the count of defects within the number of samples. Cbar can then be used to calculate the upper and lower control limits.

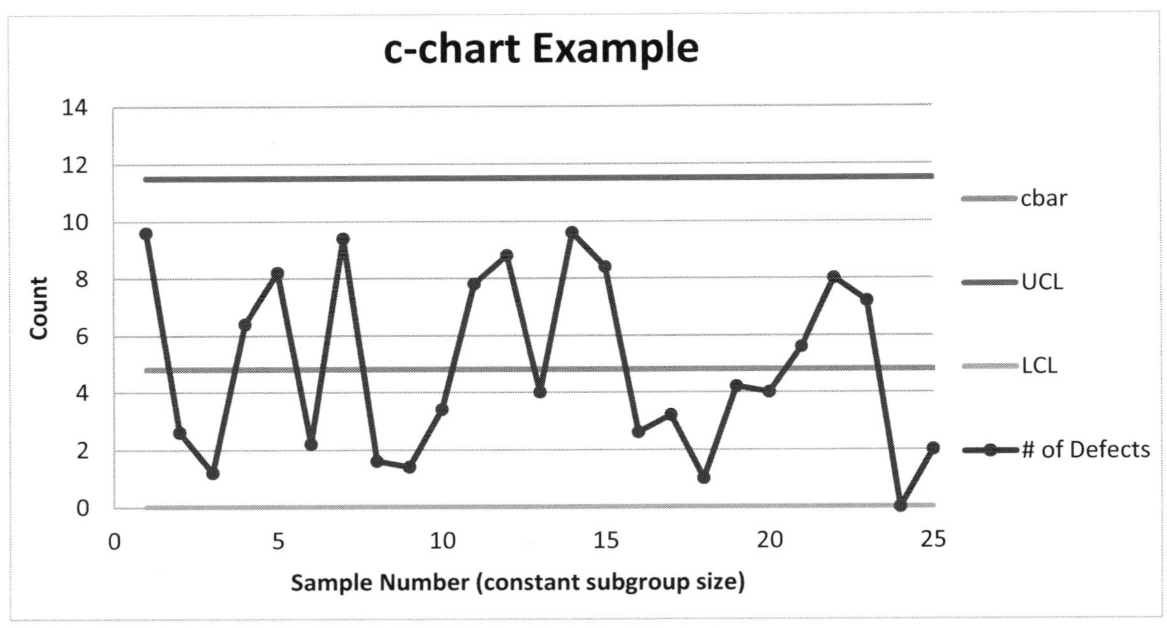

U-Chart for Attribute Data

The u-chart is also a Poisson distribution like the c-chart. The u-chart is similar to a p-chart in that it analyzes a proportion and uses a varying subgroup size. The u-chart does measure the number of defects per unit to derive an average defects per unit metric. Upper and lower control limits for the u-chart are also calculated using average defects per unit. Control limits in the u-chart fluctuate over time as the subgroup sample size changes. The resulting chart shows changing upper and lower control limits, a consistent centerline, and plotted points. Plotted points on the chart are calculated by the ratio of subgroup defects to the sample size.

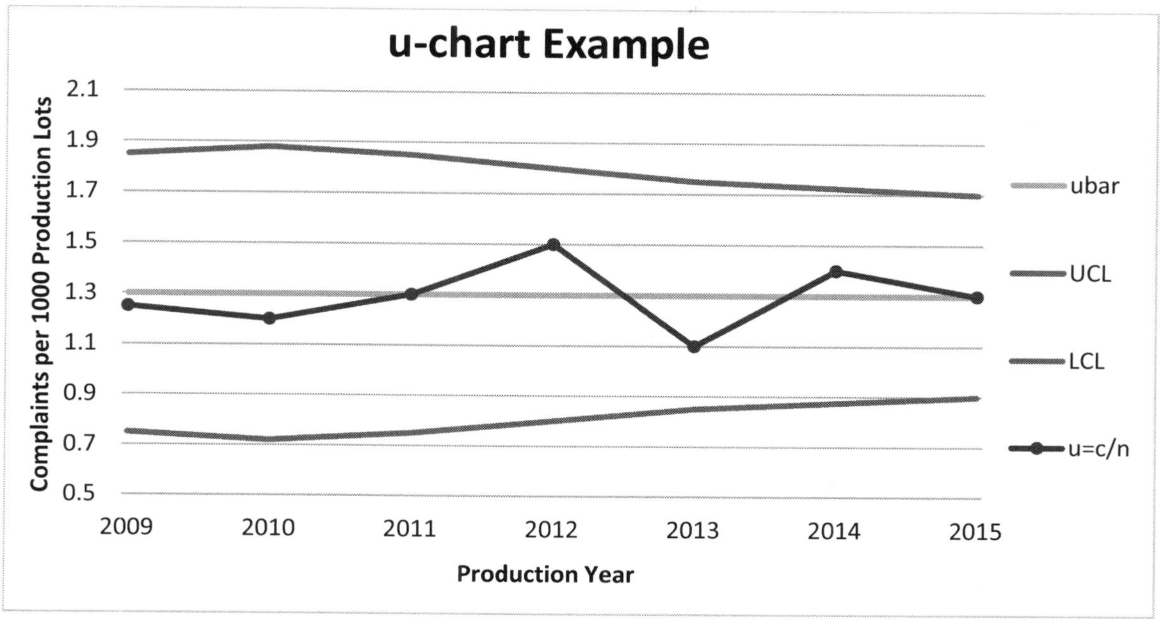

Short Run Charts for Controlling Improvements

Short-run control charts are used when the ability to take valuable SPC data on an output run is curtailed due to infrequent operation or small output volume of a process. For example, a production operation that performs many changeovers for different customers may not be able to generate longer control chart data due to a relatively high throughput process that does not take long to meet the order quantity. Short-run charts commonly use non-subgrouped datasets and thus related plot points and control limits derived from the non-subgrouped data, though subgrouping and attributes data can still be used in short-run SPC. Short-run charting can be successful when maximizing the data represented on the chart through data coding, a minimum of 20 subgroups, and common product groupings. Short-run SPC is best used when focusing on the macro-levels of the process rather than the individualized tools, materials, and products.

Special Cause and Common Cause Variation

In statistical process control (SPC) charting, special (assignable) cause variation represents changes in data points or data patterns that are a direct result of a known attributable cause, often the operator, the equipment, or material influencing the variation from target. Special cause variation will have a discernible root cause and should have corrective and preventive actions implemented to prevent recurrence. Common (random) cause variance is due to inherent variation within a normally functioning and controlled process. Such variation is not bad and does not need root cause investigation or corrective actions. Operators often mistakenly adjust processes that show common cause variance from the target. This unnecessary over-adjustment will backfire and add more variation into the previously controlled process. Alternatively, an operator failing to correct special cause variation will also be allowing variation to remain in the output of the process. Special cause variation in charting is typically represented by failing one of many run rules. Common cause variation is fluctuation of sequential data points without violating run rules.

Statistical Process Control Chart for XbarR

The XbarR chart is a very commonly used tool for statistical process control. Key elements include the Xbar chart and the R chart, generally Xbar above R. Tabular space for documenting individual measurements within a subgroup and for subgroup Xbar and R values is also needed. Chronological timestamping should be also be documented corresponding to each subgroup. Reference information such as specification limits, units of measure, operator, equipment or process being analyzed, and document control features are also important for quality assurance. Lastly, adequate space on the chart for documenting assignable cause variation and run rule violations is essential. Space to document corrective actions taken by an operator can help in determining improvement needs or acceptance of sections of a production run.

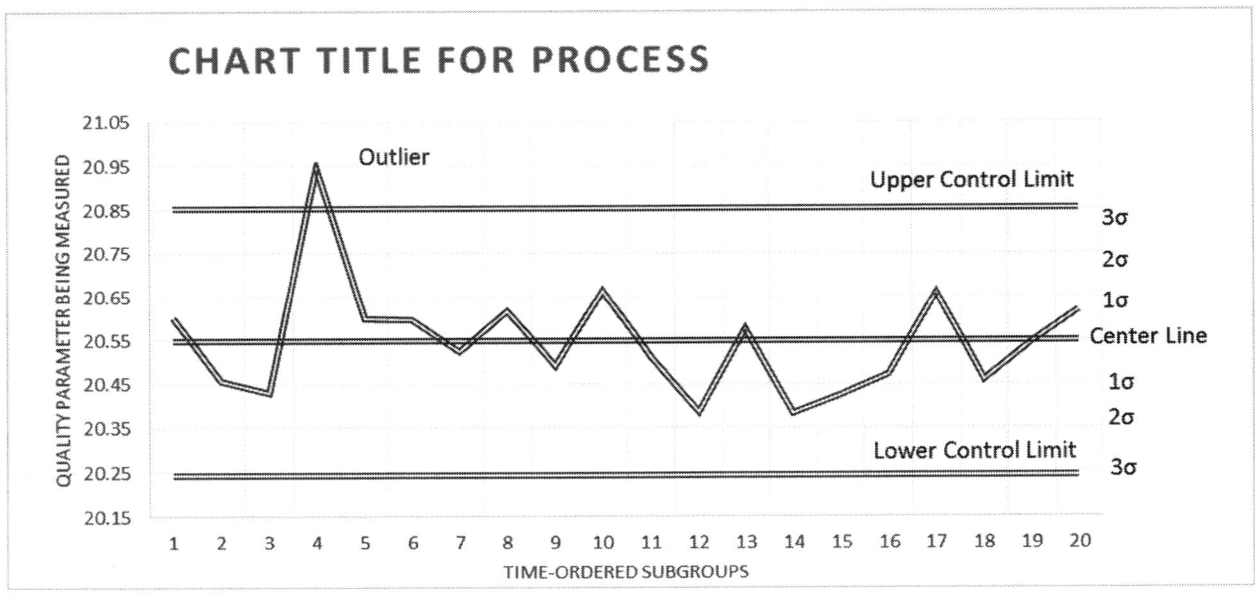

SPC Run Rule

Outliers and Two-Point Process Shifts

Outliers are data points that fall significantly beyond the upper or lower control limits and are generally followed by data points that fall back within the control limits. An outlier is defined in statistical process control (SPC) charting as one data point more than three sigmas away from the centerline. This assignable cause variance is usually due to recordkeeping error, mathematical error, severe failure of the process system or equipment, or some highly unusual occurrence. A two-point process shift run rule is defined as an SPC chart data pattern with two of three consecutive points more than two sigmas from the centerline all on the same side of the centerline. This same-side run rule is considered an early indicator that an assignable cause has occurred and the process is losing control.

Four of Five Points More Than One Sigma of the Centerline Either Side

When operators or quality assurance staff observe four or five consecutive data points at least one sigma from the centerline on their process control chart, the run should serve as an early indicator that the process is nearing an uncontrolled state. This type of run rule observation, and that of other same-side indicator rules, are presented in variables SPC charting. Observation of same-side early indicator variation should prompt the operations and quality teams to begin identifying a potential root cause and corrective action before quality and yield are lost.

Six-Points Rule

When operators review their SPC chart and observe six consecutive data points on the chart, all increasing or decreasing, there has been a process violation of the six-points rule. Generally, the assignable cause for this type of variation is equipment or operator skill level. Equipment and parts wear down over prolonged use, especially when not well maintained or worked above capacity. Six-point rule violations are generally due to gradual failure of components of equipment, tools, or chemicals used at the process. Furthermore, operators that identify perceived improvement in technique may experience a six-point rule violation as they devise ways to adjust their equipment differently. Sometimes overcorrecting poorly maintained equipment can present six-point rule data patterns.

Eight-Points Rule and Nine-Points Rule

The SPC eight-points rule indicates assignable cause variation to an operator when eight consecutive data points on a chart are all more than one sigma from the centerline on either side. This "either side" type of rule is common in variables data charts and can occur when multiples of operators or machines are used as sample sources for the charting. The SPC nine-points rule indicates assignable cause variation to an operator when nine consecutive data points on a chart are on the same side of the centerline. The root cause of the nine-points violation is a significant shift in the process mean that puts the process out of statistical control.

TPM

Total productive maintenance (TPM) is a lean tool that recognizes that equipment and workstation operators (for service industry) are best able to be the primary operator and basic maintenance specialist on their own equipment. TPM is a longer-term approach to optimizing key process stations for competitive success. TPM generally has a dedicated leader, often a lean Six Sigma black belt to coordinate the TPM process with operators. The results of TPM processes include better safety, cleanliness, education of workforce, and reduced equipment downtime. Added benefits include improved process flow, freed maintenance capacity, reduced quality failures, and a more engaged workforce.

Typical TPM Steps
1) Implement pre-requisites (downtime and planned maintenance tracking)
2) Select appropriate area
3) Define and measure downtime and utilization
4) Develop team and charter
5) Begin autonomous maintenance and 5S
6) Operator training program
7) Fine-tune planned maintenance
8) Begin focused improvement

Autonomous Maintenance

Autonomous maintenance (AM) programs are performed within a lean TPM initiative. AM transitions the majority of equipment management responsibilities to operators and away from maintenance or engineering. AM theory summarizes that equipment operators are best suited to care for and operate their equipment as well as perform basic problem solving and trouble-shooting on that equipment. More complex problem solving and periodic preventative maintenance are still performed by mechanics. Operators become responsible for the prevention of deterioration and standard operation of their assigned equipment. Standard operating procedures, cleaning procedures, and training are created to make consistency between all operators and develop their skills.

PREVENTATIVE MAINTENANCE

Preventative maintenance (PM) is a planning system where equipment and tools used for performing a process or manufacturing a good are subjected to restorative servicing before failure is reached. Manufacturers of the equipment or tools often provide reliability and PM information when such goods are purchased. PM programs are widely used in total productive maintenance systems within lean. PM programs are valuable sources of maintenance effectiveness information. Measures such as mean time between failure (MTBF) and mean time to repair (MTTR) can be calculated from strong PM recordkeeping. Preventative maintenance is often managed through paper-based service records or through scheduling software. Specific tasks, frequencies, and responsible mechanics can be assigned to each piece of equipment.

VISUAL CONTROLS

Visual controls are used to quickly convey a message to workers or stakeholders of the status of a process or workflow. The controls are meant to minimize or prevent process deviations. They are often used in manufacturing or service operations to indicate the status of elements of a process to workers and communicate that a decision has to be made. Visual controls are used widely in lean tools such as Kanban, 5S, poka-yoke, TPM, rapid changeover, and SMED. Visuals can provide a quick indication to workers, but are often limited to a small amount of information to be conveyed.

MEASUREMENT SYSTEM REANALYSIS DURING THE CONTROL PHASE OF DMAIC

Process improvements in DMAIC often result in significantly reduced process variation. Because the total variation is the sum of process variation and measurement system variation, a process reduction can increase the representative proportion of variation caused by the measurement system. The control phase is an opportunity to maximize the effect of the process improvement by reanalyzing gage R&R data as a measurement system reanalysis. Threshold values are commonly used when interpreting MSA error results. High error (over 30%) implies highly ineffective measurement. Below 10% error implies a highly capable measurement system. Values in between 10% and 30% are improvement opportunities where other influencing cost/benefit elements should be considered before making changes.

ELEMENTS TO CONTROL PLANNING IN DMAIC

A control plan is a summary document or table that highlights the key control elements that resulted from the earlier DMAIC phases. Positive improvements often revert back to failure, waste, and variation if controls are not maintained. Control planning provides clarity regarding how the inputs or outputs of the process are sustained, critical limits or tolerances, and responsible persons for each control step. Key information within control plans include related steps or dependent quality outcomes, inputs, critical limits or tolerances, measurement method, frequency and sample size, responsible person(s), corrective actions, and descriptive statements about each control method. Similar approaches are used in FMEA-based hazard analysis programs such as HACCP for food safety.

DOCUMENTING ORGANIZATIONAL LESSONS LEARNED

Documenting organizational successes from continuous improvement projects allows the organization to build upon previous work and sustain past solutions to prevent falling back into undesirable conditions. Documentation of lessons learned can also help future efforts avoid mistakes and failures that were learned in the past. With the improvement trail blazed, setting a permanent path helps the organization continue forward through the unknown opportunities ahead. Common methods to build upon previous improvements include project presentations, A3 reports, and changes to strategic planning. Methods used to prevent fallback to states of poor quality include capturing new methods in standard operating procedures or standard work. Work instructions, document control updates, employee training, audits, check sheets, and KPIs also contribute to sustaining the improvement in the control step of DMAIC. Avoiding repeat mistakes can also be achieved by the tools mentioned. Error proofing concepts like poka-yoke, statistical process control, and DFSS provide preventative controls. Strong organizations may employ knowledge management roles to feed lessons learned to key divisions and colleagues.

Training to Sustain Quality Improvements

New information and solutions to quality problems will not last if efforts are not made to sustain the improvements and cement them into the organization's knowledge base. New standard operating procedures, work instructions, operating plans, and quality recordkeeping all may require that operators, managers, and stakeholders become trained to these new approaches. Getting stakeholder commitment, awareness, and competence will ensure the improvement becomes part of the organizational culture and norms. New employees may need updated orientation training that reflects the improvements. Existing employees may need an update of past training or work instruction content because of the improvement. Competence of understanding of the new improvement should be verified by trainers; employees not grasping the new improvements should be retrained and retested. Furthermore, new practices that result from improvement efforts may require certain employees and managers to receive formal lean Six Sigma training through a certified training body.

Ongoing Evaluation Strategies to Sustain Improvements

Many of the tools used in other phases of DMAIC can be essential for the control phase when teams are looking to continuously maintain improvements and prevent fallback into states of poor quality. Measurement systems analysis (MSA) is a tool that can be continuously used to verify measurement devices and methods for consistency to validated reference standards. Gage repeatability and reliability studies should be repeated periodically so that drift and poor quality do not creep back into measurement activities. Process capability studies performed continuously as key performance indicators can help teams be constantly knowledgeable of how their process meets quality expectations of their customers. Capability and poor quality can be controlled using SPC control charts. Periodic challenging of the SPC system by an outside validator can be helpful in preventing bias and unseen drift. Lastly, key performance indicators (KPIs), with enforced corrective and preventive actions if KPIs are missed, help an organization measure performance against strategic plans.

Downtime

Production operations experience downtime when a piece of equipment or process itself was scheduled to run but, for any number of reasons, is not functioning as scheduled. More simply, downtime is when scheduled activity does not occur for an assignable cause. Organizations running lean and Six Sigma initiatives track downtime in their operations, often by piece of equipment and by production line as a whole. Downtime is a contributing factor in measuring utilization and overall equipment effectiveness (OEE). Processes with buffers and equipment redundancy may not count upstream downtime at individual equipment as long as flow continues through a downstream bottleneck or constraint in a process. However, loss of throughput due to equipment failure can never be recovered, even if line speeds are increased ahead of the bottleneck. Measuring downtime can help identify failure root causes and focus improvement efforts on the vital few sources of downtime. Measuring downtime and related concepts such as mean-time-between-failure and mean-time-to-repair help keep throughput and flow at desired rates.

Scheduled production time (hrs)	Unscheduled downtime at bottleneck (hrs)	% Downtime
13,450	567.5	=567.5/13,450 = 4.2% downtime = 95.8% utilization in OEE calculation

Design for Six Sigma Framework and Methodologies

DFSS AND ALIGNMENT BETWEEN DMAIC AND DFSS

DFSS uses a wide range of Six Sigma tools used to prevent waste and build quality into products and processes. This is performed by Six Sigma-trained design teams early in the development phases before launch or release rather than after products are being made for the market. DFSS processes reinforce quality prediction to improve performance of early designs and shorten the time from concept to commerce. DFSS creates a long-term shift in cost of quality towards design and prevention. DFSS organizations are much less likely to have high costs of internal and external failure. Quality issues, defects, and failure modes are identified through probability and testing; such deficiencies are prevented early in the development process to keep variation infinitesimal. DMAIC aligns with DFSS primarily in the common toolbox of statistics and improvement methods.

DMADV AND ALIGNMENT WITH DMAIC AND DFSS

DMADV stands for define, measure, analyze, design, verify. It is a common type of design for Six Sigma (DFSS) modelling that uses key LSS tools to create high-quality design. The first three phases are identical to DMAIC. Design in DMADV focuses on building the framework of the project, the goals, the charter, etc. It also focuses on voice of the customer (VOC) and QFD/house of quality tasks to objectively confirm the customer design expectations. Measurement in DMADV focuses on selecting CTQs, completing stakeholder analyses, and developing specifications. The analyze phase begins testing the design and process for failures, defects, poor quality, and waste. Benchmarking is often used in the analyze phase of DMADV. The design phase of DMADV is similar to the implement phase of DMAIC. The measured and analyzed knowledge is now executed into a designed product. Here, advanced tools such as modeling, DOE, process mapping, and prototyping are used. Lastly, a verification step is used as a means to control the design and ensure it meets the stated objectives and customer expectations. Six Sigma tools such as capability studies, statistical process control, and auditing help sustain these assurances.

DMADOV AND ALIGNMENT WITH DMAIC

DMADOV as a DFSS strategy is nearly identical to DMADV in steps and alignment with DMAIC. DMADOV includes an additional step of optimize after the design phase. Though this is implied in the DMADV process, the two DFSS methods differ by the formal use of improvement tools such as plan-do-check-act cycles (or similar) in DMADOV. Statistical evaluation of the performance levels against customer requirements would prompt the DMADOV team to redesign, modify designs, or modify process in order to optimize quality before product launch. Assessing statistical quality levels through the optimize and verify phases cannot be understated. Strong examples include capability studies and resulting predictive sigma values for process steps and final output against customer parameters.

DMEDI AND ALIGNMENT WITH DMAIC

DMEDI stands for design, measure, explore, develop, and implement. DMEDI is a statistical innovation approach to designing quality and customer requirements into a product or service during development. It is also widely used to redesign an existing product or service to better match customer expectations when common DMAIC approaches have failed. Redesign through DMEDI often occurs when it is just as beneficial to start from scratch. DMEDI is similar to other DFSS processes but differs in its blended use of lean Six Sigma and innovation concepts. Also,

DMEDI is typically a longer and more resource-intensive process compared to DMAIC. Often, significant process and cultural change may be required when developing the design concepts from a DMEDI process.

The design and measure phases of DMEDI are almost identical to that of DMAIC. There is no strong frame of reference with voice of the customer data in DMEDI; it must be obtained anew. The explore phase launches new tools such as ideation, innovation stage-gate, and concept discovery sessions. Develop and implement phases of DMEDI include designed experiments, prototyping, mapping, simulations, and field studies so that concepts can be evaluated and proven before further push to market.

IDOV Process

IDOV is a process similar to design for Six Sigma that relies heavily on voice of the customer and quality function deployment to establish quality design. IDOV stands for identify, design, optimize, validate. The identify phase evaluates customer quality requirements through voice of the customer tools such as CTQs and quality function deployment. The design phase serves to define the functional requirements, implement critical to quality factors, and evaluating optimal prototypes. The optimize phase involves fine tuning the design concept with the quality parameters in mind. The final phase of validation includes prototype testing and reliability evaluations.

Method of Design for Cost

Design for cost (DFC) approaches to quality design begin with the target cost and develop the customer's product or service within the cost limitations. The DFC approach is often used when customer(s) require a capped budget for development or when the producing firm has imposed expense restrictions or mandatory margins. Six Sigma and innovation concepts can be used to keep waste, variation, and failures minimal so that cost variations during production are reliable. DFC generally designs its product or service based on customer purchase cost and customer life-cycle cost. Voice of the customer, external market analysis, and benchmarking are key elements in understanding the customer market, knowing customer feature trade-offs, and creating realistic concepts to match what the market will bear. Life cycle costs include expenses paid by the customer beyond the actual acquisition; these can include infrastructure, maintenance, training, and parts.

Design for Manufacturing, Production, and Assembly Variants of DFSS

Similar to design for cost, design for manufacturing (DFM), production (DFP) and assembly (DFA) are used for quality product and process design, with the design focused on different operational functions. All seek to optimize the product or service design for ideal manufacturing capability. It would be considered limiting if these similar approaches were not used in conjunction with a customer-focused DFSS method. Optimization for processing or manufacturing alone will not inherently please customers. DFM and its related methods are performed using many lean elements. Concepts such as waste reduction, 5S, SMED, Rapid change-over, and TPM are all essential to ensuring a well-designed process for manufacturing, production, and assembly.

Design for Test Approach

Design for test (DFT) approaches to Six Sigma design focus on including product features that allow the production or quality teams to perform non-destructive functionality tests of products before reaching consumers. DFT is very common in electronics and advanced technology operations. During the design process, features not likely to add or remove value from the customer are built into the product to support such testing. Ease of testing and appropriate testing protocols support the uniform and consistent testing during or after the production process.

Design for Maintainability Approach

Design for maintainability is a DFSS concept commonly seen in industrial equipment and complex retail/consumer equipment where mechanical or electrical maintenance is likely required over time. Designing products to be easily maintained allows for more customer satisfaction and loyalty. Good designs for maintainability include concepts similar to lean and total productive maintenance. Examples of subparts to the approach include minimal time to make repairs, simplified and minimal parts, limited or no special tools needed for maintenance, ease of inspection, inherently designed safety, and failure detection. Quality metrics and specifications may be imposed upon the product in order to verify that value is being delivered to the customer.

Design for Robustness

Robust design allows for the equipment, product, or service to be flexible to a wide variance in input tolerance. A robust process or product should be able to perform as the customer expects, despite a reasonable variation in input attributes. Output of a robust design should also not show significant variance from customer expectations as a result of variable input. Another source of variance factored into robust designs includes the operating environment. Customer-related activities in the define phase of DMAIC are valuable tools to obtain customer expectations regarding robustness.

Noise Strategies Used in Design for Robustness

Noise, as a form of background variation, exists within an input variable to a process. At any point along that process, where the process generates a response, such noise variation may influence the result of an output measure within a range of likely response outcomes. The process response function can be determined using designed experiments. In other words, where a process generates a defined set of outcomes, variation in input raw materials will lead to variation in output measures of quality. The noise element can significantly disrupt the quality outcome. Knowing the response function, an effective noise mitigation strategy can be used where the optimal input level and variation can be derived so that the quality variation can be minimized in the output.

Tolerance Design, Statistical Tolerances, and Conventional Tolerances

As a continuation of noise strategy, tolerance design works backwards to identify the acceptable variation for input variables so that the process response yields ideal quality measures for the output. This ideal outcome covers a range of acceptable values; that range represents the acceptable tolerance permitted so that quality is maintained. Tolerance parameters must then be set or adjusted for the input variable with the vendor(s) so that output remains consistent. A common problem arises when trying to fit capability within tolerances. For example, stacked components to make a whole. The conventional approach to a worst case scenario is to gain unit tolerances by taking the whole tolerances and dividing by the number of stacked components. A better way to fit capabilities within tolerances is to add stack component variances through statistical tolerancing. The latter approach often yields a wider tolerance, yet still results in adequate capability.

Worst-case tolerancing for stacked parts		**Statistical tolerancing for stacked parts**	
Stacked tolerance 10.0mm ±0.100mm # of stacks = 5	Component tolerance = 10.0mm/5 = 2.0mm 0.100mm/5 = 0.02mm = 2.0mm ± 0.02mm	σ_{stack} = $\sqrt{\sigma_A{}^2 + \cdots + \sigma_n{}^2}$ recognizing each part of stack may have different dimensions.	Stack tolerance = Statistical tolerance is often greater than any individual stack part tolerance and higher than the worst-case result.

TAGUCHI QUALITY LOSS FUNCTION AND PROTOTYPING METHOD

The Taguchi loss function adds a cost to output that is produced and deviates from the central target within customer specification limits. Deviation from this central mean adds economic consequences and financial loss in the form of poor quality, potential lost sales, and lower customer satisfaction. While traditional thinking held that parts that are produced and measure within the specification range are good, the Taguchi approach introduced increasing losses as measurements diverged from optimum. The method is primarily used by Six Sigma professionals rather than financial professionals as a tool to prioritize improvement efforts.

Taguchi Loss Function Graph	Taguchi Loss Function
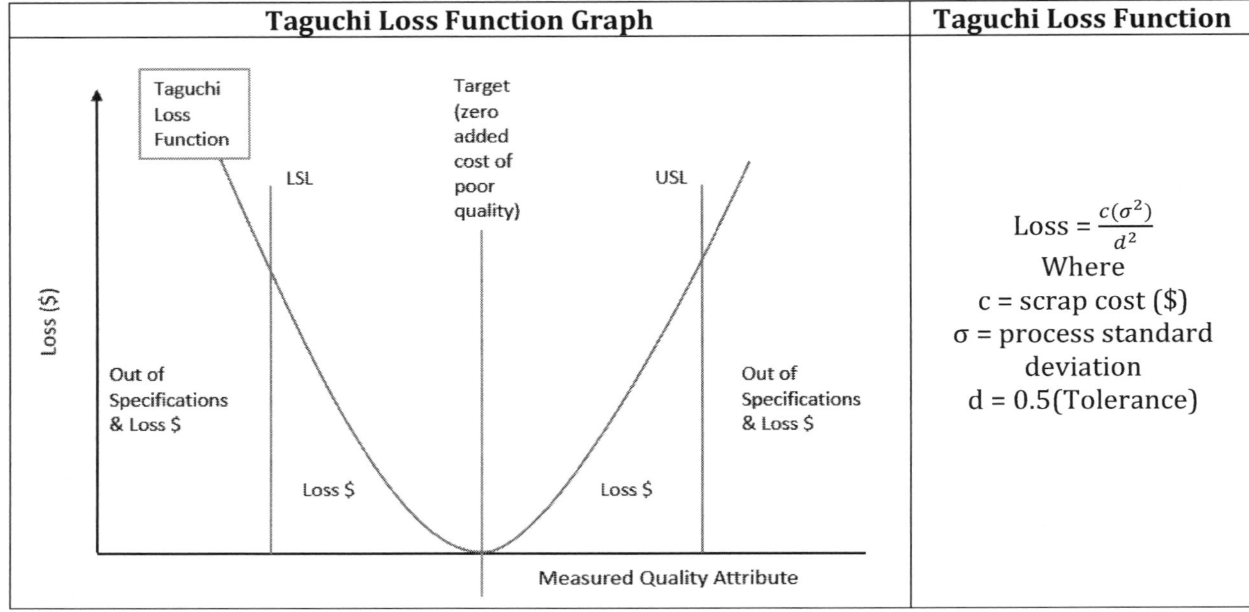	Loss = $\frac{c(\sigma^2)}{d^2}$ Where c = scrap cost ($) σ = process standard deviation d = 0.5(Tolerance)

Six Sigma Practice Test

1. Which key performance indicator is calculated by subtracting current costs from ideal costs?

a. Cost of poor quality
b. Revenue growth
c. Competitive quality
d. Performance on quality improvement

2. Which type of chart is appropriate when sample size is variable and each sample may contain more than one instance of the targeted condition?

a. P chart
b. Autocorrelation chart
c. U chart
d. X-bar chart

3. What is the purpose of PERT analysis during the analyze phase of DMAIC?

a. To identify the most influential steps in a process
b. To monitor improvements in cycle time
c. To identify the critical path of a process
d. To reduce cycle time

4. Which of the following is a disadvantage of using engineering process control devices to prevent deviation?

a. The devices must be monitored by human operators.
b. The use of these devices precludes the use of statistical process controls.
c. These devices require constant maintenance.
d. These devices cannot handle multiple inputs.

5. Which form of leveling typically includes the use of heijunka boxes?

a. Leveling by volume
b. Leveling by product
c. Demand leveling
d. Customer leveling

6. Which parameter of a statistical distribution relates to the sharpness of its peak?

a. Central tendency
b. Kurtosis
c. Skewness
d. Standard deviation

7. If a mixed-level experimental design has four factors with three levels and two factors with three levels, how many total runs are required for the experiment?

a. 24
b. 64
c. 72
d. 90

8. Which method of creating a prioritization matrix is appropriate when time is limited?

a. Partial analytical method
b. Consensus–criteria method
c. Full analytical method
d. Summary method

9. In which design is it possible to have two-factor interactions confounded with one another as well as with higher-order interactions?

a. Resolution IV
b. Resolution V
c. Resolution VI
d. Resolution VII

10. Which of the following is a disadvantage of higher-order multiple regression models?

a. These models do a poor job of defining the area around a stationary point.
b. Comprehensive and detailed experiments must be performed on the main effects.
c. These models rarely have clear peaks and valleys.
d. Small regions are difficult to perceive.

11. In response surface analysis, which of the following values for *s* and *t* weights would indicate that the upper and lower boundaries are more important than the target?

a. –0.3
b. 0
c. 1
d. 7

12. Which type of human error is typically limited to a particular task?

a. Willful
b. Inadvertent
c. Technique
d. Selective

13. If a process consists of two tasks, the first of which has a 0.04 probability of error and the second of which has a 0.03 probability of error, and these errors can occur at the same time, what is the overall likelihood of an error occurring during the process?

a. 0.0012
b. 0.0688
c. 0.0120
d. 0.1688

14. In a histogram, the number of bars is equal to

a. the square root of the total number of data values.
b. the square root of the range of data.
c. the range of data divided by the total number of data values.
d. the number of data observations.

15. Which of the following diagrams indicates the critical path of a process?

a. Gantt chart
b. Work breakdown structure
c. Value stream analysis
d. Matrix diagram

16. During which stage of DMAIC is level loading typically performed?

a. Define
b. Control
c. Improve
d. Measure

17. Which of the following increases the power of an estimation of the confidence interval on the mean?

a. A sample population with a normal distribution
b. A smaller number of samples
c. A known standard deviation
d. An unknown standard deviation

18. Which of Altshuller's eight laws for system development asserts that functions will tend toward simplicity and efficiency?

a. Law of transition to a super system
b. Law of increasing substance-field involvement
c. Law of increasing ideality
d. Law of harmonization

19. In an analysis of variance, how is the F statistic used?

a. To compare the mean square treatment with the mean square error
b. To estimate the process average
c. To find the variation within each subgroup
d. To find the variation between different subgroups

20. In a numerical matrix diagram using a ten-point scale, which of the following values would indicate the strongest relationship?

a. 9
b. 1/10
c. 1
d. –1/5

21. If there are 32 observations in an experiment, it is typical to run autocorrelations from lag 1 to

a. lag 4.
b. lag 8.
c. lag 16.
d. lag 32.

22. Which of the following is a disadvantage of using enumerative statistics?

a. It is difficult to determine whether the samples are representative.
b. These statistics do not produce an assumed distribution.
c. They cannot be applied to process baseline estimation.
d. Values are drawn from a static population.

23. Which distribution is appropriate for a continuous set of data with a fixed lower boundary but no upper boundary?

a. Johnson
b. Exponential
c. Normal
d. Lognormal

24. In metrology, what is the degree to which a measurement can be compared to a known standard with confidence called?

a. Traceability
b. Measurement uncertainty
c. Calibration
d. Engineering tolerance

25. Which of the following autocorrelation functions would indicate the strongest correlation?

a. 0.1
b. –0.8
c. 0.9
d. –0.2

26. In Porter's five forces analysis, what is the likely result of strong distribution channels?

a. Switching distributers will have no impact on cost.
b. There will be more incentive for new firms to enter the market.
c. Suppliers will have less bargaining power.
d. Firms will have a hard time maintaining competitive advantage.

27. In most cases, what is the lowest coefficient of determination that is considered acceptable in a linearity analysis?

a. 10%
b. 30%
c. 50%
d. 70%

28. Which type of Pareto chart would be the least useful?

a. One in which the bars represent costs
b. One in which the cumulative percentage line is steep
c. One in which all the bars are roughly the same height
d. One in which the bars on the left are significantly taller than the bars on the right

29. Which median test is the most appropriate for handling outliers?

a. Mood's median test
b. Kruskal–Wallis test
c. Mann–Whitney test
d. Kolmogorov–Smirnov test

30. Which distribution should be used when the targeted characteristic may appear more than once per unit?

a. Binomial
b. Exponential
c. Lognormal
d. Poisson

31. What is the final step in a kaizen event?

a. Modifying the solution after implementation
b. Celebrating success
c. Implementing a solution
d. Laying off employees

32. If all of the data points on an *Np* chart fall between the upper and lower control limits, the process is

a. representative.
b. stable.
c. efficient.
d. erratic.

33. What is the Japanese term for *inconsistency*?

a. Mura
b. Muki
c. Muda
d. Muri

34. In nominal group technique, how many pieces of paper should each participant receive if there are 40 options to be considered?

a. 2
b. 4
c. 6
d. 8

35. What is the term for the degree to which an experimental design allows all the indicated parameters to be measured independently of one another?

a. Autonomy
b. Normalization
c. Orthogonality
d. Balance

36. Which of the following factors is not included in the calculation of risk priority number?

a. Detection level
b. Severity
c. Expense
d. Likelihood

37. In an exponentially weighted moving-average chart, which of the following weighting factors would be best for detecting small shifts?

a. 0.4
b. 0.19
c. 0.38
d. 0.47

38. How many runs would be required in a complete factorial design if there are four levels and three factors?

a. 7
b. 12
c. 64
d. 81

39. In which of these scenarios would batching be appropriate?

a. Setup time for the activity is significant.
b. The process contains multiple steps.
c. Completed products must be shipped in bulk.
d. Employees must wait for a certain amount of materials before beginning a task.

40. Which of the following run tests identifies shifts in the process mean?

a. Run test 4
b. Run test 6
c. Run test 7
d. Run test 8

41. Which of the following items is NOT a part of the typical tollgate review?

a. Milestone list
b. Project deliverables document
c. Check sheet
d. Gantt chart

42. In kaizen, what is the term that refers to the idea that one step in a process should be completed only when the subsequent steps are ready?

a. Flow
b. Poka-yoke
c. Pull
d. Perfection

43. Which business performance measure is calculated by subtracting current cash outflows from current cash inflows?

a. Revenue growth
b. Net present value
c. Return on investment
d. Margin

44. Which of the following is NOT one of the phases of rapid problem resolution?

a. Resolution
b. Investigation
c. Discovery
d. Implementation

45. Which pioneer of quality control wrote *Quality Is Free*?

a. W. Edward Deming
b. Joseph M. Juran
c. Armand V. Feigenbaum
d. Philip B. Crosby

46. Which experimental design is similar to a central composite design but without corner or extreme points?

a. John's ¾ design
b. Plackett–Burman design
c. Box–Behnken design
d. Mixed-level design

47. Which of the following is NOT one of the seven classic wastes?

a. Motion
b. Transportation
c. Inventory
d. Indecision

48. In order to calibrate an instrument, one must know the ______ of both the instrument and the standard.

a. durability
b. traceability
c. tolerance
d. measurement uncertainty

49. Which of the following is an advantage of the transformation technique known as *normalization*?

a. Normalization screens irrelevant factors from a nonlinear experimental design.
b. Normalization balances the experimental array.
c. Normalization places all values on a common scale from 0 to 2.
d. Normalization is more effective in nonlinear experiments.

50. In a Kano model, what value is always on the *y*-axis?

a. Time
b. Satisfaction
c. Quality
d. Price

Answer Key and Explanations

1. A: The *cost of poor quality* is calculated by subtracting current costs from ideal costs. This is just a rough estimate as the exact value of the cost of poor quality is unknowable. The point of estimating the cost of poor quality is to get a general idea of what savings could be made available through remediation and improvement efforts. *Revenue growth* is calculated by determining the net increase in sales figures over a particular interval. *Competitive quality* is an umbrella term for a set of metrics related to the parts of performance that have the most influence on sales. Some competitive quality measures depend on obtaining information from customers. *Performance on quality improvement,* finally, is a subjective metric that includes the number of completed and active projects, the financial results of these projects, and the number of employees and hours required for the project.

2. C: A *U chart* is appropriate when sample size is variable and each sample may contain more than one instance of the targeted condition. These are control charts most appropriate for handling attributes data. A *P chart,* on the other hand, is better for measuring the percentage of samples with a particular characteristic when sample size is variable and the characteristic will either be present or absent. An *autocorrelation chart* indicates the relationships between various factors in the process. An *X-bar chart,* finally, is a control chart for variables data, in which the subgroup averages are assessed to determine the process location variation over time.

3. C: The purpose of program evaluation and review techniques (PERT) analysis during the analyze phase of DMAIC is to identify the critical path of a process. PERT analysis uses activity network diagrams and other charts to isolate the tasks on the critical path. Note that the critical path is the sequence of necessarily consecutive steps in a task, such that the sum of the durations required for each step on the critical path will be the minimum amount of time required for the total process. PERT analysis may also be used to identify the most influential steps in a process, though this takes place during the define stage of DMAIC: Likewise, PERT analysis may be used during the improve stage to monitor adjustments to cycle time. The overarching goal of PERT analysis is to reduce cycle time, but this answer choice is too general to be correct.

4. B: One disadvantage of using engineering process controls to prevent deviation is that the use of these devices precludes the use of statistical process controls. An *engineering process control* is a mechanism that automatically adjusts inputs when it detects variations in the process. A thermostat is a basic example of an engineering process control. It is not necessary for these devices to be monitored by human operators, and in most cases, engineering process controls do not require constant maintenance. The constant adjustments made by these devices, however, mean that any data related to their activities is not independent and, therefore, cannot be analyzed with statistical process control charts. However, the engineering process controls used by heavy industry are capable of handling a number of different inputs and outputs simultaneously.

5. B: Leveling by product typically includes the use of heijunka boxes. A *heijunka box* is a tool for scheduling in which the tasks to be completed and the estimated times for initiation and completion are listed. The point of leveling by product is to reduce inefficiency by adjusting the mix of products or the order in which they are produced. Leveling by volume, by contrast, is an approach to reducing inefficiency in which production is aligned with average demand. Demand leveling is a series of strategies that attempt to make customer demand more uniform and predictable. There is no such thing as customer leveling.

6. B: *Kurtosis* is the parameter of a statistical distribution related to the sharpness of the peak. In a normal distribution, where the points resemble the standard bell curve, the kurtosis value is one. If the peak is sharper, the kurtosis value will be higher than one; if the peak is less severe, the kurtosis value will be less than one. *Central tendency* is the general trend of the data: In an asymmetrical distribution, the median is roughly equivalent to the central tendency, while in an asymmetrical distribution, the mean is a better marker. *Skewness* is basically the difference between the mean and the mode of a data set. The *mode* of the data set is the value that appears most often. Finally, the *standard deviation* of the data set is the average amount of variation from the mean.

7. D: If a mixed-level experimental design has four factors with three levels and two factors with three levels, 90 total runs will be required. The formula for calculating the number of required runs for a mixed-level experimental design is similar to that used on a complete factorial design. The number of factors must be raised to the power equal to the number of levels for that factor. So, for this problem, the total number of runs is calculated as $3^4 + 3^2 = 81 + 9 = 90$.

8. B: When time is limited, the consensus–criteria method should be used to create a prioritization matrix. In this method, a group of people are each allotted 100 points, which they then allocate across a series of criteria according to perceived importance. Prioritization matrices are used to identify those projects that will create the most value improvement over the long term. Also, organizations use participation matrices to identify the projects that will contribute the most to the achievement of the organizational goals. Besides the consensus–criteria method, the other method for creating a prioritization matrix is called the *full analytical method*. In this method, all of the various options are listed, and the members of the team assign a numerical value to each.

9. A: In a resolution IV experimental design, it is possible to have two-factor interactions confounded with one another as well as with higher-order interactions. The point of design resolution is to determine the types of interactions that may be estimated independently within a particular design. When factors and interactions are confounded, they may not be estimated. Resolution V designs feature main-factor and two-factor interactions that are not confounded with one another, though it is possible that these interactions may be confounded with higher-order interactions. In a resolution VI experimental design, main-factor and two-factor interactions are not confounded with one another or with three-factor interactions, but three-factor and higher-order interactions may be confounded with one another. In a resolution VII design, main-factor, two-factor, and three-factor interactions are not confounded with one another, but each of these interactions may be confounded with higher-order interactions. It is also possible for four-factor and higher-order interactions in a resolution VII design to be confounded.

10. B: One disadvantage of higher-order multiple regression models is that comprehensive and detailed experiments must be performed on the main effects. Otherwise, it will not be wise to assume that the results of the higher-order multiple regression models are useful or accurate. However, higher-order multiple regression models have a number of advantages. For one thing, they are excellent at clearly defining the area around a stationary point. They typically have well-defined peaks and valleys, which enable analysis. Also, they are very effective at mapping small regions in the process, so they are able to achieve a high level of precision and detail.

11. D: In response surface analysis, values of 7 for the *s* and *t* weights would indicate that the upper and lower boundaries are more important than the target. In phase 2 of response surface analysis, the *s* and *t* weights are based on the relationship between the target and the boundary. When the target and the boundary have equal value, the *s* and *t* weights are 1. When the target is more important than the boundary, the *s* and *t* weights are between 1 and 10. When the boundary is more important than the target, the *s* and *t* weights are between 0.1 and 1.

12. C: Technique error is typically limited to a particular task. Six Sigma experts identify three categories of human error: technique, inadvertent, and willful. Technique errors are the result of a lack of comprehension or poor training. It is more likely that technique errors will occur on difficult tasks. Inadvertent errors are slightly different because they occur by accident even when an employee is experienced and understands the task. It is impossible to entirely eliminate inadvertent errors so long as there are human operators. A willful error is made intentionally by an employee. The best way to reduce willful errors is to maintain high morale and incentivize high performance.

13. B: If a process consists of two tasks, the first of which has a 0.04 probability of error and the second of which has a 0.03 probability of error, and these errors can occur at the same time, the overall likelihood of an error occurring during the process is 0.0688. The formula for the probability of two events that can happen at the same time is $P(A \cup B) = P(A) + P(B) - P(A \cap B)$, meaning the probability of A or B occurring is equal to the probability of A plus the probability of B minus the probability of A and B. In this case, then, the probability would be calculated as $0.04 + 0.03 - (0.04 \times 0.03) = 0.0688$.

14. A: In a histogram, the number of bars is equal to the square root of the total number of data values. Histograms look like bar graphs, but the bars on a histogram represent the number of observations that fall within a particular range. Histograms are often used to locate multiple distributions or apply a distribution to capability analysis. The width of each bar in a histogram is calculated by dividing the range of data by the number of bars. The range of data is determined by subtracting the minimum data value from the maximum data value. On a histogram, the x-axis represents the data values of each bar, and the y-axis indicates the number of observations.

15. A: A *Gantt chart* indicates the critical path of a process. The *critical path* is the sequence of steps that have a direct bearing on the overall length of the process. Some steps can be delayed without elongating the overall duration of the process: These steps are not considered to be on the critical path. A *work breakdown structure* depicts the organization of a process. To create a work breakdown structure, one isolates the various components of a problem and then considers the various contingencies associated with each component. A *value stream analysis* determines the elements of a process that add value to the finished product. These elements are targeted for special attention. Finally, a *matrix diagram* depicts the relative strengths of the relationships between the items in different groups. A matrix diagram might indicate causal relationships between various factors in a process or might simply indicate which of the factors are related.

16. C: Level loading is typically performed during the improve stage of DMAIC. The intention of level loading is to make the flow of orders in a process more regular and predictable. When level loading is effective, fewer inventory checks and less wait time should be required during the course of a process. Level loading depends on careful measurement of takt time earlier in the DMAIC process.

17. C: A known standard deviation increases the power of an estimation of the confidence interval on the mean. Indeed, when the standard deviation is known, the z tables may be used to find the confidence interval on the mean; when the standard deviation is unknown, the t tables must be used. The confidence interval on the mean is the percentage of samples that will contain the true population mean. It is assumed that the sample population will follow a normal distribution. When there are more samples, this increases the power of the estimation of the confidence interval on the mean.

18. C: Altshuller's law of increasing ideality asserts that functions will tend toward simplicity and efficiency. Genrich Altshuller is famous for devising eight basic laws of system development, which form the philosophical core of his theory of inventive problem solving (TRIZ). These laws were created to solve engineering problems, though Altshuller contended that they could be applied in any situation. The *law of increasing ideality* is essentially an optimistic vision of the evolution of functions over time. The *law of transition to a super system* asserts that the individual solutions created for specific systems will eventually become components of a larger, comprehensive system. The *law of increasing substance-field involvement* asserts that engineers will treat design problems as two individual materials interacting through a field, and the results of these interactions will be system improvements. *The law of harmonization* suggests that, as a system improves, energy will be transferred throughout it more efficiently.

19. A: In an analysis of variance, the *F statistic* is used to compare the mean square treatment with the mean square error. The *mean square treatment* is the average variation between the subsets, while the *mean square error* is the sum of the squares of the residuals. In order to trust the results of the F statistic, one must assume that the subsets have a normal distribution and unequal variance. The variation within each subgroup is calculated by taking repeated samples from the subgroup. The variation between different subgroups is found by comparing the averages of each subgroup.

20. B: In a numerical matrix diagram, a value of 1/10 would indicate the strongest relationship. Numerical matrix diagrams assign relationships values on a scale to indicate the strength of the interactions between variables. This diagram indicates the direction of the relationship by expressing the value as either a whole number or a fraction: That is, on a 10-point scale, a 10 would indicate the strongest possible relationship in one direction and 1/10 would indicate the strongest possible relationship in the other. Therefore, a value of 1/10 would indicate a stronger relationship than a value of 9. Negative values do not appear on a numerical matrix diagram.

21. B: If there are 32 observations in an experiment, it is typical to run autocorrelations from lag 1 to lag 8. The basic calculation for the number of autocorrelations in an experiment is lag 1 to lag $x/4$, in which x is the number of observations. Because there are 32 observations in this experiment, autocorrelations should run from lag 1 to lag 8. The lag is the difference between correlated observations. In lag 1, for instance, observation 1 is correlated with observation 2, observation 2 is correlated with observation 3, observation 3 is correlated with observation 4, and so on. In lag 8, observation 1 would be correlated with observation 9, observation 2 with observation 10, observation 3 with observation 11, and so on. An experiment with 32 observations would include all of the intervening correlations between lag 1 and lag 8 (i.e., lags 2 through 7).

22. D: One disadvantage of using enumerative statistics is that values are drawn from a static population. If a dynamic process is to be measured, as is often the case in Six Sigma, it is necessary to use analytical statistics. The other answer choices allude to advantages of enumerative statistics. For instance, one advantage of enumerative statistics is that they make it easy to determine whether samples are representative. A representative sample is one extracted from the population without any bias. Enumerative statistics provide an assumed distribution as well as a confidence level and a set of confidence intervals. Finally, enumerative statistics may be applied to process baseline estimation, namely for the purpose of assessing random samples.

23. D: A *lognormal distribution* is appropriate for a continuous set of data with a fixed lower boundary but no upper boundary. In most cases, the lower boundary on a lognormal distribution is zero. These distributions can be tested with a goodness-of-fit test. A *Johnson distribution* is more appropriate for continuous data that, for whatever reason, is inappropriate for a normal or exponential distribution. An *exponential distribution* is appropriate for any set of continuous data, though these distributions are most often used for frequency data. A *normal distribution* is appropriate for a set of continuous data with neither an upper nor a lower boundary. The normal distribution follows the pattern of the classic bell curve.

24. A: In metrology, the degree to which a measurement can be compared to a known standard with confidence is called *traceability*. Experts on measurement are aware that every gauge is to some extent inaccurate (i.e., it contains measurement uncertainty), but it is important that these inaccuracies themselves be measurable. Six Sigma projects require a number of different measurements taken at different times and in different conditions, and it is essential that these measurements have essentially the same level of traceability.

25. C: An autocorrelation function of 0.9 would indicate the strongest correlation. The range of autocorrelation functions and partial autocorrelation functions extends from −1 to 1. The strength of the correlation is indicated by the distance from 0 (i.e., the absolute value) regardless of whether the value is on the positive or negative side. Therefore, an autocorrelation function of 0.9 would indicate a stronger correlation than would functions of 0.1, −0.8, and −0.2.

26. C: In Porter's five forces analysis, the likely result of strong distribution channels is that suppliers will have less bargaining power. This is because firms that feel confident in their supply chains will be less likely to accept disadvantageous terms from their vendors. Five forces analysis was developed by Michael E. Porter as a tool for assessing the potential for success in a given market. The five forces are the likelihood of new competition, the threat of substitute products, the bargaining power of customers, the bargaining power of suppliers, and the level of competition within the industry. The existence of strong distribution channels would indicate that switching distributers would have an impact on cost and that new firms would be discouraged from entering the market. Also, strong distribution channels would tend to reinforce competitive advantage.

27. D: In most cases, the lowest coefficient of determination that is considered acceptable in a linearity analysis is 70%. The coefficient of determination indicates the adequacy of the measurement system. A *linearity analysis* is a study of the potential for bias error for a particular measurement system at different points in the equipment's operating range. It is important that the Six Sigma team know that the measurement system will be roughly as accurate at all points during a process.

28. C: The least useful type of Pareto chart would be one in which all the bars are roughly the same height. A *Pareto chart* is used to identify the most important and urgent problems in a process. It is based on the *Pareto principle,* which is the idea that a process can be improved dramatically through attention to the few most important problems. It is essential that the bars on a Pareto chart represent tangible values, like cost or count. A Pareto chart will not be useful if it is based on percentages or rates. The most useful Pareto charts have several large bars on the left, indicating problems that are significantly more important than others. Similarly, a steeply ascending line on a Pareto chart indicates that a few of the identified factors are very important and, therefore, that the chart will be useful. If all of the bars on a Pareto chart are roughly the same height, no one factor is more important than another, and therefore, it will be impossible to generate an unusual amount of benefit by solving a single problem.

29. A: Of the given tests, the Mood's median test would be the most appropriate for handling outliers. A *Mood's median test* is a method of nonparametric estimation similar to a chi-square test. This form of test is better at handling outliers, but the *Kruskal–Wallis* does a better job of evaluating certain distributions. In both the Mood's median and Kruskal–Wallis tests, the null hypothesis is that all population medians are equal, while the alternative hypothesis is that not all of the medians are equal. The *Mann–Whitney test* is closer to the Kruskal–Wallis. The *Kolmogorov–Smirnov* is a goodness-of-fit test that provides more specific results than a chi-square test.

30. D: A *Poisson distribution* should be used when the targeted characteristic may appear more than once per unit. In order for a Poisson distribution to be effective, the data should consist of positive whole numbers, and the experimental trials should be independent. A *binomial distribution* is appropriate for situations in which the units in the population will only have one of two possible characteristics (e.g., off or on). An *exponential distribution* is appropriate for measurement data, especially frequency. A *lognormal distribution* is appropriate for continuous data with a fixed lower boundary but no upper boundary. In most cases, the lower boundary of a lognormal distribution is zero.

31. B: The final step in a kaizen event is celebrating success. Kaizen experts insist that this is an important part of the process because it builds organizational morale and establishes proper conditions for success on similar projects in the future. In general, the steps in a kaizen event are providing employees with basic training, defining the problem, measuring performance, brainstorming, deciding upon a solution, implementing the solution, making adjustments, gathering results, and celebrating.

32. B: If all of the data points on an *Np* chart fall between the upper and lower control limits, the process is stable. So long as all of the variation is within these limits, it can be assumed to be the result of common causes. Assuming the chart is reliable, data points that fall outside the upper and lower control limits are the result of special-cause variation. At the least, the presence of data points outside the upper and lower control limits identifies areas where employees will need to conduct further research. *Np* charts are control charts for analyzing attributes data. These charts are used when the sample size is regular and the targeted condition may only occur once per sample.

33. A: The Japanese term for inconsistency is *mura*. Eliminating *mura* often requires a comprehensive redesign of the process, for which reason many Six Sigma programs have focused instead on reducing *muda*, which is wasteful or unproductive activity. *Muri*, or overloading, is the third form of waste identified by the Toyota Production System. *Muki* is not a term in quality management.

34. D: In nominal group technique, each participant should receive eight pieces of paper if there are 40 options to be considered. Each participant will then write one of the options down on each piece of paper, along with its rank (first through eighth). It is typical for each participant to receive eight pieces of paper when there are more than 35 options. When there are from 20 to 35 options, the typical number of papers for each person is six. When there are fewer than 20 options to be considered, it is typical for each member of the group to receive four pieces of paper. Once all of the group members turn their rankings in, the various options are compared, and the most popular are given further consideration.

35. C: The term for the degree to which an experimental design allows all the indicated parameters to be measured independently of one another is *orthogonality*. This is an essential characteristic of experimental design. Balance, on the other hand, is not necessary. An experiment may have either *design balance,* when the design array has columns with equal numbers of levels for each parameter, or *data balance,* when each data point has roughly the same influence on parameter definition. *Autonomy* is not a characteristic of experimental design. *Normalization* is a technique of transformation in which data values are placed on a common range for easier comparison.

36. C: Expense is not one of the factors included in the calculation of risk priority number. Risk priority number is calculated by multiplying severity, likelihood, and detection level. The severity of the risk is the significance of its occurrence. Various industries have created standardized tables for indicating the severity of common risks. The likelihood of a risk is simply the chances of it happening. Finally, the detection level is based on the number of modes for identifying the error or failure as well as the chances that any one of these modes will be successful in detection. A common formula for calculating risk priority number is to place all of these categories on a scale from 1 to 10 and then multiply them together. In this scenario, the maximum risk priority number would be 1,000.

37. B: In an exponentially weighted moving-average chart, a weighting factor of 0.19 would be best for detecting small shifts. Generally, a weighting factor around 0.2 is most appropriate for detecting small shifts. Larger shifts may be most effectively detected with a weighting factor of between 0.2 and 0.4. Exponentially weighted moving-average charts establish a weighting factor so that values can receive different emphases depending on their ages.

38. C: If there are four levels and three factors in a complete factorial design, 64 runs would be required. The number of required runs is calculated by raising the number of levels to a power equal to the number of factors. In this case, then, the calculation is performed as $4^3 = 64$. If the complete factorial design had five levels and three factors, the number of runs would be calculated as $5^3 = 125$.

39. A: Batching would be appropriate in a scenario where setup time is significant. It was long thought that batching was a foolproof way to improve efficiency, but Six Sigma research indicated that batching strategies often lead to an increase in wait time and overall cycle time. One of the only situations in which batching would be appropriate would be when the preparation time for the activity is significant because there would then be a disincentive to set up and break down the equipment frequently.

40. B: Run test 6 identifies shifts in the process mean. The other run tests provide information about sampling errors. Run tests 1, 2, 3, and 5 also identify shifts in the process mean. Run tests are typically used in statistical process control programs to identify errors in data collection. Unfortunately, run tests are only able to identify the presence of errors and are not very good at pinpointing their locations.

41. D: A Gantt chart is not a part of the typical tollgate review. A *tollgate review* is a gathering of all the participants in a Six Sigma project, during which an assessment of the overall success of the project is made. Specifically, the participants in a tollgate review will identify whether the planning objectives have been met. In order to make this judgment, they may use basic check sheets, milestone lists, or project deliverables documents. However, a *Gantt chart,* which is used to identify the critical path of a project, is used exclusively during the define stage of DMAIC and is more aimed at improving efficiency then measuring the success of improvement efforts.

42. C: In kaizen, the idea that one step in a process should be completed only when the subsequent steps are ready is referred to as *pull.* This is opposite to the typical arrangement in manufacturing processes, in which materials are pushed through the process chain as they are completed. Kaizen recommends instead that materials be drawn along by vacuums created in the production chain. A process chain in which this occurs is said to have pull. *Flow,* meanwhile, is the continuous completion of a process. Organizations that adopt the kaizen philosophy attempt to make flow constant in every department and stage of processes. *Poka-yoke* is a Japanese system for error proofing, based on the premise that avoiding errors in the first run is worth a slightly higher cost.

Perfection is the kaizen ideal of continuous improvement. Perfection is a goal that can never be attained but should be strived toward regardless.

43. B: *Net present value* is calculated by subtracting current cash outflows from current cash inflows. Net present value is an important variable when considering whether to make a particular investment. *Revenue growth,* meanwhile, is the change in sales figures over a particular interval. *Return on investment* is the amount of money received back by the company after an initial outlay of funds. Measuring return on investment is an effective way to determine whether an improvement or investment program has been worthwhile. *Margin,* finally, is the amount of funds a business must create in order to maintain its operations.

44. D: Implementation is not one of the phases of rapid problem resolution (RPR). RPR is an effective method for solving recurrent problems. The core process of RPR has three phases: discovery, investigation, and resolution. In the discovery phase, the team gathers information. In the investigation phase, the root cause of the problem is isolated. In the resolution phase, an appropriate solution is applied.

45. D: Philip B. Crosby wrote *Quality Is Free*, a book that revolutionized quality management by placing an explicit emphasis on getting processes right the first time. Crosby insisted that businesses are better served by investing more money in quality control on the first run and, thereby, avoiding the costs of defective products. W. Edwards Deming is famous for enumerating the seven deadly diseases of the workplace and 14 points of emphasis for management. Joseph M. Juran stressed the importance of customer satisfaction as a goal of quality control. Armand V. Feigenbaum is known for emphasizing four key actions in the implementation of quality management: establishing standards, creating metrics for conformance to these standards, resolving issues that impede conformance, and planning for continuous improvement.

46. C: A *Box-Behnken design* is similar to a central composite design but without corner or extreme points. For this reason, the Box-Behnken design can fully cover the experimental space without requiring as many points as a complete factorial design. Extreme factor-level combinations are not required for this design. A *Plackett-Burman design* is often used in lieu of a fractional factorial design when the number of runs in the experiment is equal to a factor of four. The *John's ¾ design* is so called because it only requires three-quarters of the runs of the typical fractional factorial design. This design is most often used when running a fractional factorial design indicates the need for further exploration of a limited set of interactions. A *mixed-level design* is used when factors have different numbers of levels.

47. D: Indecision is not one of the seven classic wastes. In the Japanese waste reduction system of *muda*, seven classic wastes are identified. These are transportation, inventory, motion, waiting, overprocessing, overproduction, and defects. The Toyota Production System emphasizes reducing each of these seven sources of waste as a means to improving efficiency.

48. D: In order to calibrate an instrument, one must know the *measurement uncertainty* of both the instrument and the standard. In most instances of calibration, the standard can have a maximum of 25% of the measurement uncertainty of the instrument. When this is the case, variations in standard will not significantly affect calibration. *Traceability* is a similar concept to measurement uncertainty, but it is the degree to which an instrument can be compared to a known standard, meaning that the standard itself will not have a defined traceability. In measurement, *tolerance* is the extent to which a measurement instrument will maintain its capability over a long duration. This is similar to the *durability* of the measurement instrument and standard.

49. A: One advantage of normalization is that it screens irrelevant factors from a nonlinear experimental design. However, normalization is more often used for linear experimental models. The process of normalization does not balance the experimental array; rather, the experimental array must be balanced in order for normalization to be a success. Normalization does place all the values on a common scale, but the scale ranges from –1 to 1. Finally, as indicated above, normalization may be used in nonlinear experiments, but it is typically more effective for linear experimental models.

50. B: In a Kano model, satisfaction is always on the y-axis and quality is always on the x-axis. In other words, increases in quality are tied to increases in satisfaction. One of the insights of the Kano model is that customer expectations and needs are always shifting and that, in order to maintain a constant level of satisfaction, a business needs to continuously improve processes and products.

How to Overcome Test Anxiety

Just the thought of taking a test is enough to make most people a little nervous. A test is an important event that can have a long-term impact on your future, so it's important to take it seriously and it's natural to feel anxious about performing well. But just because anxiety is normal, that doesn't mean that it's helpful in test taking, or that you should simply accept it as part of your life. Anxiety can have a variety of effects. These effects can be mild, like making you feel slightly nervous, or severe, like blocking your ability to focus or remember even a simple detail.

If you experience test anxiety—whether severe or mild—it's important to know how to beat it. To discover this, first you need to understand what causes test anxiety.

Causes of Test Anxiety

While we often think of anxiety as an uncontrollable emotional state, it can actually be caused by simple, practical things. One of the most common causes of test anxiety is that a person does not feel adequately prepared for their test. This feeling can be the result of many different issues such as poor study habits or lack of organization, but the most common culprit is time management. Starting to study too late, failing to organize your study time to cover all of the material, or being distracted while you study will mean that you're not well prepared for the test. This may lead to cramming the night before, which will cause you to be physically and mentally exhausted for the test. Poor time management also contributes to feelings of stress, fear, and hopelessness as you realize you are not well prepared but don't know what to do about it.

Other times, test anxiety is not related to your preparation for the test but comes from unresolved fear. This may be a past failure on a test, or poor performance on tests in general. It may come from comparing yourself to others who seem to be performing better or from the stress of living up to expectations. Anxiety may be driven by fears of the future—how failure on this test would affect your educational and career goals. These fears are often completely irrational, but they can still negatively impact your test performance.

Review Video: 3 Reasons You Have Test Anxiety
Visit mometrix.com/academy and enter code: 428468

Elements of Test Anxiety

As mentioned earlier, test anxiety is considered to be an emotional state, but it has physical and mental components as well. Sometimes you may not even realize that you are suffering from test anxiety until you notice the physical symptoms. These can include trembling hands, rapid heartbeat, sweating, nausea, and tense muscles. Extreme anxiety may lead to fainting or vomiting. Obviously, any of these symptoms can have a negative impact on testing. It is important to recognize them as soon as they begin to occur so that you can address the problem before it damages your performance.

Review Video: 3 Ways to Tell You Have Test Anxiety
Visit mometrix.com/academy and enter code: 927847

The mental components of test anxiety include trouble focusing and inability to remember learned information. During a test, your mind is on high alert, which can help you recall information and stay focused for an extended period of time. However, anxiety interferes with your mind's natural processes, causing you to blank out, even on the questions you know well. The strain of testing during anxiety makes it difficult to stay focused, especially on a test that may take several hours. Extreme anxiety can take a huge mental toll, making it difficult not only to recall test information but even to understand the test questions or pull your thoughts together.

Review Video: How Test Anxiety Affects Memory
Visit mometrix.com/academy and enter code: 609003

Effects of Test Anxiety

Test anxiety is like a disease—if left untreated, it will get progressively worse. Anxiety leads to poor performance, and this reinforces the feelings of fear and failure, which in turn lead to poor performances on subsequent tests. It can grow from a mild nervousness to a crippling condition. If allowed to progress, test anxiety can have a big impact on your schooling, and consequently on your future.

Test anxiety can spread to other parts of your life. Anxiety on tests can become anxiety in any stressful situation, and blanking on a test can turn into panicking in a job situation. But fortunately, you don't have to let anxiety rule your testing and determine your grades. There are a number of relatively simple steps you can take to move past anxiety and function normally on a test and in the rest of life.

Review Video: How Test Anxiety Impacts Your Grades
Visit mometrix.com/academy and enter code: 939819

Physical Steps for Beating Test Anxiety

While test anxiety is a serious problem, the good news is that it can be overcome. It doesn't have to control your ability to think and remember information. While it may take time, you can begin taking steps today to beat anxiety.

Just as your first hint that you may be struggling with anxiety comes from the physical symptoms, the first step to treating it is also physical. Rest is crucial for having a clear, strong mind. If you are tired, it is much easier to give in to anxiety. But if you establish good sleep habits, your body and mind will be ready to perform optimally, without the strain of exhaustion. Additionally, sleeping well helps you to retain information better, so you're more likely to recall the answers when you see the test questions.

Getting good sleep means more than going to bed on time. It's important to allow your brain time to relax. Take study breaks from time to time so it doesn't get overworked, and don't study right before bed. Take time to rest your mind before trying to rest your body, or you may find it difficult to fall asleep.

Review Video: The Importance of Sleep for Your Brain
Visit mometrix.com/academy and enter code: 319338

Along with sleep, other aspects of physical health are important in preparing for a test. Good nutrition is vital for good brain function. Sugary foods and drinks may give a burst of energy but this burst is followed by a crash, both physically and emotionally. Instead, fuel your body with protein and vitamin-rich foods.

Also, drink plenty of water. Dehydration can lead to headaches and exhaustion, especially if your brain is already under stress from the rigors of the test. Particularly if your test is a long one, drink water during the breaks. And if possible, take an energy-boosting snack to eat between sections.

Review Video: How Diet Can Affect your Mood
Visit mometrix.com/academy and enter code: 624317

Along with sleep and diet, a third important part of physical health is exercise. Maintaining a steady workout schedule is helpful, but even taking 5-minute study breaks to walk can help get your blood pumping faster and clear your head. Exercise also releases endorphins, which contribute to a positive feeling and can help combat test anxiety.

When you nurture your physical health, you are also contributing to your mental health. If your body is healthy, your mind is much more likely to be healthy as well. So take time to rest, nourish your body with healthy food and water, and get moving as much as possible. Taking these physical steps will make you stronger and more able to take the mental steps necessary to overcome test anxiety.

Review Video: How to Stay Healthy and Prevent Test Anxiety
Visit mometrix.com/academy and enter code: 877894

Mental Steps for Beating Test Anxiety

Working on the mental side of test anxiety can be more challenging, but as with the physical side, there are clear steps you can take to overcome it. As mentioned earlier, test anxiety often stems from lack of preparation, so the obvious solution is to prepare for the test. Effective studying may be the most important weapon you have for beating test anxiety, but you can and should employ several other mental tools to combat fear.

First, boost your confidence by reminding yourself of past success—tests or projects that you aced. If you're putting as much effort into preparing for this test as you did for those, there's no reason you should expect to fail here. Work hard to prepare; then trust your preparation.

Second, surround yourself with encouraging people. It can be helpful to find a study group, but be sure that the people you're around will encourage a positive attitude. If you spend time with others who are anxious or cynical, this will only contribute to your own anxiety. Look for others who are motivated to study hard from a desire to succeed, not from a fear of failure.

Third, reward yourself. A test is physically and mentally tiring, even without anxiety, and it can be helpful to have something to look forward to. Plan an activity following the test, regardless of the outcome, such as going to a movie or getting ice cream.

When you are taking the test, if you find yourself beginning to feel anxious, remind yourself that you know the material. Visualize successfully completing the test. Then take a few deep, relaxing breaths and return to it. Work through the questions carefully but with confidence, knowing that you are capable of succeeding.

Developing a healthy mental approach to test taking will also aid in other areas of life. Test anxiety affects more than just the actual test—it can be damaging to your mental health and even contribute to depression. It's important to beat test anxiety before it becomes a problem for more than testing.

Review Video: Test Anxiety and Depression
Visit mometrix.com/academy and enter code: 904704

Study Strategy

Being prepared for the test is necessary to combat anxiety, but what does being prepared look like? You may study for hours on end and still not feel prepared. What you need is a strategy for test prep. The next few pages outline our recommended steps to help you plan out and conquer the challenge of preparation.

Step 1: Scope Out the Test

Learn everything you can about the format (multiple choice, essay, etc.) and what will be on the test. Gather any study materials, course outlines, or sample exams that may be available. Not only will this help you to prepare, but knowing what to expect can help to alleviate test anxiety.

Step 2: Map Out the Material

Look through the textbook or study guide and make note of how many chapters or sections it has. Then divide these over the time you have. For example, if a book has 15 chapters and you have five days to study, you need to cover three chapters each day. Even better, if you have the time, leave an extra day at the end for overall review after you have gone through the material in depth.

If time is limited, you may need to prioritize the material. Look through it and make note of which sections you think you already have a good grasp on, and which need review. While you are studying, skim quickly through the familiar sections and take more time on the challenging parts. Write out your plan so you don't get lost as you go. Having a written plan also helps you feel more in control of the study, so anxiety is less likely to arise from feeling overwhelmed at the amount to cover.

Step 3: Gather Your Tools

Decide what study method works best for you. Do you prefer to highlight in the book as you study and then go back over the highlighted portions? Or do you type out notes of the important information? Or is it helpful to make flashcards that you can carry with you? Assemble the pens, index cards, highlighters, post-it notes, and any other materials you may need so you won't be distracted by getting up to find things while you study.

If you're having a hard time retaining the information or organizing your notes, experiment with different methods. For example, try color-coding by subject with colored pens, highlighters, or post-it notes. If you learn better by hearing, try recording yourself reading your notes so you can listen while in the car, working out, or simply sitting at your desk. Ask a friend to quiz you from your flashcards, or try teaching someone the material to solidify it in your mind.

Step 4: Create Your Environment

It's important to avoid distractions while you study. This includes both the obvious distractions like visitors and the subtle distractions like an uncomfortable chair (or a too-comfortable couch that makes you want to fall asleep). Set up the best study environment possible: good lighting and a comfortable work area. If background music helps you focus, you may want to turn it on, but otherwise keep the room quiet. If you are using a computer to take notes, be sure you don't have any other windows open, especially applications like social media, games, or anything else that could distract you. Silence your phone and turn off notifications. Be sure to keep water close by so you stay hydrated while you study (but avoid unhealthy drinks and snacks).

Also, take into account the best time of day to study. Are you freshest first thing in the morning? Try to set aside some time then to work through the material. Is your mind clearer in the afternoon or evening? Schedule your study session then. Another method is to study at the same time of day that you will take the test, so that your brain gets used to working on the material at that time and will be ready to focus at test time.

Step 5: Study!

Once you have done all the study preparation, it's time to settle into the actual studying. Sit down, take a few moments to settle your mind so you can focus, and begin to follow your study plan. Don't give in to distractions or let yourself procrastinate. This is your time to prepare so you'll be ready to fearlessly approach the test. Make the most of the time and stay focused.

Of course, you don't want to burn out. If you study too long you may find that you're not retaining the information very well. Take regular study breaks. For example, taking five minutes out of every hour to walk briskly, breathing deeply and swinging your arms, can help your mind stay fresh.

As you get to the end of each chapter or section, it's a good idea to do a quick review. Remind yourself of what you learned and work on any difficult parts. When you feel that you've mastered the material, move on to the next part. At the end of your study session, briefly skim through your notes again.

But while review is helpful, cramming last minute is NOT. If at all possible, work ahead so that you won't need to fit all your study into the last day. Cramming overloads your brain with more information than it can process and retain, and your tired mind may struggle to recall even previously learned information when it is overwhelmed with last-minute study. Also, the urgent nature of cramming and the stress placed on your brain contribute to anxiety. You'll be more likely to go to the test feeling unprepared and having trouble thinking clearly.

So don't cram, and don't stay up late before the test, even just to review your notes at a leisurely pace. Your brain needs rest more than it needs to go over the information again. In fact, plan to finish your studies by noon or early afternoon the day before the test. Give your brain the rest of the day to relax or focus on other things, and get a good night's sleep. Then you will be fresh for the test and better able to recall what you've studied.

Step 6: Take a practice test

Many courses offer sample tests, either online or in the study materials. This is an excellent resource to check whether you have mastered the material, as well as to prepare for the test format and environment.

Check the test format ahead of time: the number of questions, the type (multiple choice, free response, etc.), and the time limit. Then create a plan for working through them. For example, if you have 30 minutes to take a 60-question test, your limit is 30 seconds per question. Spend less time on the questions you know well so that you can take more time on the difficult ones.

If you have time to take several practice tests, take the first one open book, with no time limit. Work through the questions at your own pace and make sure you fully understand them. Gradually work up to taking a test under test conditions: sit at a desk with all study materials put away and set a timer. Pace yourself to make sure you finish the test with time to spare and go back to check your answers if you have time.

After each test, check your answers. On the questions you missed, be sure you understand why you missed them. Did you misread the question (tests can use tricky wording)? Did you forget the information? Or was it something you hadn't learned? Go back and study any shaky areas that the practice tests reveal.

Taking these tests not only helps with your grade, but also aids in combating test anxiety. If you're already used to the test conditions, you're less likely to worry about it, and working through tests until you're scoring well gives you a confidence boost. Go through the practice tests until you feel comfortable, and then you can go into the test knowing that you're ready for it.

Test Tips

On test day, you should be confident, knowing that you've prepared well and are ready to answer the questions. But aside from preparation, there are several test day strategies you can employ to maximize your performance.

First, as stated before, get a good night's sleep the night before the test (and for several nights before that, if possible). Go into the test with a fresh, alert mind rather than staying up late to study.

Try not to change too much about your normal routine on the day of the test. It's important to eat a nutritious breakfast, but if you normally don't eat breakfast at all, consider eating just a protein bar. If you're a coffee drinker, go ahead and have your normal coffee. Just make sure you time it so that the caffeine doesn't wear off right in the middle of your test. Avoid sugary beverages, and drink enough water to stay hydrated but not so much that you need a restroom break 10 minutes into the test. If your test isn't first thing in the morning, consider going for a walk or doing a light workout before the test to get your blood flowing.

Allow yourself enough time to get ready, and leave for the test with plenty of time to spare so you won't have the anxiety of scrambling to arrive in time. Another reason to be early is to select a good seat. It's helpful to sit away from doors and windows, which can be distracting. Find a good seat, get out your supplies, and settle your mind before the test begins.

When the test begins, start by going over the instructions carefully, even if you already know what to expect. Make sure you avoid any careless mistakes by following the directions.

Then begin working through the questions, pacing yourself as you've practiced. If you're not sure on an answer, don't spend too much time on it, and don't let it shake your confidence. Either skip it and come back later, or eliminate as many wrong answers as possible and guess among the remaining ones. Don't dwell on these questions as you continue—put them out of your mind and focus on what lies ahead.

Be sure to read all of the answer choices, even if you're sure the first one is the right answer. Sometimes you'll find a better one if you keep reading. But don't second-guess yourself if you do immediately know the answer. Your gut instinct is usually right. Don't let test anxiety rob you of the information you know.

If you have time at the end of the test (and if the test format allows), go back and review your answers. Be cautious about changing any, since your first instinct tends to be correct, but make sure you didn't misread any of the questions or accidentally mark the wrong answer choice. Look over any you skipped and make an educated guess.

At the end, leave the test feeling confident. You've done your best, so don't waste time worrying about your performance or wishing you could change anything. Instead, celebrate the successful completion of this test. And finally, use this test to learn how to deal with anxiety even better next time.

Review Video: 5 Tips to Beat Test Anxiety
Visit mometrix.com/academy and enter code: 570656

Important Qualification

Not all anxiety is created equal. If your test anxiety is causing major issues in your life beyond the classroom or testing center, or if you are experiencing troubling physical symptoms related to your anxiety, it may be a sign of a serious physiological or psychological condition. If this sounds like your situation, we strongly encourage you to seek professional help.

Thank You

We at Mometrix would like to extend our heartfelt thanks to you, our friend and patron, for allowing us to play a part in your journey. It is a privilege to serve people from all walks of life who are unified in their commitment to building the best future they can for themselves.

The preparation you devote to these important testing milestones may be the most valuable educational opportunity you have for making a real difference in your life. We encourage you to put your heart into it—that feeling of succeeding, overcoming, and yes, conquering will be well worth the hours you've invested.

We want to hear your story, your struggles and your successes, and if you see any opportunities for us to improve our materials so we can help others even more effectively in the future, please share that with us as well. **The team at Mometrix would be absolutely thrilled to hear from you!** So please, send us an email (support@mometrix.com) and let's stay in touch.

If you'd like some additional help, check out these other resources we offer for your exam:
http://mometrixflashcards.com/SixSigma

Additional Bonus Material

Due to our efforts to try to keep this book to a manageable length, we've created a link that will give you access to all of your additional bonus material.

Please visit http://www.mometrix.com/bonus948/sixsigmabb to access the information.

Made in the USA
Middletown, DE
16 May 2021